Ethnic Politics in Europe

Ethnic Politics in Europe

THE POWER OF NORMS AND INCENTIVES

Judith G. Kelley

PRINCETON UNIVERSITY PRESS   PRINCETON AND OXFORD

Library of Congress Cataloging-in-Publication Data

Kelley, Judith Green.
Ethnic politics in Europe : the power of norms and incentives / Judith Kelley.
p. cm.
Includes bibliographical references and index.
ISBN: 0-691-11798-5 (cloth: alk. paper)
1. Europe, Eastern—Politics and government—1989–. 2. Europe,
Eastern—Ethnic relations. 3. International agencies—Europe, Eastern.
4. Europe, Eastern—Foreign relations. 5. International relations. I. Title.
JN96.A58K45 2004
323.147—dc22   2003066412

British Library Cataloging-in-Publication Data is available.

This book has been composed in Janson

Printed on acid-free paper. ∞

pup.princeton.edu

Printed in the United States of America

10 9 8 7 6 5 4 3 2 1

To Michael

Contents

Figures and Tables

Preface

THIS PROJECT developed from my initial interest in conflict prevention issues into a larger inquiry about the mechanisms that international actors use to influence domestic politics. Interaction with such scholars as Kalypso Nicholaidis and Graham Allison led me to ask questions about the role of external actors in early efforts to address ethnic tensions. After reviewing efforts by various regional institutions, the European case posed the most rewarding inquiry because of the variation in types of involvement as well as in state responses. With my first, basic questions I grappled with the ethnic politics, how to understand the different kinds of engagements, and how these practices related to the broader compliance theory. As the mechanisms of influence became clearer, questions of effects and the role of domestic factors demanded the further attention of conflict theory, international organization theory, and socialization theory. At the same time, the theoretical inquiry became directed toward international institutions more generally and their tools of influence more specifically. Academically, I came of age when international relations scholars were moving from the debate about whether institutions matter to the more interesting debate about the conditions, mechanisms, and results of their influence. Thus, when and how international organizations could influence domestic politics became a fascination for me.

Writing about ethnic issues risks stirring multiple sentiments from various parties. Thus, I feel I ought to disclose the angle of my observations. Inevitably, observers will have different versions of the truth. This is particularly the case when different parties occupy different sides of the issue. Thus, for example, ethnic Hungarians are likely to view any account of ethnic politics in Romania as too timid an interpretation of ethnic relations, whereas ethnic Romanians will likely charge that the account is over dramatized. I think that I can accurately describe my own leanings on the different ethnic situations in the countries included in this study as neutral. I have little stake in the ultimate outcomes of any of these issues. Indeed, it would not have been academically counterproductive for me to conclude that international efforts had no effect; such a finding would have been as informative as the one ultimately presented in this book. Thus, I had no motivations to portray the processes and outcomes in any certain light. Naturally, my interests motivated me to portray the situations as interesting, but in doing so I do not believe that I have systematically biased the accounts.

I am grateful for a four-year grant from the Danish government and what was then called the Danish Research Academy (Forskerakademiet), which generously supported me at Harvard University. Research Travel Grants from the Weatherhead Center for International Affairs in 1999 and 2000 aided my fieldwork. Finally, my years as a graduate student associate at the Minda de Gunzburg Center for European Studies as well as the Weatherhead Center for International Affairs provided me with invaluable logistical and professional support as well as a vibrant intellectual community in which to work.

My gratitude also goes especially to certain other people who helped along the way. Most of all, Lisa Martin has been a steadfast, forthright, and a caring advisor. Always returning messages and offering solid constructive advice, she was an intellectual anchor whose contribution went far beyond the obligations of a dissertation advisor. She is integrity defined. I also owe a special thanks to Robert Putnam for his confidence in me, and his willingness to lend a hand at the right time. I am also grateful to those who offered comments on the project, including, among others, Liliana Botchava, Jeffrey Checkel, Alexandra Gheciu, Frank Schimmelfennig, Milada Vachudova, Stephen Walt, Steven Wilkinson, and Michael Zürn, as well as to my colleagues in the Public Policy and Political Science departments here at Duke for their support.

The book gained tremendously from the generous cooperation from all the persons interviewed. EU commission representatives, national delegations to the EU, as well as members of the European parliament were helpful in offering information and insights. The OSCE HCNM office in The Hague gave me generous access to a great part of their records and took time to improve my understanding of the OSCE efforts. This was also true of the OSCE missions in Riga and Tallinn. Finally, I am most indebted to all the decision makers and policy experts who made the in-country research so rewarding.

My research has also benefited from the comments of American Political Science Association and International Studies Association panel participants and attendees over the years. At Harvard, two years of participation in the Performance of Democracy Workshop under Robert Putnam's leadership provided a forum for inspiration and input: I am grateful to those involved in that workshop between 1997 and 1999. In Europe, a European Union–sponsored project, IDNET, allowed for extensive feedback on my work through a serious of workshops in Florence and Oslo. Finally, I am grateful to the Massachusetts Institute of Technology's Steven Van Evera, who turned a course on the causes of war into a thorough and invaluable training in methods.

In my personal life, my fellow Harvard students Lisa Sanbonmatsu and Alma Cohen not only helped me through the greater challenges of graduate school, but more importantly they were there during the twists and turns of life outside academia, helping me to keep things in proper perspective.

Finally, my deep gratitude goes to my mother, Maria Barking, and my late father, Enok Green Jensen, who sacrificed to give me the best of opportunities during my childhood. But without Michael Kelley, my husband, the entire academic endeavor would not have been possible. Labeled by Stanford University as "trailing spouse," he has followed me from Oxnard College, a small community college in Los Angeles, to Stanford, to Harvard, and now to Duke University. He has been by my side, sometimes bewildered by my endeavor but never failing in his dedication and faith.

Ethnic Politics in Europe

CHAPTER 1

Introduction

In 1991 LATVIA had only recently regained independence from Russia. After years under Soviet rule ethnic Latvians comprised just slightly more than half the population of 2.6 million, while Russian speakers made up more than a million. How should Russian speakers be accommodated? On October 15, 1991, Latvia's supreme council issued a resolution restoring citizenship only to those who had been citizens of Latvia before 1940 and their descendants, leaving about 700,000 inhabitants without citizenship. At the same time, naturalization requirements were extremely strict. Two years later, in October 1993, with a new citizenship law on the table, an opinion poll showed that 39 percent of Latvians favored annual quotas for granting Latvian citizenship such that ethnic Latvian citizens would form 75 percent of the population. Such a plan would effectively mean little to no naturalization for years to come. By early 1994 a proposal by the Latvian National Independence Movement set the main terms of the debate, including a strict key requirement limiting the future rate of naturalization to 1 percent of the total number of citizens, or about 2,000 per year—in effect, barring hundreds of thousands of people from ever receiving Latvian citizenship.

Meanwhile, emphasizing language as a proof of loyalty, in 1994 parliament passed a law that limited the participation of almost half of Latvia's population—noncitizens—from voting or standing in local elections. The law did not legally contradict international norms. Because of Latvia's large noncitizen population, however, vast numbers of people were now without any form of political participation. As a result, several regions with Russian-speaking majorities would be governed exclusively by ethnic Latvians. Even more problematic, the law barred from running for office anyone who was not proficient in the state language at the highest official testing level. This meant that even many ethnic non-Latvians who *were* citizens could not run for local office.

June 1994 brought much activity on the citizenship issue. On June 9 the parliament approved a law on citizenship in the second of three readings. On June 21, after nationalists scored a victory in local elections, the parliament passed the final version of the law on citizenship with strict quotas. But in a turnaround on June 24 the president sent the law back to parliament. A month later, contrary to prior party preferences, parliament replaced the controversial quotas with a more liberal "window system," allowing different categories of people to nationalize in stages until year 2003, after which all groups would be handled equally.

The spirit of compromise did not transfer to the national election law, however. In the spring of 1995 parliament adopted a national election law similar to the local election law. The law barred Communist Party members and non-Latvian speakers from running for national office, and required candidates who had not completed education in a school with Latvian as the language of instruction to submit a notarized document indicating the highest level of Latvian language skills. Thus, Latvia had curbed ethnic Russian political representation on both the local and the national levels.[1]

What explains the difference in Latvia's degree of compromise on the citizenship law and the election laws?[2] Why in general did governments in eastern Europe sometimes accommodate ethnic minorities while at other times restricting their rights or ignoring them? Even more curiously, why did governments sometimes outright *reverse* their policies after fighting hard to pass them in the first place, while at other times similar attempts to revoke policies failed?

Scholars of ethnic minority issues have traditionally focused on three factors to explain such puzzles, namely, the roles of the ethnic minority, of the ethnic majority, and of the external homeland (Brubaker 1995). Given that the topic of ethnic minorities is inherently international, dating back at least to secessions from the Ottoman Empire in 1878 and later to the League of Nations (Reitz 1999), ethnic politics in eastern Europe in the 1990s cannot be explained without examining the unique role of international institutions as domestic policy actors. This introduces another round of questions. How do international institutions use traditional tools of states to influence domestic policies? What strategies are most effective? How do domestic factors influence international efforts? With the growing policy scope and increasing membership of international organizations, the influence of such organizations could eventually preclude harsher actions to enforce international will, such as military intervention. To accurately assess whether an international institution actually influenced domestic policy, however, is extremely challenging: some policy change might instead be related to domestic political incentives; in other instances, governments may make hollow promises to the international organizations. Thus, the key challenge is to isolate the effect of the institutions.

To assess when and how the Organization for Security and Cooperation in Europe (OSCE), the Council of Europe (CE), and the European Union (EU) have influenced governments to pass certain legislation on ethnic minorities, I have analyzed ethnic minority policy in Latvia, Estonia, Slovakia, and Romania from 1990 to 1999.[3] Although the EU, the OSCE, and

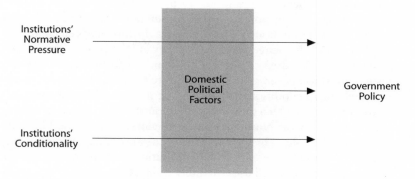

Figure 1.1. Basic analytical framework.

the CE made many specific recommendations on ethnic policy during this time, there has been little systematic examination of the policy effects within specific countries.[4]

Whereas previous studies have focused on one of these institutions and its particular methods and effects, this is the first to examine all three as well as two distinct institutional strategies for influencing behavior: "normative pressure," and conditionality. Briefly, normative pressure occurs when an institution advises a government on the direction a policy should take, offering no reward other than the approbation of the institution. Conditionality, on the other hand, involves explicitly linking the change advocated to an incentive, a particular benefit provided by the institution. I specifically examine the use of institutional membership as an incentive and the benefits that accompany progress toward admission, paying particular attention to the timing and design of conditionality strategies.[5]

Further, I ask how domestic factors, for instance, opposition in parliament to international policy preferences, shape policy outcomes and the overall effectiveness of international efforts. Some have protested that scholars operate in a shallow political environment when thinking about compliance and have thus failed to consider historic and domestic contexts (Collier 1997, 54; Killick 1998, 156). To avoid this pitfall, I examine how domestic politicians—nationalist politicians and parties, authoritarian leaders, or ethnic minority politicians—influence policy outcomes. (See figure 1.1.)

THE ARGUMENT

I argue that European institutions have been significant, active participants in shaping domestic policy on ethnic issues. I make three claims about their effects. First, membership conditionality by the EU and occasionally by the CE motivated most policy decisions, but normative pressure often guided them. That is, case after case illustrates the link between conditionality and decisions to change policies, but they also show how the CE and especially the OSCE often shaped the substance of the solutions. Second, domestic opposition posed greater obstacles to normative pressure than it did to membership conditionality. When European institutions used only normative pressure—which they did quite frequently—governments rarely changed their behavior. Normative pressure alone failed to build a sufficient coalition for policy change when the domestic opposition was strong. Subsequently, in the few cases in which normative pressure influenced ethnic policy without the added use of conditionality, the domestic opposition was usually low and the effect was only moderate. Third, as domestic opposition to concessions on ethnic policy grew, membership conditionality was not only increasingly necessary to change behavior, but it was also surprisingly effective. Membership conditionality enticed policymakers to compromise, whether they agreed in principle or not. Willingness to compromise, however, depended less on the initial position of policy makers than on how much they wanted the reward. Thus, given the countries' high desire to join the CE and EU, these institutions were well positioned to exercise political conditionality and were able to overcome surprising levels of opposition to their proposed policy changes. This was especially true on ethnic minority issues, which presented credible concerns about regional ethnic stability, and thus appeared as highly credible requirements. In addition, membership conditionality was particularly effective, because the prolonged multiple-step process of joining the EU provided multiple levers of influence over time and diverse ways of building confidence within the applicant states through gradual rewards for partial accomplishments.

Why Study Ethnic Issues in Europe?

There are several reasons to focus on ethnic issues in Europe. First, ethnic issues facilitate a good research design for understanding the role of international actors on the domestic scene. Ethnic issues subject institutions to a stringent test, because ethnic reforms are generally more difficult for international actors to influence than technical or economic reforms; while technical or economic issues may face powerful domestic lobbies and the like, they do not address core identity the way ethnicity does (Hardin 1995). Further, ethnic issues lend themselves to analysis because good variation marks the independent variable: involvement by international institutions. Although ethnic issues have tended not to hit the international radar screen until tensions turned violent, European institutions have been involved in many of these issues at preconflict stages, in large part because of concerns raised by the war in former Yugoslavia, coupled with the process of how such issues could affect institutional enlargement and integration in Europe—if cooperation between postcommunist and western Europe were to increase, western Europe wanted to minimize potential instability. International institutions, however, could not and did not get involved in every ethnic issue, nor did they have the political will to engage equally in all countries. Furthermore, each institution had unique resources and strategies for engagement. Such variety in the methods and degrees of institutional involvement thus provides excellent material for studying the role of international institutions as domestic policy actors and for examining the compelling questions surrounding early intervention in ethnic issues.

Second, ethnic issues hold high priority on the international agenda. At the 1919 Peace Conference, President Wilson said, "Nothing . . . is more likely to disturb the peace of the world than the treatment which might in certain circumstances be meted out to minorities" (quoted in Macartney 1934, 297). Indeed, the roots of ethnic politics can be traced to religious minorities as far back as the thirteenth century and more recently to the Berlin Congress in 1878. With the establishment of League of Nations, the issue of minority protection reached a new level (Rosting 1923; Claude 1955). The peace settlements that followed World War I firmly linked territorial transfers to obligations for international protection of ethnic minorities.[6] After World War II, however, the emphasis shifted from minority protection to the promotion of individual human rights. Human rights standards have unfortunately proven insufficient to address ethnic minority problems. Today, laws on citizenship and national minorities continue to be matters of public debate in Europe, as in the rest of the world. What are the membership principles of citizenship? What rights do immigrants have? Are they aliens or citizens-in-waiting? How should states treat national minorities? Do states assimilate or recognize difference and encourage separateness?[7]

In Europe, such issues became hot policy topics after the fall of Communism and after the war in the former Yugoslavia. The shifting occupations and geopolitical influences of twentieth-century Europe left large ethnic minority groups outside their national homelands; indeed, in central and eastern Europe, about one in four persons lived as minorities (Weidenfeld 2000). In Slovakia Hungarians comprised nearly 10 percent of the population of five million, and in Romania they comprised 7 to 8 percent of the population of twenty-two million. Both countries also had considerable numbers of Roma or gypsies and other minority groups. Several Russian-speaking peoples from the former Soviet Union constituted almost a third of Estonia's population and half of Latvia's population. Thus, in the 1990s, such "host" countries—especially Baltic and central European states—

struggled to address ethnic minority issues including residency rights, citizenship, language and education rights, and so forth, with significant variation in solutions and results. Furthermore, the timing for the resolution of issues varied among countries, just as degrees of accommodation varied among issues. Thus, the ethnic conflicts of the last decades demonstrate that the relationship between a state and its ethnic minorities is of pressing practical relevance to issues such as democracy and conflict (Dixon 1993).

Finally, how the international community can calm ethnic issues is a growing field of interest to regional organizations, nongovernmental organizations, and others. Although ethnic issues in Europe illuminate the role of international actors in domestic politics, however, research on the role of such institutions in shaping domestic politics on ethnic issues is scarce and tends to focus on a single institution (Michalchuk 1999; Kemp 2001; Ratner 1999).[8] While journalists and observers in general have tended to credit, for example, EU enlargement with policy reforms in the candidate states, little theorizing and systematic inquiry has explored the specific effects on ethnic minority policies or on how different institutional efforts have contributed to outcomes. Studying several mechanisms of influence side by side thus delivers both practical and theoretically valuable insights.

EXPLAINING COMPLIANCE

The literature offers several alternative explanations for a state's choice of ethnic minority policies. To understand domestic policymaking, political scientists examine domestic factors and how domestic redistribution of power among social groups and political actors leads to certain outcomes. Thus, scholars of ethnic issues emphasize the role of a nation's demographics, political system of representation, and the relationship among the ethnic groups within a country.[9] While such factors naturally represent an important part of the puzzle of explaining ethnic policy, outcomes were nevertheless more compatible with international norms than with the preferences of the dominant domestic actors, even when domestic opposition was quite strong. Gaining a more detailed understanding of how the domestic politics interacts with other factors is therefore important.

Another set of influences on a state's ethnic minority policies comes from homelands such as Russia or Hungary, which may use economic or military leverage to influence states to moderate their treatment of ethnic minorities (Brubaker 1995; Brubaker 1996; Van Heuten 1998). I explore such homeland pressures but find that they do not account fully for the pattern of legislative changes that occurred. While Russia in particular had a complex and influential relationship with the Baltic States, little evidence supports that Russia motivated legislation to accommodate ethnic minorities. Indeed, in several instances Russia's efforts created more resentment than cooperation. Russia and Hungary, however, did play an indirect role by using international institutions to call attention to ethnic issues. This may at times explain why institutions became involved but does not explain the outcomes.

Finally, ethnic policies may simply improve over time, perhaps because general democratic improvements within the state lead to policy improvements, perhaps because the *type* of institutional involvement matters less than the duration of involvement. Since institutions tend to use normative pressure as a first resort and add incentives only later, the analysis could thus erroneously credit incentives when the real cause of change may be persistence. This explanation, however, is also unsatisfactory; several cases contradict such a time-based pattern, as evidenced both by aggregate data analysis and in the policy issues I carefully trace in chapters 4 through 7. (I return to these alternative explanations in chapter 8.)

Thus, prior explanations for compliance in the area of ethnic minority policies are insufficient. Indeed, after discussing Brubaker's classic triangular nexus of minority, majority, and homeland, van Houten acknowledges that "extending the theory by incorporating the role of other states and international organizations (including the interaction between [homeland] state and these external actors) is a promising direction for further research" (1998, 140).

The Role of International Institutions

International relations theory offers several mechanisms through which international institutions may influence state behavior. This study focuses on two specific mechanisms, which are defined according to whether or not they rely on membership incentives. First is straight membership conditionality, whereby institutions link admission directly to behavior; this is akin to the conventional use of conditionality and incentives. With this mechanism, states respond to incentives and sanctions imposed by international actors, thereby maximizing a (mostly) constant set of preferences or interests. Such theory corresponds with a rationalist set of assumptions that defines actors as cost-benefit-calculating, utility-maximizing creatures. A comment by Bulgarian Prime Minister Ivan Kostov in April 2000 fits well with this theory: "The West does not really interest me. . . . So, with all my respect for the West, I am watching there only the opinion of the structures, which finance Bulgaria. All the others, whatever they say, are of no importance."[10]

The second mechanism, normative pressure, groups a broader set of socialization processes that may include social influence or persuasion efforts. The defining feature of this mechanism is that external actors do not link any concrete incentives to behavior but rely solely on the use of norms to persuade, shame, or praise actors into changing their policies. Several causal mechanisms can thus be at play.[11] Along the line of more constructivist explanations, normative pressure may operate by changing actors' beliefs and ultimately their behavior (Johnston 2001, 488). Normative pressure, however, also describes other forms of socialization such as social influence that can lead actors to display pro-norm behavior in the absence of exogenous material incentives (ibid., 495). Actors may, for example, rely on a more calculating use of norms as a way to solicit behavior change through a state's concern for its reputation (Schimmelfennig 2001). While reputational concerns are essentially focused on benefits of future exchange (Kreps 1992), social influence is still a much softer method than outright conditionality. As I discuss in chapter 2, this study does not evaluate which of these causal pathways is at work but instead uses this theory to derive hypotheses about when normative pressure is likely to result in behavior change.

Conditionality and normative pressure are thus similar to enforcement and managerial explanations of compliance. As Kal Raustiala and Anne-Marie Slaughter (2002) note, tying aid or other concrete benefits to a discursive process corresponds with managerial theory, while linking compliance and payoff corresponds with enforcement theory. In reality, however, the two mechanisms are by no means mutually exclusive, as actors presumably base their actions on a combination of normative and rationalist considerations. This, indeed, is what makes studying both under the same framework so compelling.[12]

Doing so, however, requires a strategy for sorting out the effects of norms and incentives. This is tricky because rational choice scholars who study incentives tend to focus on behavior change, while constructivists who study norms tend to study belief change. With the proper caution, though, it is possible as well as productive to study both mechanisms in terms of their policy effects. Therefore, I treat the theories and relevant variables side-by-side, develop testable hypotheses about the policy effects of both mechanisms, and subject them both to extensive empirical analysis in the context of domestic politics.

This study builds on mutual theoretical concessions that constructivists and rationalists have recently hinted at but have not fully developed (Fearon and Wendt 2002). While the economic models of compliance traditionally assume that inducing compliance "is a matter of getting the incentives right" (Checkel 2000a, 4), some rational choice scholars suggest that norms influence how actors maximize their interests. Thus, Judith Goldstein and Robert Keohane (1993) argue that under conditions of uncertainty or incomplete information, instrumentally rational actors can use ideas as road maps or signposts indicating how they could best realize their interests under given circumstances. At the same time, several constructivist scholars emphasize that instrumental and normative actions work in tandem or that instrumental action may dominate the early stages of socialization or even trigger the effects of socialization (Finnemore and Sikkink 1998, 909; Ikenberry and Kupchan 1990, 284). Thus, this study feeds into the debate about the respective role of norms and incentives, and advances beyond the either/or debate between rationalists and constructivists.

Policy Tools: Achieving Compliance

Many scholars and practitioners question the effectiveness of non-incentive-based methods that rely on persuasion or social pressure. Talk is cheap, but do results follow (Shannon 2000)? Organizations such as the OSCE and the CE have been praised for easing ethnic tensions, but few comparative studies systemically evaluate the effectiveness of their efforts toward persuasion in terms of achieving policy goals. The level of detailed case studies required often leads to one- or two-country case studies, which makes it harder to extrapolate general implications from the findings. And because these studies tend to have belief change, not policy change, as the dependent variable, applying the findings to policy is harder. This study, on the other hand, examines cases of non-incentive-based methods in the light of their policy results. By so doing, this study is less able to speak to the causal mechanisms of norm-based methods but is better equipped to inform policy choices about when to use such methods.

The policy effects of different kinds of conditionality are also ambiguous. Research on aid conditionality identifies several weaknesses of the approach, such as recidivism (Bird 2001a; Bird 2001b; Vermeersch 2002), moral hazard, lack of ownership, and pure ineffectiveness (Martinez-Vasquez et al. 2001; Bird 2001a; Bird 2001b; Baehr 1997; Collier et al. 1997; Killick 1996). Similarly, some scholars of sanctions find them blunt and slow (Drezner 2000), while others conclude that sanctions can be effective (Hufbauer, Scott, and Elliot 1990).

Although aid conditionality and sanctions differ from membership conditionality, membership conditionality may very well suffer from similar weaknesses. Most relevant to the goals of this book, EU scholars have specifically criticized EU conditionality (Grabbe 2001). Some point out that EU conditionality is too externally imposed and thus causes anger within applicant states (Fierke and Wiener 1999), or that western Europe's "missionary" attitude endangers the social and political progress of eastern Europe.[13] Others point out that the EU preaccession strategy is too broad and difficult to measure in practice among different applicants (Grabbe and Hughes 1998, 41 ff). Most often, however, critics argue that EU advice has sometimes been internally inconsistent, either because different institutional actors have contradicted one another or because individual member states have instituted policies that violated EU-espoused norms (Amato and Batt 1998; Grabbe 2001; De Witte 2000).

To understand the practical domestic implications of conditionality in general and political membership conditionality in particular, more research is necessary.[14] Empirical analysis of the effectiveness of positive incentives in various fields such as development, international trade, environmental policy, and arms control has emerged only in the last decade (Oye 1992; Keohane and Levy 1996; Bernauer and Ruloff 1999). Davis notes, "Positive incentives, defined here as transfers of positively valued resources from one actor to another with the aim of influencing the recipient's behavior, are among the most understudied if frequently employed tools of international statecraft" (2000, 312). Bernauer similarly notes, "Theorizing about the conditions under which positive incentives are used and are effective or efficient lags far behind developments in the 'real world' " (1999, 157). For example, can institutions apply conditionality to require "peace reforms" that will decrease conflict (Boyce and Pastor 1998; Reinicke 1996; World Bank 1997; Boyce 1996)?

Furthermore, the potential benefits of positive incentives warrant continued study. While a promise can be turned into a threat and vice versa, as argued by Shelling (1960, n. 24), positive and negative incentives cannot always be reduced to two sides of the same coin. The key difference is in actors' baseline expectation and whether others' actions represent a gain or a loss relative to that baseline (Baldwin 1971, 24–27). The distinction is important because positive incentives have different behavioral implications than do negative incentives. Because they create less resentment in the recipient, positive incentives are more likely to facilitate constructive dialogue and greater interaction and understanding (Cortright 1997, 11; Long 1996). Indeed, Baldwin notes, "B's immediate reaction to sticks usually differs from his immediate reaction to carrots. Whereas fear, anxiety, and resistance are typical responses to threats, the typical responses to promises are hope, reassurance, and attraction" (1971, 32).[15] Whereas sanctions and negative incentives are usually applied as a punishment in response to an action, positive incentives have the advantage that they can be employed preemptively (Hurlburt 1997, 226), which makes them better suited to a range of issues where avoidance of conflict is a high priority.

Finally, existing organizations such as the World Trade Organization (WTO), the Organization of Economic Cooperation and Development (OECD), the North Atlantic Treaty Organization (NATO), and others have opportunities to put knowledge about membership incentives to use. New organizations also emerge at a considerable rate and can design admission policies to optimize leverage (Shanks et al. 1996). In addition, this study may also have implications for general membership organizations.

Ongoing approval by an institution may also be a useful incentive, as became evident when the EU in 2000 condemned the Austrian government, which included the nationalist Freedom Party; although furious, the Austrian government took EU concerns seriously and made efforts to commit itself to a course of action compatible with EU wishes to maintain normal relations with the institution.[16] Thus, in a world of growing interdependence, the ability to include and exclude remains a potent tool.

METHODOLOGY

Because this study seeks to understand the role of international institutions as domestic policy actors, it assesses most rigorously and productively the effectiveness of international institutions by examining policy as a dependent variable (Ruggie 1998, 880–84). Chapter 2 discusses this decision in much greater depth, including the ramifications for theoretical and practical inferences as well as the relationship between compliance and implementation. I evaluate policy in terms of compatibility of legislation with international recommendations and international standards in general.[17] *Compatibility* or *compliance* indicates when state policy accords with the recommendations that international institutions express (Simmons 2000, 1). Measurement of compatibility rests on a thorough examination of the legislative outcome and implementation, not of the attitudes of actors or their willingness to comply.

Country Selection

Because domestic factors are an essential part of understanding policy outcomes, appropriate case selection is crucial; herein are case studies from Latvia, Estonia, Slovakia, and Romania from 1990 to 1999. These four countries provide a good analytical set; Latvia and Estonia share several historical, cultural, and economic traits, as do Slovakia and Romania, although to a lesser extent. Also, the main ethnic minority group in both Latvia and Estonia is the Russian-speaking population, while the largest ethnic group in both Romania and Slovakia is the Hungarian population. Thus, good grounds for comparison exist. At the same time, when one examines the individual policy of each government, the variation in how European institutions treated each country becomes evident. For example, the institutions tended to use conditionality more frequently in Slovakia than in the Baltic States. Sometimes institutions pursued one strategy in one of the four countries, while pursuing a different strategy in another. Sometimes an institution pursued similar strategies in different countries simultaneously but achieved either different results or differently timed results. And several cases did not involve institutions at all. Naturally, too, domestic factors varied over time and between issues. In particular, Slovakia and Romania had periods of authoritarian leadership, while Latvia and Estonia did not. On the other hand, while Latvia and Estonia had larger proportions of ethnic minorities, only Slovakia and Romania had actual minority representation in government.

These four countries represent a balanced empirical sampling and thus afford analysis with good variation in both dependent and independent variables. The data also allow the hypothesis about normative persuasion and conditionality to be rejected, because about half the cases included herein are not cases of successful policy adaptation. At the same time, I have included an approximately equal number of cases that completely lack institutional involvement (as a control group) and those that involve the two institutional mechanisms under consideration.

Domestic Contexts

Latvia and Estonia both enjoyed independence in the interwar period. In June 1940, however, the Soviet Union annexed both countries, followed a year later by German invasion and at the end of World War II by Soviet reoccupation. After World War II Moscow encouraged large-scale immigration to Estonia and Latvia from other parts of the USSR, and in 1949–1950 deported many Estonians and Latvians to Siberia. Russians immigrants arrived either as workers or as part of the Soviet military. Since Moscow did not encourage Russian immigrants to integrate, few learned to speak Estonian or Latvian, and two separate ethnic communities emerged in each country. By 1989 the Latvian share of Latvia's population had declined from 82 percent in 1943 to 52 percent, and the Estonian share of Estonia's population had declined from 98 percent in 1945 to 62 percent.[18]

When Latvia and Estonia regained independence, they faced the challenges of dealing with large non-Latvian and non-Estonian populations, including questions of citizenship, residency, education, elections, and language.[19] Ethnic tensions naturally emerged. Decades of Soviet occupation left many Latvians and Estonians with ethnic nationalist preferences, and few of the proposed solutions favored the Russian-speaking ethnic minorities. For example, Latvia's initial resolution and law on citizenship prevented a third of the country's population from acquiring citizenship. These so-called noncitizens not only lacked citizenship in Latvia or Estonia, but most were essentially stateless because the collapse of the Soviet Union.[20] They faced critical restrictions on their rights, including limits on travel, the inability to pursue certain professions (e.g., as firefighters or airline pilots), and the denial of certain state benefits. Many noncitizens had voted for independence and felt cheated when they were denied citizenship and voting rights in the newly independent countries. Latvians and Estonians, on the other hand, were weary of fifty years of "occupation," as they called the period of Soviet rule, and felt a need to assert their cultural and linguistic identity.

Although the situation was generally similar in Latvia and Estonia, the influence of nationalists varied.[21] Latvian politicians wanted to reestablish and protect the Latvian state. While this was on its face a positive agenda, many party programs included specific policies that were less benign. Many politicians, for instance, supported limiting naturalization so that "Latvians" constituted about 75 percent of the population. Thus, parties such as Fatherland and Freedom (FF) and the Latvian National Independence Movement (LNIM) opposed the Russian population.[22] Initially, even the leading Latvia's Way party, which was not perceived as nationalist, strongly opposed citizenship rights for the Russian population.

Although Estonia's share of nonnationals was less than Latvia's, ethnic relations were acute throughout the transitional period. Only a third of the Russian-speaking population favored independence, while another third categorically opposed it. After decades of repression of national identity, Estonian politicians urged caution about language and other rights for noncitizens and ethnic non-Estonians. The Estonian National Independence Party (ENIP) and the Fatherland coalition, which came out of the independence movement, were representative of the nationalist trend in Estonia. Although their programs were less extreme than the nationalist parties in Latvia, and although Estonia adopted a technically more liberal citizenship law than Latvia, Estonian reluctance to accommodate noncitizens was pervasive. Nationalism did not simply wane over time.[23] Comparison of Latvia and Estonia is particularly fruitful because the governments' degree of opposition to accommodating ethnic minorities varied, as did the timing of policy issues and the actions of the European institutions.

Slovakia and Romania share the key feature of having about a 7 to 10 percent Hungarian minority, many of whom live concentrated in regions or in border areas with Hungary. Before the 1990s both countries were strongly Communist, downplaying ethnic identity in favor of party identity, and both countries had long-term relationships with Hungary. In Romania, the key region for ethnic Hungarians is Transylvania. During the Communist period Romania denied ethnic Hungarians minority privileges and bulldozed many Hungarian villages in the name of land reform. By the mid-1980s not a single Hungarian secondary school remained open and bilingual signs had all but disappeared. Ironically, it was ethnic minorities who initiated the overthrow of the Communist dictator Nicolae Ceausescu. The revolutionary move toward democratization fueled—not decreased—ethnic tension (Verdery 1993; Stan 1997). When tensions flared in Transylvania, they led to a deadly encounter in March 1990.[24] This was the first serious interethnic flare-up in eastern Europe following the collapse of communism. "Once again Transylvania seemed to be the paradigm example of an ethnically-based territorial dispute in Eastern Europe," as Tom Gallagher wrote (quoted in Stan 1997, 29). Anti-Hungarian sentiment continued throughout the 1990s, accompanied by controversies about language rights and education, and continued even after election losses in 1996 (Gross and Tismaneanu 1997, 30).[25] Indeed, although Ion Iliescu won the 2000 presidential election with 67 percent of the vote, even more telling was extremist Corneliu Vadim Tudor's capture of 33 percent of the vote.

Slovakia has shared some traits with Romania, although historical, economic, and cultural differences abound. After World War II Czechoslovakia turned Communist and, in accordance with urban integration policy, built houses only in so-called central settlements, not in smaller villages, resulting in school mergers and closure of countryside schools that had benefited ethnic minorities. Thus, the number of students in schools with Hungarian-language teaching almost halved between 1970 and 1989. When Soviet influence collapsed in 1989, problems emerged in ethnically mixed regions. In the 1992 elections, the Movement for a Democratic Slovakia (PSDR) secured overwhelming support and quickly created a coalition government with the nationalist and xenophobic Slovak National Party (SNS). In July 1992 the new Slovak National Parliament proclaimed Slovakia's sovereignty—in contrast to Romania, where borders did not change. With the January 1993 dissolution of Czechoslovakia, Hungarians became a much more visible minority group, their proportion rising from 3 percent in Czechoslovakia to about 9 percent in the new Slovakia. With only a brief interlude, Vladimir Meciar's nationalist government ruled until the 1998 elections. Romania and Slovakia thus provide good cases for comparison because the ethnic population has similar proportions as well as some shared cultural and historical traits.

The foursome of countries also offers some opportunities for larger scale comparison and contrast. Unlike Latvia and Estonia, for instance, both Slovakia and Romania have had periods of authoritarian leadership in the 1990s. In Romania during Iliescu's reign the postcommunist secret service directly influenced political personalities, publication of secret service files, and surveillance of journalists and other critics of the government (Tismaneanu 1996). Iliescu depended on nationalist parties and his own renowned use of nationalist rhetoric to gain popularity. As one analyst noted in 1996, "The country has been governed primarily by decrees. Pressures on local officials to toe the government line intensified after 1993. . . . [T]he real center of power is thus located in the presidential palace, rather than in the government or in the two parliamentary chambers" (ibid., 8, 10).

Meciar ran Slovakia in a manner similar to Iliescu—only worse. He too depended on nationalists and nationalism to keep power. In the early-to-mid-1990s, he became a political outcast from the West, his authoritarian arrogance stemming in part from his belief that Slovakia was too important for the West to shun; he repeatedly reassured the citizenry that the West "has no other option than to embrace Slovakia" ("Constitution Watch" 1997). Also like Iliescu, Meciar was reluctant to join the EU. As a Slovak policy expert put it, "There was no compatibility between the national government under Meciar and the declared foreign policy goals."[26] Meciar was more comfortable with his relations with Russia.[27] He despised EU meddling in his governing style and feared, correctly, that following EU standards of democracy would undermine his hold on power.[28]

The cases studied herein further detail the influence of domestic opposition in the four countries. Table 1.1 summarizes the changes of governments and the varying influence of more nationalist-leaning politicians in domestic politics. While table 1.1 makes an overall evaluation of domestic opposition to minority rights during each government period, the larger study allows for greater consideration of the details. Furthermore, table 1.1 evaluates the influence of nationalist-leaning parties in parliament, not the level of racism in the country, which may be very different. For this period, Slovakia has demonstrated a strong nationalist influence for the greatest percentage time, followed closely by Romania. For most of the time, Latvia has experienced a strong or moderately strong influence by politicians and parties opposed to extended minority rights, with Estonia having the mildest overall influence of nationalist-leaning parties.

Type of Institutional Engagement

The study design herein relies on understanding the variation of institutional engagement in the four countries. The EU, OSCE, and CE were the most engaged in ethnic issues, and they operated with different resources and strategies. Sometimes the institutions engaged heavily, while at other times ethnic issues went seemingly unnoticed. Sometimes institutions made clear links between behavior and institutional membership, while at other times they relied primarily on persuasion of policy actors. The real independent variable was not the institutions themselves, however, but their mechanism of influence. Institutions and mechanisms are not congruent but can work with both normative pressure and membership incentives, except in the case of the OSCE. Thus, the variable is not only the identity or function of the institution, but what it does.

The OSCE admitted most new states quickly, and thus never directly used membership conditionality as a mechanism for influence.[29] Rather, it used normative pressure in the form of persuasion and social influence as its primary method. The OSCE has several lengthy texts that specify educational

TABLE 1.1

General influence of parties opposed to extended minority rights in Slovakia, Romania, Estonia, and Latvia, 1990–1999

Country and Dates	Majority government	Ethnic Minorities in government?	Seats in parliament	Position in parliament	General influence	Percent time influence
Slovakia						
June 1992–Mar. 1994	no, then yes	no	91/150	In government	Strong	Strong 77%
Mar. 1994–Dec. 1994	no	support	less than 91/150	In opposition	weak to moderate	
Dec. 1994–Nov. 1998	yes	no	83/150	In government	Strong	weak, or weak to moderate 23%
Dec. 1998–present	yes	yes	56/150	In opposition	weak	
Romania						
May 1990–Sept. 1992	yes	no	263/396 deputies 92/119 senators	In government	Strong	Strong 72%
Nov. 1992–Oct. 1996	yes, then no	no	176/341 deputies 74/143 senators	In government	Strong	
Dec. 1996–April 1998	yes, then no	Yes	128/341 deputies 56/143 senators	In opposition	weak	Weak 28%
April 1998–Dec. 1999	Yes	Yes	128/341 deputies 56/143 senators	In opposition	weak	
Estonia						
Aug. 1991–Sept. 1992	*	No	Poorly defined	Poorly defined	Moderate	Moderate 76%
Oct. 1992–Mar. 1995	Yes	No	41/101	In government	Moderate	
April 1995–Mar. 1997	Yes, then No	No	8/101	In opposition	Moderate	Weak to moderate 24%
Mar. 1997–Mar. 1999	No	No	8/101	In opposition	Weak to moderate	
Mar. 1999–present	Yes	No	18/101	In government	Moderate	
Latvia						
May 1990–Aug. 1993	Yes	No	Poorly defined	Poorly defined	Moderate to strong	Strong 30%
Aug. 1993–July 1994	No	No	21/100	In opposition**	Moderate to strong	
Sept. 1994–Dec. 1995	No	No	21/100	In opposition**	Moderate	Moderate to strong 56%
Dec. 1995–July 1997	Yes	No	22/100	In government	Strong	
Aug. 1997–Nov. 1998	yes, then No	No	22/100	In government	Strong	
Nov. 1998–July 1999	No	No	17/100	In government	Moderate to strong	Moderate 14%
July 1999–present	Yes	No	17/100	In government	Moderate to strong	

Source: Coding based on the qualitative case studies by author.

* Difficult to speak of majorities within this government as individual party affiliations were unclear.

** During the Vahi and Siimann governments, the moderate character came from the coalition agreement to not change the laws on citizenship, language and residency. This locked the government into retaining poor policies–a preference equivalent to that of a parliament with a moderate nationalists influence and language rights for ethnic minorities. Since these are not legally binding and since the OSCE was quite liberal in granting admission in the late 1980s and early 1990s, countries initially paid little attention to the OSCE's comments. Nevertheless, the OSCE has gradually gained stature from the EU's reliance on the OSCE High Commissioner on National Minorities as an expert on minority rights. Finally, the OSCE has had the highest degree of "on the ground" involvement and thus perhaps the highest level of in-country expertise and political dialogue; it has also made the greatest effort to normatively persuade policymakers to change their behavior.

The OSCE has three primary instruments for addressing minority rights issues. Fact-finding and rapporteur missions are short-term visits by experts and personalities from OSCE-participating states to ascertain how well recently admitted states are progressing with OSCE commitments.[30] Missions, or field offices, are the OSCE's principal instrument for long-term conflict prevention, crisis management, conflict resolution, and post-conflict rehabilitation in its sphere of influence. The purposes of the missions usually are to facilitate the political processes that are intended to prevent or settle conflicts, and to inform the OSCE. The OSCE has not deployed missions in Romania or Slovakia, but it did open missions in Latvia and Estonia in 1993.

Most relevant to this study, however, was the OSCE's creation in 1992 of the position of High Commissioner on National Minorities (HCNM) as "an instrument of conflict prevention at the earliest possible stage."[31] Netherlands Minister of State Max van der Stoel was appointed as the first high commissioner in December 1992, and throughout the 1990s he worked with all four countries examined in this study. He visited them frequently—often two or three times a year, sometimes twice in a month—and wrote several letters with specific comments on legislation. He operated primarily within the framework of normative pressure, using persuasion and social influence.

The CE admitted Estonia, Romania, and Slovakia in 1993, and Latvia in 1995. Although the CE did at times pursue the strategy of using admission to solicit changes in the behavior of states, as in the case of Latvia, this was not its primary approach. Instead, the CE obtained "commitments" from states to take certain actions by specific dates with regard to human rights and the treatment of noncitizens.[32] The council chose this strategy in the belief that it could most effectively influence states that were inside rather than outside the council. Thus, the CE's approach has mostly been one of persuasion and social influence rather than use of incentives.

As an institution with an extensive human-rights mission, the CE has generated specific documents related to the protection of minorities. The first and most controversial document on minority issues is Recommendation 1201. Drafted in 1993, it refers to the rights of ethnic minorities in

CE member states.[33] Since 1993 it has been included as a "commitment" in the assembly's officially issued "opinions" on the admission of new member states to the CE.[34]

In addition, the CE has two treaties related specifically to minorities. The first is the 1992 European Charter on the Protection of Minority Languages.[35] CE member states, however, protective of their own legislation, have been slow to ratify the charter.[36] Neither Slovakia, Romania, Latvia, nor Estonia has signed this treaty, and all the signatories have attached reservations to their ratification of the treaty.[37] The second is the 1993 Framework Convention for the Protection of National Minorities.[38] The committee of ministers is called on to "monitor" the implementation of the convention, with the assistance of a committee of experts.[39] A delegation of the official advisory committee, created to oversee the convention, can visit the countries, but only after the contracting state provides a required initial report.[40]

In addition, the CE has several practical tools for interacting with states on minority issues. The CE sends fact-finding missions and monitors (or rapporteurs, in CE terms) to the target countries. A series of visits occurs before admission, followed by another series of monitoring mechanisms after admission that trace how states work to fulfill the promises they made on joining the CE. Monitoring mechanisms can be closed and then reopened when there are causes for concern. Visits normally result in a written report stating causes for concern and stressing the changes needed to address deficiencies. Another, more distinct CE function is to send teams of legislative experts to aid in the drafting of legislation. The CE also offers a special guest status to engage nonmembers in institutional activities.

The EU differs most starkly from the OSCE and the CE in that its substantive background in ethnic issues is quite thin. Until the 1990s EU references to human rights and democracy were not explicit and did not emphasize minority rights.[41] In 1993, however the Copenhagen European Council laid down more specific political criteria for the associated countries of central and eastern Europe that wished to accede. The war in the former Yugoslavia contributed to the redefinition, particularly in western Europe, of the nature and importance of minority issues; it also lent credibility to addressing these issues as more than rhetoric. Among the binding political criteria was the ensurance of respect for human rights as well as *respect for and the protection of minorities*.[42] Thus, more than any other institution in Europe, the EU has practiced political membership conditionality.

The EU's explicit linkage of political criteria, including minority rights, to admission was credible because it made sense from a security perspective. Candidate states knew that current member states had to address very real concerns stemming from the conflict in the former Yugoslavia. The emphasis on democracy, human rights, and minority rights was also increasingly obvious to candidate states as the EU developed enlargement processes and mechanisms, such as annual reports and official "accession partnerships," by which the EU could publicly review the issues. Nevertheless, at least until the mid-1990s, how the EU would weigh such political issues in comparison to other EU concerns such as agriculture and economic reforms remained unclear.

The commission opinions—the EU Commission's official evaluation of countries preparedness to join the EU, released in July 1997—clearly emphasized political criteria. The commission systematically considered whether candidate countries had adhered to the European Convention on Human Rights and to the primary UN instruments related to human rights and ethnic minority rights, among other conventions. The commission opinions furthermore took a broad conception of what constituted a minority, including in its definition that part of the permanent population that does not hold citizenship in its given country. The opinions made it clear that political criteria, including human rights and minority rights, would be considered in the admission process. The principal legal advisor to the EU Commission said, "I was surprised in [the] 1997 [opinions] that the commissioners allowed as much of the human rights material to remain in the final reports produced as they did."[43]

The seriousness of these political criteria gained credibility when, based on the July 2000 commission opinion, the EU chose not to open negotiations with the politically offensive Slovakia. The December 1997 summit had already confirmed the importance of the Copenhagen criteria for opening accession negotiations, and the official accession partnerships that had been forged in the spring of 1998 included further conditionality clauses to be applied if an applicant country breached the initial criteria.[44] The accession partnerships also set out practical short- and long-term political goals for candidate states.

The EU's primary tools for addressing minority concerns have been annual reports and various official declarations, such as presidency declarations, demarches, and EU parliamentary resolutions.[45] Dialogue has remained open through local missions, visits by EU presidents and commissioners, the commission country-desk personnel in Brussels, and interaction in joint-committee meetings at various levels in EU candidate countries. The EU has also used key events, such as the issuance of reports or the holding of European Council meetings, to prompt and accelerate policy change. In sum, the EU has clearly practiced concrete conditionality but has lacked the depth of political dialogue characteristic of the CE and OSCE.

While these European institutions have different strategies, resources, and levels of engagement, their activities can nonetheless be divided into two fundamental mechanisms: normative pressure and membership conditionality. While the OSCE used only the first, and the EU mastered the latter, the

TABLE 1.2
Institutional mechanisms

Tools associated with normative pressure:

Direct official statements and declarations expressing opinion about current state and desired direction of policy.
Guidance and argumentation in written follow up reports from fact-finding visits.

Missions in the field/and hoc visits

Numerous personal interaction opportunities
Observation in policy process on political committees and parliament
Production of reports

Legal expert teams to guide and advise the policy as it is forming
Providing treaties and recommendations that outline the general standards for laws
Participation by national officials in institutional fora
Twinning: secondment of officials from EU countries to work in CEE ministries and the public administration

Tools associated with conditionality

Gate-keeping: accessing to negotiations and further steps in the accession process
Privileged trade and additional aid
Signing and implementing an enhanced form of association agreement

Benchmarking and monitoring
Ranking of applicants overall progess in annual reports (regular reports)
Decisions at important meetings that provide deadlines for action
Accession partnerships before negotiations identify gaps in legislation
Dialogue and interaction

Opening of negotiations
Opening and closing of 31 chapters
Signing of an accession treaty
Ratification of the accession treaty by national parliaments and European parliament

Adapted partly from Grabbe 2001.

CE straddled the divide by using both methods at various times. Further, the institutions often joined forces to apply both persuasion and conditionality. Table 1.2 outlines the practical tools associated with the two mechanisms.

The Membership Incentive: What's the Attraction?

The argument of this book is based on the assertion that membership in European institutions alters the payoff calculations of domestic policy actors, that is, that such membership is a valuable and unique asset. "Membership has its privileges," as the saying goes. But what exactly are they?

In the early 1990s membership was a positive incentive for postcommunist states, which were just then forming expectations and hopes about joining the "West" (Checkel 2000a; Schimmelfennig 2000). With the exception of some more extremist nationalist groups, for most policymakers membership served as proof of being modern or liberal and as a sign of their states' return to Europe as a democratizing, lawful country.[46] In James Baldwin's terms, membership was a positive incentive because it represented a gain from the baseline condition of having been outside the institutions for so long. Membership clearly had utilitarian benefits as well; emaciated by communism, states wanted to gain not only recognition and security but also prosperity by joining the "club" of institutions (Chayes and Chayes 1996, 118–127).

Most policymakers value EU membership in large part because of its economic advantages, but membership in the CE—and less so in the OSCE—also has concrete benefits, given the signals it sends to investors about political stability. Because information on government performance is costly, private agents may find it preferable to free ride on the decisions of international institutions and donors who are known to have invested considerable resources in monitoring performance (Collier 1997). Thus, joining the OSCE and the CE sends a signal of political stability, which is beneficial for investments, economic growth, and eligibility for international assistance. Catherine Lalumiere, who became the secretary-general of the CE in May 1989, stated that membership in the CE provides a "seal of respectability," offers proof that the member state is a pluralist parliamentary democracy and therefore eligible for Western support and benefits.[47]

Illustrating the benefits of membership, the president of the CE parliamentary assembly, Miguel Angel Martinez, assured Latvian parliamentarians that Latvia would receive extensive support from international organizations following its acceptance to the CE.[48] The CE secretary-general also discussed economic reform issues extensively on a visit to Romania.[49] Indeed, in June 1993 Slovakia was simultaneously negotiating with the International Monetary Fund (IMF) about funding and with the CE about membership. Prime Minister Meciar said that during his talks with the IMF in Switzerland, the issue of CE membership arose. He emphasized the significance of CE membership, saying

> Our admission to the Council of Europe does not just have the symbolic importance of a membership ticket. . . . As in the case of the IMF, which provides creditworthiness with banks, such an acknowledgement by the Council of Europe is a sign of confidence in the political system existing within the state. This is why we have been struggling to be accepted as a member of the Council of

Europe. We see in it a logical continuation of our endeavors to join the structures of more advanced states, more advanced political *and economic systems*. (emphasis added)[50]

Thus, in 1994 the head of the Latvian delegation to the CE, Andrei Panteleev, stressed that CE membership was of great importance to Latvia in securing already-promised investments from European institutions and as a first step toward joining the EU and NATO.[51] In sum, the majority of policymakers in aspiring member states clearly saw admission to the CE not only as an end in itself but as a means to other ends.

In the 1990s, however, OSCE and CE membership was primarily beneficial as a gateway to EU membership, good standing with the CE and the OSCE being an acknowledged requirement for admission to the EU.[52] As early as 1993, heads of state stressed that CE membership was a prerequisite for EU membership.[53] Thus, many eastern European countries applied for admission to get the CE stamp of legitimacy as a step toward integration with Europe (Manas 1996). Given the size of the candidate pool and the logistical restrictions on EU enlargement, candidates raced against one another to move forward. This competitive environment encouraged candidate states to meet compliance requirements to preserve their place in the accession queue (Grabbe 2001).[54] Thus, in several ways membership offered states improvements.

Design and Analysis

This study uses both quantitative and qualitative tools. To increase the number of observations beyond four large national cases and to enable a quasi-experimental design, I divide the country studies into sixty-four subcases, using different issues and governments over time to define cases (King, Keohane, and Verba 1994, 34).[55] Indeed, treating each country as one case would make it impossible to code, as there are multiple issues and types of intervention and outcomes within one country. Thus, how a specific government in power addresses education, for example, is a separate issue from how it addresses election laws; how a different government addresses these two issues again represents two different cases. Such division utilizes the variation within the four countries to make the analysis more efficient and systematic.

To examine how effective normative pressure and conditionality are at achieving compliance, I compare twenty-five cases in which normative pressure was used alone with nineteen cases in which institutions combined it with conditionality, and then again with twenty cases in which institutions were not involved at all. Statistical analysis makes it possible to isolate

Table 1.3
Basic study design

	Socialization	No socialization
Conditionality	(19 cases) Quantitative analysis can determine combined effectiviness of conditionality and socialization efforts. Case studies can probe the relative casual power.	(No cases) Counterfactual and other analysis must be used to consider how conditionality efforts would have fared in the absense of socialization efforts.
No conditionality	(25 cases) The study can determine the effectiveness of persuasion and social influence when used alone.	(20 caes) Control cases.

the independent effect of normative pressure and the combined effect of normative pressure and conditionality, and to control for other factors. Since conditionality is always used as an extension of normative pressure, however, evaluating the effectiveness of conditionality alone is more difficult. Thus, when drawing conclusions about conditionality, one should be cautious about how much the effectiveness is the result of normative pressure and how much is the result of conditionality itself (Checkel 2000a, 9). While I can infer the effectiveness of combining efforts, it may be that conditionality is completely responsible for achieving the outcome. On the other hand, even if I show normative pressure to be ineffective when used alone, I cannot conclude that, when combined with conditionality, it is not contributing to the outcome. In other words, statistically I can test if normative pressure is sufficient, but I cannot test if it is necessary. Conversely, I can test if conditionality is necessary, but I cannot test if it is sufficient. Finally, I can test if the combined use of conditionality and normative pressure is sufficient, but I cannot test if it is necessary. Table 1.3 shows the comparison of cases and the conclusions it facilitates.

Fortunately, the power of inference increases with the additional use of detailed case studies, which provide insights into the effects of each institution's individual actions. Here, it becomes somewhat possible to distinguish between responses to normative pressure and responses to conditionality by, for example, examining timing.

Thus, in detailed case studies, I rely on process tracing that may reveal the timing of events and action, the motives and attitudes of actors, and the substantive overlap between advice and policy outcomes. This helps me overcome Checkel's criticism that standard rationalist assumptions "lead many scholars to portray the roles of language and communication in purely strategic/informational terms and to erect a 'black box' around the interaction context from which decisions to comply emerge" (2001, 556). Furthermore, case studies help overcome the design issues discussed above in that, although I am still not able to separate the use of conditionality from the use of normative pressure, the examination of individual legislative cases through process tracing helps distinguish between different temporal phases in the influence process, phases characterized by no intervention, normative pressure only, and normative pressure plus conditionality. If behavioral change occurs only when conditionality comes into play, and if policy actors stress the need to adapt to meet the membership criteria, this strengthens claims that conditionality really was the efficient cause. In addition, in the conclusion I also employ counterfactual analysis to disentangle the effects. I discuss the variables and measurements more in chapter 3.

Data and Caveats

This study relies on careful analysis of all the legislative issues related to ethnic minorities from 1990 to 1999 in Latvia, Estonia, Slovakia, and Romania. I followed each issue over time and observed how international institutions were or were not involved in the issue, how the legislature addressed the issue, and how the issue in general fit into larger events such as parliamentary changes, elections, institutional developments, and the like. I examined all formal communication from each institution to the governments, including press releases, letters from officials or offices, fact-finding reports and regular opinions, special resolutions or declarations by institutional bodies, and statements by officials to the media. When possible I also considered informal or confidential communication, although I am not able to refer directly to it. To evaluate the players' preferences I used party platforms and other party documents; the rhetoric displayed in public and published in the media, including during political campaigns; texts of relevant parliamentary discussions; records of prior legislative proposals by parities; and numerous interviews with party officials and other domestic elites as well as with representatives of the international organizations.

While all theorizing is a dynamic process between deduction and induction, some cases were still developing as the study was ending, thus presenting clear opportunities to test new data rather than to rationalize from existing cases. The subhypotheses, however, are mostly later developments prompted by initial examination of the data.

Data are rarely perfect and are even less so in studies such as this. First, there are data limitations regarding sources and selection biases. Chapter

3 discusses how these affect the analysis. Since this study does not examine cases in which institutions used incentives without normative pressure, it can at best identify the combined effect of using normative pressure and conditionality. Separating these effects is difficult. Furthermore, the way that quantitative data are created prompts some caution to take findings as suggestive rather than conclusive, which is why qualitative analysis is a crucial component of this study. This is particularly true when it comes to testing interactive effects, as chapter 3 also discusses further.

PLAN OF THE BOOK

The book proceeds as follows. Chapter 2 discusses the theoretical framework more in-depth. I analyze the decision to examine behavior as the dependent variable and discuss the implications and inherent limitations of such a focus. Furthermore, I situate the mechanisms clearly in the context of previous scholarship by outlining how they connect to other concepts in the field. I pay particular attention to a discussion of normative pressure, since this term covers a range of traditional socialization mechanisms. Although the study does not aim to test the causal pathway of the different mechanisms, chapter 2 does debate the theoretical underpinning of each to derive a set of consistent theoretically rooted hypotheses.

Chapter 3 accomplishes two tasks. First, it discusses the data and clarifies how I transformed the qualitative case studies for the quantitative data. It also reveals the data sources and discusses the inherent limitations of the analysis. It includes an extensive examination of selection bias as well as a discussion about testing interactive relationship. The quantitative analysis then proceeds first by providing simple tabular overviews of the relationships between variables and then, when possible, by applying ordered logit analysis. The chapter's conclusion summarizes the quantitative findings in a discussion of predicted probabilities and discusses the relationships suggested by the data.

Chapters 4 through 7 present the bulk of the case-study evidence, the goal being to examine the findings suggested by the qualitative analysis. Each of these chapters begins with a brief introduction to the country under discussion, as well as an overview of domestic politics in each of the four countries during the 1990s. The chapters then discuss the inclusion of particular cases and what they illustrate analytically. Each case study, as well as each chapter, concludes with a brief summary.

Chapter 8 discusses alternative hypotheses. In line with more realist arguments, I examine the role of the homelands, such as Russia or Hungary, in using economic or military influence to direct policies. I also examine the hypothesis that, regardless of international efforts, the policies can be explained by the fact that the countries simply improved over time as ethnic tensions decreased and as democracy in the countries was consolidated. I address, too, the hypothesis that the type of involvement is less significant than its duration in explaining outcomes.

Chapter 9 concludes the book, discussing the findings more in depth and uses counterfactual analysis to sort out the effects of normative pressure and conditionality. It then extends the analysis to the existing relevant theory, draws some policy lessons, and discusses several questions raised by the findings. Thus, I examine issues such as durability of compliance, the *sui generis* question, as well as the relationship between compliance and implementation. I conclude by suggesting further research.

PART I

Theory and Data

CHAPTER 2

Theoretical Framework

WHILE INTERNATIONAL ACTORS historically have engaged in the protection of ethnic minorities through various treaties and through the minority protection system developed under the League of Nations, international institutions' involvement in the 1990s had a quite different character. In this chapter I examine institutional efforts to influence legislation on ethnic issues as well as how institutional factors may shape the effectiveness of such efforts and how domestic factors may influence the outcome of ethnic issues.

WHY STUDY BEHAVIOR AS THE OUTCOME?

Past efforts to study the effects of international institutions have tended to focus on one particular mechanism—sanctions, conditionality, use of force, or various socialization processes such as persuasion or shaming—and for good reasons. First, a narrow focus is often necessary to uncover micro processes of causality. Second, comparison of mechanisms is difficult because they often have different dependent variables. Whereas persuasion tends to focus on beliefs and identity, sanctions, conditionality, use of force, and even shaming mostly focus on behavior. Treating these outcomes as comparable would be methodologically flawed. Internalization and behavior change are not identical, and while they may influence each other they do not necessarily occur simultaneously or in a particular order (Levy 1994).[1] The challenge is thus how to perform a more comprehensive study that takes both processes into account yet retains consistency.

Since this study primarily examines the role of international institutions as domestic policy actors, I choose as the dependent variable actual policy behavior and implementation. While one might argue that this slights the norm-based approach—indeed, as Payne points out, "Persuasion . . . cannot be revealed by studying behavior" (2001, 42)—I do not consider it irrelevant to examine the ability of norm-based methods to produce behavior change. Where I discuss the success or failure of norm-based methods, however, such conclusions should be understood to apply only to behavioral outcomes, not to the more traditional dependent variables of beliefs and preferences.

Using behavior as the dependent variable is advantageous for three reasons. First, it does address an important part of the overall socialization puzzle, which includes the effects of norm-based methods. Thus, according to Johnston (2001, 487), for example, assessing whether socialization processes actually lead to cooperative behavior is important. Checkel likewise emphasizes the link between internalization and behavior, arguing, "Norms become internalized and constitute a set of shared understandings that make behavioral claims" (1999, 88). And Risse and Sikkink write that "to endorse a norm not only expresses a belief, but also creates impetus for behavior consistent with the belief" (1999, 7). From this perspective, then, a behavior-based assessment of the effectiveness of norm-based methods is essential to any complete picture. Second, studying behavior actually facilitates the goal of the actors—in this case, the three European organizations—that is, is to change policy. As Ruggie (1998, 880–84) notes, the aim of policy conformance both to influence theories that inform policy choices and to serve as a measure of success; therefore, the most rigorous assessment of a theory's effectiveness emerges from the utilitarian perspective of examining behavior as a dependent variable. Third, using a consistent and parsimonious dependent variable enables the simultaneous study of different institutional mechanisms without the either/or rhetoric of rationalists and constructivists.

RELATIONSHIP TO EXISTING THEORY

In evaluating the effectiveness of various institutional efforts to affect policy, this study speaks to two categories of theory. First, the study fits into research on conditionality and the larger debate about the use of incentives to change state behavior.[2] Conditionality is a technique by which an actor makes the transfer of positively valued resources contingent on the recipient behaving consistently with the actor's preferences.[3] Conditionality theory uses rational choice arguments to explain state behavior in response to incentives, assuming that policy makers choose based on utilitarian reasoning whether to meet the requirements of, in this case, international institutions. Previous research has focused mostly on the use of negative incentives such as trade sanctions and threats of force. While recent research on aid conditionality has begun to address more positive uses of incentives and has identified several deficiencies specific to aid conditionality, studies on political conditions set by institutions other than the IMF and the World Bank are scarce, although such conditionality is on the rise (Killick 1996). Thus, this chapter elaborates on the theory of using positive incentives to achieve political reforms.

Second, this study joins a larger body of research about the role of norms in changing state behavior. European institutions have applied considerable effort to encouraging political reforms outside the conditionality framework, appealing instead to a set of norms on ethnic minority issues, as spearheaded by the OSCE and the CE but also practiced behind the scenes by the EU. "Normative pressure," as I call it, brackets a set of socialization mechanisms, such as persuasion and social influence, that can operate through a variety of constructivist and rationalist microprocesses, as elaborated by Johnston (2001), Checkel (2001), and others. Normative pressure thus allows decision makers to be both strategic and social. Policy makers *may* change their beliefs, but they may also respond rationally to the constraints that norms impose on them in terms of maintaining or obtaining international approval. The unifying element of the activities associated with normative pressure, however, is that external actors try to influence the direction of the a policy within a state *without* connecting the policy change to rewards other than the approval of the external actor. Normative pressure thus applies much less traditional "muscle" than conditionality, and studying it addresses the question of the role of softer mechanisms of influence. This chapter discusses the underlying theory of such norm-based efforts in more depth and derives hypotheses about the ability of such efforts to change policy.

The main goal of this study, though, is not to adjudicate between different socialization theories or to uncover the causal pathways of normative pressure.[4] Rather, the study develops hypotheses about when and how institutions can influence domestic policies on ethnic minorities by selectively deploying techniques such as normative pressure and conditionality, that is, which approaches result in compliance and when. More practically, by learning from successes and failures, this study contributes to vital efforts to develop tools with which the international community can intervene constructively and at an early stage in tense ethnic situations.

The choice to examine normative pressure versus conditionality reflects the two types of efforts actually being used by European institutions to address issues related to ethnic minorities. In this context, an institution exerts normative pressure when it expresses concern about a policy and makes recommendations on the policy without linking this to membership in the institution. An institution exerts membership conditionality when it links institutional membership to the fulfillment of such a recommendation. In other words, normative pressure alone could be described as soft diplomacy, persuasion, or social influence. The combination of normative pressure and membership incentives could be described as conditionality or issue-linkage. Throughout the study I refer to the two types of efforts as either "normative pressure" or "conditionality," conditionality thus herein referring to the combination of normative pressure and conditionality.

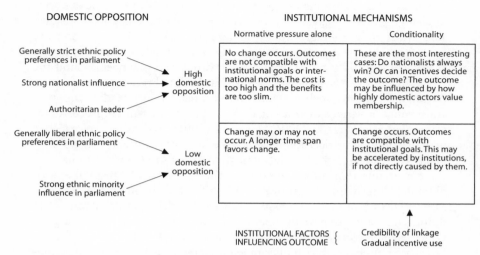

DOMESTIC OPPOSITION | INSTITUTIONAL MECHANISMS

Figure 2.1. Model of theoretical framework and predictions for policy change.

Figure 2.1 shows the analytical framework that rests on these two mechanisms, and also illustrates how domestic factors may influence the outcomes of institutional involvement. The rest of this chapter explains this framework in greater depth. First, I discuss the two institutional methods and what affects their effectiveness. Second, I discuss the role of domestic factors and how they influence the size of the normative gap and the policy outcome. Finally, I summarize the hypotheses.

Normative Pressure without Linkage to Membership Incentives

Many scholars have focused on international norms and rules in the last decades, with recent interest focusing in particular on the influence of international norms on domestic actors and policies (Axelrod 1986; Nadelman 1990; Goertz and Diehl 1992; Finnemore 1993; Goldstein and Keohane 1993; Sikkink 1993b; Klotz 1966; Cortell and Davis 1996; Legro 1997; Ikenberry and Kupchan 1990). While much of this research falls under the study of socialization, I instead refer to institutional activities as normative pressure, since there is some disagreement about whether socialization can also refer to mechanisms like conditionality that employ concrete incentives.[5] The absence of concrete incentives is consistent with Ikenberry and Kupchan's definition of "normative persuasion," in which "the hegemon is able to secure the compliance of secondary states without resorting to material sanctions and inducements" (1990, 290). Axelrod

(1997a, 58–59) also notes a series of mechanisms such as "identification," "authority," "social proof," and "voluntary membership" that may lead to pro-norm behavior without exogenous material manipulation. A discussion of the different types of engagement in the countries and the possible causal processes at work both clarifies how normative pressure relates to the existing field of socialization and aids development of useful theories by identifying the conditions under which normative pressure may and may not result in the dependent variable of behavioral change.

How have institutions deployed normative pressure? To solve ethnic problems, international institutions have used various "verbal" means to convince a country to change its policy. At times, such verbal pressure has been quite formal, with institutions making official reprimands of a country's behavior, as when the EU issued a démarche openly criticizing Slovakia in November 1994.[6] In other cases institutions have released various public declarations or reports that openly ask a country to change its behavior on a certain issue. The CE issues such reports intermittently to follow-up on commitments countries make at admission. The EU has issued regular reports and statements from joint meetings that were used to flag EU concerns on ethnic issues. Such methods of normative pressure are most akin to methods of social influence that incorporate praise and social opprobrium (Johnston 2001) aimed at the desire for legitimacy (Cortell and Davis 1996), to simple learning that changes means but not ends (Levy 1994), or to rhetorical action in which actors strategically use statements to manipulate other actors (Schimmelfennig 2001). The causal mechanism is rational. For example, Johnston defines social influence as "a number of sub-processes—backpatting, opprobrium or shaming, social liking, status maximization, etc." (ibid.). Also, Darren Hawkins argues that international pressure can "shame" and "punish offenders by invoking human rights norms" (1997, 403).[7] Similarly, Kathryn Sikkink and Martha Finnemore argue that states conform to "peer pressure" because of their desire for "legitimization, conformity and esteem" (1998, 897). According to Risse and Sikkink, shaming occurs when "norm-violating states are denounced as pariah states which do not belong to the community of civilized nations, as was the case with South Africa," and they note that "some repressive governments might not care. Others, however, feel deeply offended, because they want to belong to the 'civilized community' of states" (1999, 15). Several other scholars also focus on shaming and social pressure as methods for eliciting treaty compliance (Chayes and Chayes 1996; Young 1992; Susskind 1994; Moravcsik 1995). Such actions influence outcomes primarily because actors adjust their behaviors to preserve their reputations.

In reality the line between persuasion and social influence is blurred, or the two processes are simultaneous. Indeed, institutions rarely limit themselves to such hands-off approaches but often pay ad hoc visits to the country in question, with representatives privately discussing options with policy makers and urging them to conform to institutional—and international—norms.[8] These more intimate meetings between OSCE and CE representatives and national policy makers are often confidential and thus rely less on adjustments motivated by reputation. Rather, the actors put a premium on dialogue, the purpose being not to convey new information but to teach and persuade. While such dialogue has undoubtedly contained arguments for the strategic advantages of making policy adjustments, the records of the letters from the High Commissioner on National Minorities (HCNM), who was the OSCE's primary emissary on such issues, indicate a high level of effort to appeal to and explain the reasoning behind international norms. Indeed, Ratner notes that van der Stoel was a "normative intermediary . . . an agent dispatched by a norm-concerned community with the authority and tools to communicate norms and persuade states to comply with them" (1999, 668). Indeed, van der Stoel has remarked that his "blueprints are OSCE principles and commitments and international legal norms and standards" (1999, 429). The CE secretary general has also stressed that the CE philosophy has been to work to influence the norms of states through day-to-day interaction inside the CE after admission.[9] Thus, it is reasonable to assume that attempts at genuine persuasion and complex learning took place (Levy 1994; Risse-Kappen 1995; Risse 2000; Payne 2001; Finnemore 1996). Ad hoc visits were often followed by written communication enforcing the normative arguments. Addressing such processes of persuasion, John Ikenberry and Charles Kupchan comment, "Elites in secondary states buy into and internalize norms that are articulated by the hegemon and therefore pursue policies consistent with the hegemon's notion of international order" (1990, 283; see also Nadelman 1990, 524; Duffield 1992, 838).

Other forms of engagement have included sending experts to help draft legislation, presenting formal declarations from high-level bodies of the institutions, or issuing public statements by member states when their leaders visited the candidate countries. In the spirit of a dual constructivist and rationalist framework of soliciting change, institutions have also combined formal monitoring mechanisms that influence reputational concerns with regular fact-finding visits (with activity similar to ad hoc visits) that involve more direct forms of persuasion. Indeed, this fits with Finnemore and Sikkink's suggestion that international organizations socialize by "pressuring targeted actors to adopt new policies and laws and to ratify treaties and by monitoring compliance with international standards" (1998, 897). As instruments for shaming or praising the country, the CE used formal reports on the results of such visits and monitoring activities. These reports were approved in the CE in an institutional forum to amplify the reputational effects. Thus, again, one can track a constant dynamic between socialization mechanisms that rely on both constructivist and rationalist pathways of change.

This study, however, is not designed to adjudicate between the mechanisms of socialization, although that is a very interesting current debate among scholars (Johnston 2001; Checkel 2001).[10] Instead, this study places both incentive- and norm-based efforts in a comparative framework of how institutions influence behavior, to assess whether normative pressure by the institutions actually does achieve behavior change. Thus, what light does this theory cast on the question of when normative pressure alone produces policy change?[11]

When or Why Normative Pressure Might Not Work

Whether constructivist or rationalist in their approach, scholars argue that normative pressure does work at times. For example, Checkel (1999) argues that the CE successfully socialized key Ukrainian leaders on citizenship and nationality issues, and that Ukraine subsequently adopted legislation in accordance with CE norms. Similarly, Finnemore (1993) points to a case of educational ministries as promoted by the United Nations as an illustration of how institutions and international norms about the role of such national level ministries changed traditional preferences of states and state actors, who then in turn changed their behavior. Indeed, the specific factors that scholars list as favorable to the effectiveness of persuasion and social influence were present in Europe in the 1990s; that is, the external actors, in the form of western European institutions, wielded considerable geopolitical influence and used a publicly visible process of influence, which in theory should have resulted in effective use of social influences such as shaming and praise. Likewise, because the target states were in transition and had a great desire to be accepted by the external actors, and because the external actors engaged in intense normative lobbying, persuasive efforts should have been quite useful.[12] Furthermore, the very prevalence of normative pressure campaigns would also suggest its effectiveness. Indeed, Johnston points out that "most non-coercive diplomatic influence attempts by most actors most of the time are aimed at 'changing the minds' of others, of persuading, cajoling, or shaming them to accept, and hopefully internalize, new facts, figures, arguments, norms, and causal understandings about particular issues" (2001, 489). Certainly, several institutions (including the OAU, the OAS, the OSCE, and the CE) and various nongovernmental organizations (Amnesty International, Human Rights Watch) have institutionalized diplomatic mechanisms akin to normative pressure to address conflict and democracy issues, including minority concerns. In general, tools of normative pressure, such as international agreements and conventions on human rights issues, have proliferated in the last decades. Also, although different from research that assesses the success of normative pressure in changing legislation, some scholarly and practical arguments suggest that the type of soft diplomacy practiced by the OSCE is quite worthwhile in preventing conflict (Chigas 1996; Huber 1994; Munuera 1994; Wright 1996; Flynn and Farrell 1999).

Despite the theoretical and practical reasons to expect normative pressure to be effective, however, several reasons explain why normative pressure may not work well as a singular strategy. For instance, one might dismiss the constructivist notion that state actors change their beliefs because of external normative contact; since belief change is an intervening variable in the process leading to policy change, behavior would not change unless it were in the interests of the state actors for reasons identified by the more rationalist school of socialization theory. Reputational concerns, on the other hand, may be too mild to prompt policy change. As realists argue, the power relationship between a state and its national minorities is asymmetrical. In many cases domestic politicians gain political capital from staunch positions against accommodating ethnic minority; thus, if the minority does not pose a threat, politicians may not consider external social pressure reason enough to accommodate minorities. That is, their domestic gain from standing firm on their ethnic policy preferences may outweigh whatever they may lose in international reputation. Rewards stemming from reputation payoffs are likely to be too vague and uncertain to overcome key identity issues. Thus, normative pressure, be it based on efforts to persuade or to shame or praise, may be insufficient to change preferences on ethnic policy.

Questioning the validity of the link between changes in preference and changes in policy is also possible. That is, even were individual domestic policy actors to actually change their policy preferences because of social influence or persuasion, it would not necessarily translate into policy change. While this point of view does not deny the validity of various theories about normative pressure, it does suggest that such socialization alone may work only under certain conditions.[13] Such conditions are intricately intertwined with domestic factors. Perhaps, for instance, policy makers do modify their opinions but not enough to warrant, in their minds, a change in policy. Or perhaps the number of policy makers who want to enact a policy change does not ultimately add up to a winning coalition (Risse-Kappen 1994, 208). Or domestic constituents may constrain policy makers who want to be reelected. In such cases the change in policy *preferences* effected by normative persuasion efforts is not enough to produce actual policy *change*.

With regard to both persuasive and strategic causality, normative pressure as a sole initiative may be said to work only in "easy cases," that is, when domestic opposition to the proposed behavior change is minimal.

For example, the UN's campaign to create national education ministries, as studied by Finnemore (1993), was not met with fervent domestic resistance; furthermore, in the long run one could see that it is in the interest of the parties and states involved. Thus, beliefs did not need to change greatly, and cost-benefit calculations were easier to tip by gains in reputation and status. In line with this reasoning, Checkel (2000a, 15) argues that the CE successfully socialized key Ukrainian leaders on citizenship and nationality issues because Ukraine did not have a strong domestic opposition to these issues. Thus, normative pressure alone might not work when external institutional norms meet with considerable domestic resistance, but could work when opposition is low. Opposition might be low when the issue itself is not controversial, when opponents have little voting power in parliament, and when advocates of the issue form a government coalition and thus wield influence over the preferences of the government.

Hypotheses about Normative Pressure

In sum, normative pressure may succeed alone in certain instances, as some scholars have argued (Risse 2000; Checkel 1997). Because of the difficulty of changing policy preferences through persuasion or social influence and the additional difficulty of translating changes in policy preference into behavior, however, normative pressure alone rarely changes policy in more diverse political processes. But normative pressure may work in easy cases, as described above, when the domestic opposition to the proposed behavior change is low.

Of course, low domestic opposition could arise when ethnic minorities are a controlling part of the government, in which case their preferences, and thus indirectly those of the government, may already align with institutional norms. One could argue, however, that such minority influence is not actually representative of successful normative pressure, but only that it is indistinguishable from a case in which normative pressure alone had an effect. The actual cause of the change in such a case lies less with the institution than with the bargaining power of the ethnic coalition partner—a purely domestic political explanation. In any case, only when these domestic factors prevail would the study predict positive outcomes associated only with the presence of normative pressure.

CONDITIONALITY

Conditionality is the use of positive incentives to alter a state's behavior.[14] In addition to normative pressure, which naturally is the method of first resort, international institutions frequently use political conditionality to promote certain policies.[15] This practice has been particularly common in post–Cold War Europe (Checkel 2000a; Killick 1998). In what Schimmelfinnig calls "reinforcement by rewards," "International organizations offer material and political rewards in return for norm compliance but do not coerce non-compliant governments" (2002, 1). Practices that use military threats or other direct interventions as coercion to supercede the sovereign nation are thus inconsistent with the definition of conditionality. While some scholars argue that the use of normative pressure alone (particularly in the form of social influence) also presents some rational incentives to or places constraints on policy makers, conditionality is a much more clear-cut exchange of rewards and behavior, relying on cost-benefit calculations and material incentives rather than norms. The rewards are more tangible than the praise and recognition associated with normative pressure. Indeed, membership in an institution is often an official ticket to influence, funds, and increased prosperity, even if only indirectly, as membership in the OSCE or CE often leads to membership in institutions such as the EU or NATO that offer those rewards.[16]

Although conditionality has many variants, restraint and enticement are most relevant to this study. Restraint is defined as the government's using conditionality as a mechanism of either commitment to or locking in of a particular government policy. A government can protect itself against pressures for policy change by agreeing to lock in a policy as a condition for receiving a payoff. The institution applying conditionality acts as an agency of restraint (Collier et al. 1997, 1401). With enticement—by far the most common use of conditionality in this study—the aim is to lure the government to do something it would not have chosen to do without the offer of a payoff (ibid., 1400–1401). The two types of conditionality are two sides of the same coin, with the only difference being where the target state perceives the baseline policy.

Theories about conditionality assume that actors maximize utility based on exogenous, self-interested political preferences.[17] Thus external actors and the policy makers in target states weigh the costs and benefits of compliance to optimize their own fixed interests (Elster 1982, 22). Whether actors alter their beliefs after altering their actions is not of concern to the study of this mechanism.[18] Political conditionality thus relates to bargaining theory, which argues that incentives can alter states' behavior by changing the international payoff structure facing states.[19] For example, Putnam (1988, 447) refers to international issue-linkage that domestically alters feasible outcomes. Similarly, Long argues that "economic incentives can affect a state's definition of its preferences by changing its external payoff environment and its domestic politics and, in some cases, alter its chosen policies" (1996, 11). Conditionality thus relies on the logic of consequentialism as defined by March and Olsen (1989; 1998). As Elster notes,

"Rational choice is instrumental: it is guided by the outcome of action. Actions are valued and chosen not for themselves, but as more or less efficient means to a further end" (1982, 22).

Why Conditionality?

To actually change policy, conditionality is in most cases not only effective but also *necessary* (Gilbert et al. 1997; Gilbert, Powell, and Vines 1999). Indeed, even constructivist case studies suggest that incentive manipulation is often the key to action. For example, Keck and Sikkink (1998) clearly show how transnational actors trying to persuade target states used material levers to gain support for their positions. Thus, they write that advocates make "implied or explicit threat of sanctions or leverage if the gap between norms and practices remains large. Material leverage comes from linking the issue of concern to money, trade, or prestige, as more powerful institutions or governments are pushed to apply pressure" (1998, 201). Sikkink (1993) made a similar point in her work on the influence of the human rights network on Argentina's and Mexico's policies, arguing that the combination of moral pressure and material pressure changes state behavior (Ikenberry and Kupchan 1990; Klotz 1996; Chayes and Chayes 1995). Similarly, Checkel's work on the death penalty in Ukraine reveals that "incentives offered by the CE and careful, strategic calculations by Ukrainian elites were factors, for membership in the Council would legitimize both Ukraine's return to Europe and its independence from Russia" (2000a, 9)

Why Might Conditionality Fail?

Despite the appeal of the logic of rationality, that institutions or other international actors can fix domestic policy problems by manipulating the payoffs of state actors is far from clear. First, despite conditionality's widespread use, the practical record for its most common application—aid conditionality—is mixed at best. While aid conditionality has been a basic strategy of the World Bank and the IMF for promoting compliance by national governments on economic reforms, many scholars and practitioners argue that it is ineffective. One study concludes that conditionality leads to compliance only 60 percent of the time (Gilbert, Hopkins, Powell, and Roy 1997, 509n). Indeed, a growing body of econometric, statistical, and case-study research finds only a weak connection between conditionality and national compliance (Nelson 1996; Collier 1997; Killick 1998; Gilbert, Hopkins, Powell, and Roy 1997). Killick points out several implementation flaws that lead to the frequent failure of aid conditionality.[20] Practitioners confirm such criticism. Thus, for example, the chief economist of the World Bank, Joseph Stiglitz, resigned in November 1999 because, "There is increasing evidence that it [conditionality] was not [an effective way of changing national policy]. Good policies cannot be bought."[21] Indeed, the financial institutions themselves are now rethinking their use of conditionality.[22]

Second, research on sanctions, which similarly relies on changes in payoff structure to alter decision makers' cost-benefit calculations, also questions whether issue linkage works. In the 1960s and 1970s scholars argued that while sanctions were more humane than military force, they were not as effective (Galtung 1997; Doxey 1971; Losman 1979). Doxey (1995) noted that sanctions sometimes sparked a nationalist reaction that could actually strengthen a regime to withstand economic hardship. Sanctions have had a wide range of effects in countries such as South Africa and Rhodesia, but as the world struggled with imposing sanctions on Iraq in the 1990s, more scholars argued that sanctions were ineffective (Pape 1997; Haass 1997). A large 1990 study argued, however, that sanctions were at least partially effective (Hufbauer, Scott, and Elliot 1990). Thus, while more research is emerging on positive incentives and aid conditionality, conclusions remain ambiguous, especially in the still relatively new realm of achieving political reforms that can contribute to peace (Cortright 1995; Long 1996; Nelson 1992; Reinicke 1996; World Bank 1997; Boyce 1996).

Finally, the bottom line is that conditionality will only work if the cost-benefit calculations come out in favor of a policy change, which may not happen for several reasons. First, once one starts to relax assumptions about the rational capacities of actors, it becomes quite clear that actors often have difficulties evaluating cost and benefits, especially if they are mired in deep ethnic rifts.[23] Indeed, external pressure on ethnic issues could even backfire politically, just as Doxey (1995) suggested that sanctions could do, because politicians do not want to appear to have been pushed around on such issues. Second, when taking into account the domestic costs of justifying change, the payoff might be insufficient for policy makers to consider compromising their policy preferences. Built into the policy makers' evaluation of the benefit is an estimate of the size, certainty, and future value of the payoff. Third, individual policy makers likely have different costs and benefits, depending on their constituency base and the compromises they will have to make in their governing styles. They also may value the benefits variously, have different discount rates, or assorted estimations of the credibility of the institutional strategy. Therefore, policy makers who do calculate a net benefit from compromise may still be unable to form a winning coalition to change the policy in question, as other policy makers might prefer the status quo. Thus, several sources of failure may help account for political conditionality: factors related to the institutions' themselves and independent factors on the domestic scene in the target state.

The Credibility of International Institutions

The first institutional factor that influences efficacy is the credibility of the conditionality (Checkel 2000a, 4).[24] Naturally, the effectiveness of conditionality decreases if the target state does not perceive as credible the linkage between behavior and institutional membership (Shelling 1966; Putnam 1988).[25] Indeed, studies note that conditionality may fail first and foremost because the institutions are inconsistent in their application of requirements and rewards. As is particularly evident in IMF lending programs to Russia, the IMF and the World Bank have often given "something for nothing," thus undermining the entire logic of incentives behind conditionality. The credibility of the linkage may suffer for several reasons.

First, while the member states of international institutions and other international actors strive to be objective in their application of conditionality, the commonly acknowledged reality is that member states frequently politicize conditionality, as when Europe needed Romania's cooperation for the war in Bosnia. Six months before the European Council decided on the progress of Romania in the accession process, British Prime Minister Tony Blair essentially promised to support Romania in exchange for cooperation on Bosnia.[26] Such promises, which indicate that extraneous bargains can be made, naturally weaken the credibility of the purported direct connection between specific policy changes and advancement through the admission process.

Second, as theory on two-level games argues, disagreements within states can lower their credibility in international negotiations. Similarly, internal disagreements within an institution can lower the institution's credibility vis-à-vis external actors. Putnam argues that "the credibility of an official commitment may be low, even if the reputational costs of reneging are high, for the negotiator may be unable to guarantee ratification" (1988, 439). This is certainly relevant in an institutional setting in which members have to reach unanimity on admission decisions. Thus, since institutions are not unitary actors with carefully executed strategies aimed primarily at improving minority rights, their credibility may be undermined by internal politics of current members of the institutions (Krasner 1977; Mansfield 1995).

Furthermore, institutions have multiple goals, and one goal may at times overshadow others. For example, should the EU reward progress on agriculture despite political concerns? Should the CE admit a state before all conditions are met in the hope that it can influence a state more after admission than before?

Finally, shifting institutional designs and other internal challenges can also distort an institution's messages. If an institution is not designed to absorb new members, the credibility of the membership offer naturally

TABLE 2.1.
The conditionality game

Institution	State	
	Comply	*Do not comply*
Admit	$NB_j + B_c$, $A–C_d$	$NB_j — C$, A
Do not admit	$B_c — c$,$–C_d$	0, 0

suffers; this is one of the reasons the EU, for example, has had to work simultaneously on enlargement and internal institutional reforms.

A simplified model containing only two states—compliance and non-compliance, admission and nonadmission—clarifies what factors influence the effectiveness of conditionality. A is the state's benefit of admission, and C_c is the state's domestic cost of compliance, where $A > C_c > 0$. The state's preferences are thus $A > A – C_c > 0 > – C_c$. That is, the state prefers to be admitted without having to comply, but given the choice between comply-ing and being admitted versus not complying and not being admitted, it prefers the former. Its fear, of course, is to comply without being admitted. Table 2.1 illustrates the payoff structure for an institution using member-ship conditionality and for a state deciding whether to comply with mem-bership requirements.

Since membership conditionality by definition means that the state has to choose whether to comply before the institution decides whether to admit, the state faces the decision tree illustrated in figure 2.2, where α is the probability that the institution will admit given compliance and ß is the probability that the institution will admit given noncompliance.

Assuming risk neutrality,[27] the state will comply if the expected value of complying exceeds the expected value of not complying. Thus, the state will comply if

$$\alpha (A – C_c) + (1 – \alpha) (– C_c) > \beta A$$

Multiplying out

$$\alpha A – C_c > \beta A$$

This means that the state will comply if

$$A (\alpha – \beta) > C_c$$

or, expressed differently

$$\alpha – \beta > C_c / A$$

where $\alpha – \beta$ is a measure of the institution's credibility ranging from −1 to 1. It is also an expression of the state's marginal increase in the probability

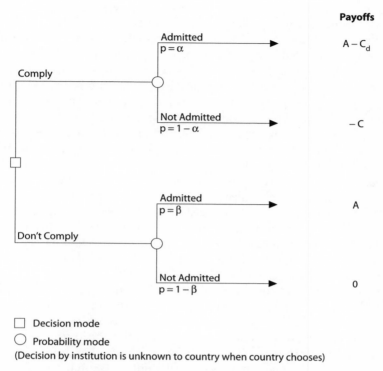

Payoffs

Admitted
$p = \alpha$ → $A - C_d$

Comply ○

Not Admitted
$p = 1 - \alpha$ → $-C$

□

Admitted
$p = \beta$ → A

Don't Comply ○

Not Admitted
$p = 1 - \beta$ → 0

□ Decision mode
○ Probability mode
(Decision by institution is unknown to country when country chooses)

Figure 2.2. The state's decision tree.

of admission from complying. If $\alpha = 1$ and $\beta = 0$, then $\alpha - \beta = 1$, and the institution is completely credible, and the state has a dominant strategy to comply given that $A > C_c$. Indeed, as long as $\alpha > \beta$, then the state *may* comply, depending on the ratio of compliance cost to admission benefits and the marginal gain in the probability of admission from complying, $\alpha - \beta$. The greater the institution's credibility, $\alpha - \beta$, the greater the likelihood that the state will comply. The likelihood of compliance also grows as the ratio of C_c / A approaches zero. This may occur either because the cost of compliance, C_c, approaches zero, or if the benefit of admission, A, grows very large. As β approaches α, however, the institution's credibility diminishes. When $\beta \geq \alpha$, then the institution seriously lacks credibility and the state prefers not to comply since $C_c / A > 0$, that is, there is some cost associated with complying. This means that it is not sufficient for the institution to make it perfectly credible that admission will follow compliance. If admission seems assured, or at least just as likely given noncompliance, then the state will not comply.

If we lift the assumption that C_c must be positive (that is, the state has an independent benefit of compliance), then the state will also comply regardless of the value of $\alpha - \beta$. In most instances this is not the case, because the institutions would not make the issue a prerequisite and it therefore would not be a point of contention between the state and the institution.

The core of the state's decision problem thus arises because it cannot precisely know $\alpha - \beta$, the institution's credibility. The state must deduce these probabilities from the entire payoff structure of the conditionality game. What are the payoffs to the institution? There are at least three important inputs. First, the institution gains some benefit from the state joining (in the case of the EU, e.g., this might be a larger future market, greater weight in international negotiations, increased regional stability, etc.). The institution also incurs costs, however, when admitting a state, which might take the form of transfers to the new state, or difficulties associated with accommodating the new member in the institutional forum. Considering both of these, the institution therefore has some net benefit of admitting a state, NB_a, which is presumably positive but could potentially be negative, at least in the short run.[28]

Next, the institution must reap some benefit from the state's compliance, B_c. If this were not the case, then it would not bother to request the action. In the case of the CE, for example, B_c may be the benefit of meeting its mandate. Finally, and most importantly for assessing the institution's credibility and making the compliance decision, the institution suffers a reputational cost, $R_{a|not\,c}$ of admitting a state that did not comply, and $R_{not\,a|c}$ of rejecting a state that complied. These reputational costs are particularly important for the institution because it will exercise conditionality with several states. Figure 2.3 shows the full payoff matrix.

Given that the game is sequential and that the state goes first, the state knows that the institution can reduce its choice to a simple comparison of payoffs for each state strategy. If the state complies, the institutions will admit the state if $NB_a > - R_{not\,a|c}$. If the state does not comply, the institutions will admit the state if $NB_a > R_{a|not\,c}$. If the state knew precisely how the institution assessed its payoffs, it could solve its decision dilemma through simple backward induction. It does not know, however, and at best can therefore estimate α, the probability of being admitted if it complies = $P(NB_a > - R_{not\,a|c})$, and β = the probability of being admitted if it does not comply = $P(NB_a > R_{a|not\,c})$. In both cases, the probability depends on the relationship between the net benefit of admitting and the reputational cost of acting contrary to the conditionality principle.

As discovered when first examining figure 2.2, the state's decision tree, to make the conditionality strategy effective, the institution needs the state to believe that $\alpha - \beta$ is as close to 1 as possible, and definitely greater than

C_c / A, the ratio of the state's cost of compliance to the state's benefits of compliance. This means that, for the state to comply

$$P(NB_a > - R_{not\,a|c}) > C_c / A + P(NB_a > R_{a|not\,c})$$

Thus, the decision to comply depends on three factors: the ratio C_c / A, the NB_a and the two reputational costs. What does this mean for the institution if it wants to make the conditionality strategy as effective as possible? The institution cannot manipulate its NB_a, since this largely is a function of exogenous economic factors and other given benefits and nonavoidable (is there such a word?) costs. It presumably cannot manipulate C_c / A very much either (though it could conceivably promise additional benefits of joining). Thus, all the institution really can do to enhance compliance is manipulate its reputational costs. Since $\alpha = P(NB_a > - R_{not\,a|c})$, α increases as $R_{not\,a|c}$ increases. Further, if the net benefits of admission are small, or even negative, it then becomes increasingly necessary that the reputational costs of the institution rejecting a compliant state are large. Thus, in general, states that believe that they will provide an institution with lower net benefits because of geography, economy, or other challenges will be less likely to meet entry requirements, especially if the institution has not made effort to increase its reputational cost of rejecting a compliant state. A state that needs much financial aid after admission will therefore need more assurances from an institution to believe that it will indeed be admitted if it complies, as was true for Romania with its struggling economy.

Similarly, β needs to be kept as low as possible. Indeed, it needs to be lower than $\alpha - C_c/A$. Unless the institution has created high reputational cost of admitting a noncompliant state, conditionality will fail if the target state believes that it will be admitted irrespective of its behavior because it is in the institution's interest, for other reasons, to admit the state. That is, if NB_a the net benefits of admission, are high, then, given that $\beta = P(NB_a > R_{a|not\,c})$, the reputational costs to the institution of admitting a noncompliant state have to be very high for the conditionality strategy to work by driving down β. If it seems that a candidate state will actually enhance the trade or security of an institution—as, for instance, Slovakia believed for a while—then the institution must emphasize the conditional nature of admission even more and, if possible, commit itself in binding documents or decisions. By so doing, the institution raises its cost of admitting the state if the state does not comply, because its reputation will be damaged more if it has been very explicit about the linkage. To avoid promoting overconfidence among prospective member states, the institution must avoid sending the wrong signal by giving cooperation, aid, and other types of approval in general when a state violates the institutional norms. This does not mean that the institution must outright criticize norm-violating behavior, but it does mean that at a minimum the institution should be careful not to proceed with aid and cooperation and other positive benefits as if nothing had occurred.

In sum, the state faces a decision under uncertainty. For the conditionality strategy to work, the *higher* the NB_a, the greater the reputational costs of admitting a noncompliant state must be, and the *lower* the NB_a, the greater the reputational costs of the institution rejecting a compliant state must be. The necessity of these relationships holding increases as the C_c/A approaches 1, or as the cost of compliance to the state approaches the benefit of admission. This means that the greater the concessions the institutions require of states, the greater the institutions' credibility also must be. The credibility, however, refers not only to how credible it is that admission follows compliance, but also to how credible it is that rejection follows non-compliance.

The institutions can bolster their reputational costs in several ways, such as increasing their official commitment to minority rights both by incorporating relevant norms into their founding treaties and other documents and, most important, by behaving toward all candidate states in a way that is consistent with their claims. A gradual admission procedure also demonstrates credibility as well as decreases the state's uncertainty, as the next section discusses.

A Gradual Admission Process

Institutions can also bolster credibility by creating an admission process in which candidates can progress to various levels. Such gradualism resembles Schelling's (1996) "continuous negotiations" concept, in which each stage of the admission process is a negotiation with consequences for future stages, which increases compliance.[29] Each step is also a signal that the reward is obtainable, which increases credibility. Thus, institutions can maximize the effectiveness of conditionality by creating a gradual payoff structure in the form of a tiered admission process. Clear, gradual steps also add more political weight to admission process decision points, because real consequences can flow from them. Subsequently, any meeting, report, or event related to the process of moving closer to the reward of membership provides opportunities for "dangling the carrot" while also addressing outstanding issues. The EU has been particularly effective at creating a gradual admission process, a gradualism born out of both necessity and desire. Given the challenges facing EU member states in relation to enlargement, a gradual process has provided both necessary assurances for candidate states that they were moving in the right direction and the desired braking mechanisms for member states worried about too hasty an enlargement (Schimmelfennig 2001). A problem associated with a long admission process, of course, is that the offset timing of costs and benefits, where reward is distant while costs are proximate, can be counterproductive. The long accession process may give policy makers incentive to lag behind, thinking that they can catch up later. Thus, intermediate rewards in terms of candidacy status are important.

Hypotheses Derived from the Theory on Conditionality

For international institutions to achieve their preferred policies in a target state, then, incentives are effective and, in most cases, necessary. Linking issues to membership is increasingly effective if institutions can administer the admission in stages. Further, the linkage to membership incentives may fail to produce the desired policy changes if the linkage is not credible either because the state believes that the institution will admit it even if the state does not make the specific policy change or because the state believes that the institution will withhold admission even if the state does make the specific policy change. Failure of the institutions' efforts, be they normative pressure or issue-linkage to membership, may also originate in the domestic political situation.

DOMESTIC OPPOSITION

Collier has commented critically that scholars have operated in a "shallow political environment" when thinking about conditionality and compliance (1997, 54). Killick similarly notes that scholars erroneously tend to assume that conditionality is "ahistorical" (1998, 156). Nevertheless, several scholars have noted domestic hindrances to the use of conditionality. Pridham argues that "international factors are dependent variables, their influence or impact largely conditional on opportunities presented by domestic developments . . ., and how a recipient states links up with the wider international system" (1997, 13). Scholars focusing on soft persuasion methods also note the importance of accounting for the domestic political landscape. Thus, Risse-Kappen (1994) argues that differences in domestic structures account for the variation in the impact of policy ideas.

Several scholars have pointed out that domestic politics may indeed hinder external influence. Speaking specifically about EU conditionality, Pridham notes, "Pressures from Brussels are not likely to help overturn a negative dynamic in regime change" (1999, 1223). Michael Ross argues that "conditionality's impact in hard cases, when powerful domestic interests oppose reforms, is unclear" (1996, 197). Others specifically point out the difficulty of nationalist opposition. While they argue that attitudes of elites are affected by participation in EU institutional forums—making elites more disposed to consider external pressures—they note that the strongest limit to such attitude change is a strong nationalist influence (Pridham 1999).

A quite different argument, however, suggests that domestic politics may actually facilitate outside influence. Moravcsik (2000), for instance, contends that certain domestic politics may render some governments eager for external mechanisms that lock in their preferences. That is, governments actually "delegate self-interestedly to combat future threats to domestic democratic governance" (Moravcsik 2000, abstract). According to this theory, new and less-established democracies will be the most receptive to external human-rights obligations. This assumes, however, that the governments in office consider their interests aligned with external actors and norms, and think they will benefit from locking them in (as may have been the case for human rights during the founding years of the CE). But it is not clear that governments run by ethnic majorities in fledgling democracies benefit from locking in ethnic minority rights the same way new democracies may benefit from locking in democratic or basic human rights standards that benefit the broader population and their own political ambitions. Nor does it appear common in the case of ethnic minority politics that legislatures want to lock in ethnic minority rights to circumvent conflicts of interests with the executive (Martin 2000, 48). Indeed, in some cases the executive appears more supportive of ethnic minority rights that the legislature. Nevertheless, it may be the case, as Checkel (1997) stresses, that transitions themselves do facilitate the receptivity to external ideas and actors by creating windows of opportunity for external actors. Given that the countries in this study are mostly states in transition, this would suggest that politicians should be open to adopt new ideas from the Western institutions.

Governments that rely on the cooperation of ethnic minority parties may gain swing votes from such parties on other key issues in exchange for minority policy concessions. In such cases, the international institution may provide credible ways for the ethnic majority parties to make commitments to the ethnic minority parties, thus increasing the chance of compliance. In such a case, however, a large part of the policy adjustment rests on the bargaining power of the ethnic minorities, and the international institutions become a facilitating mechanism for locking in such bargains.

To evaluate the myriad domestic influences, several studies examine macrolevel structural domestic factors, such as the nature of party systems, the domestic institutional composition, and economic influences (Vachudova 2004; Schimmelfennig 2002). These are all legitimate factors to consider. The structure of party systems, the historical developments of a country, its democratic background, and other such path-dependent or structural explanations, however, suffer from lack of variation across time and issues. Such studies thus provide explanatory leverage only on the macrolevel. Institutions do not operate in a vacuum; domestic factors have direct bearing on policy outcomes and thus may override institutional efforts. Analysis gains leverage, however, by examining precise circumstances at the decision-making level for each policy at a given time, since the preferences and actions of the political elite in a given situation determine the policy outcomes.[30] Studies have found that external attempts to push reforms depend to a large degree on whether the relevant special interest groups are part of a government coalition at a given time (Ross 1996; Martin and Sikkink 1993). A similar argument contends that transnational actors can only translate ideas into policy change if they can find domestic partners able to build winning coalitions (Risse-Kappen 1994). Putnam (1988) suggests that an existing coalition constrains a leader because that leader has invested a certain fixed cost in it. Constructing a different coalition may either be impossible or too politically costly. In general, then, the greater a group's political representation, the more pivotal its role for the government, and the more general support it can find for its views, the greater its influence is likely to be.

When studying domestic politics as an intervening variable, the challenge clearly is to identify whose opposition matters, how much it matters, and the conditions for overcoming such resistance. Thus, my empirical inquiry asks what the disposition of parliament was to a specific issue at a specific time. Who opposed the recommended change? What was their influence in parliament? How opposed were they? That is, were the differences between international policy preferences and domestic policy preferences minor and thus fairly easily reconciled, or were they fundamentally in conflict with the defining characteristics of the policy reputations of the domestic actors? Thus, to understand when states will adopt the institutions' desired policies, I ask how doing so will influence the domestic power balance among different political actors. Several actors may influence the process and policy outcome.

Ethnic Minorities

Ethnic minority groups naturally favor liberal policies that tend to be in line with international standards that protect them. Indeed, in some cases ethnic minority groups want more rights or protections than international institutions promote, which is particularly evident in regard to the issue of collective rights (favored by minorities) versus individual rights (favored by institutions). Nevertheless, if minority politicians are in the government coalition, they are likely to lobby for favorable outcomes generally aligned with the goals of international institutions. Thus, strong political influence by ethnic minority groups should facilitate, perhaps even make superfluous, the efforts of international institutions.

Nationalists

Several groups in target states have strong stakes in policies related to ethnic minorities. In young democratic states with ethnic minorities, parties often organize along ethnic lines.[31] Nationalist politicians and parties, who by definition are concerned with the preservation of their own nation and peoples, and consider other ethnic groups a threat, can, however, represent a strong opposition.[32] Thus, nationalist efforts are likely to diminish the effectiveness of international institutions. For example, strong nationalist opposition to reform could threaten government stability if the government reverses nationalist policies. Studies have found that states fail to make international agreements if a narrow but well-organized group bears the costs of making such agreements. If that group also holds a politically privileged position, agreement is even less likely.[33] And indeed, nationalists are often strongly organized and often hold strategic positions, such as membership on critical committees or ministerial posts, because leaders of postcommunist transitions in several states have often used ethnic nationalism to build political support. Thus, scholars suggest that it is the nationalist element that has kept Romania, Slovakia, and Bulgaria behind Poland, Hungary, and the Czech Republic on political reforms (Vachudová and Snyder 1997).

General Parliamentary Disposition

Decision makers may resist a particular issue even when they are not vested in nationalist rhetoric on other issues. History or current events may elicit staunch nationalist views on select issues in a large spectrum of politicians and the public, although those actors may otherwise take a more conciliatory line than outright nationalist politicians. Such a prevailing general attitude can undermine institutional efforts. Thus, if most parliamentarians have a restrictive view on, say, language rights for minorities, then institutions are less likely to be effect agreements on that issue.

Authoritarian Leadership

Recently, scholars have focused more on the role of elites and leadership (see, e.g., Brown 1997c; Schraeder 1994). The quality of leadership can be critical to shaping relations domestically and internationally, particularly in authoritarian states, where leaders have more relative influence. An authoritarian regime is defined as a "domestic political system with limited, not responsible, political pluralism, varying degrees of social and economic pluralism, and a government leadership consisting of a leader, or small group of leaders, who exercise power within ill-defined formal limits" (Linz 1970,

255; Gottlieb 1997). Thus, leaders may contribute individually to political outcomes based on their personalities, beliefs, and preferences (Linz and Stepan 1996, 35; Vachudová and Snyder 1997, 5). Others argue that the quality of leadership is significant because of the difference in decision-making structures in democratic versus authoritarian states. Ironically, research on economic conditionality by the IMF and the World Bank suggests that traditional conditionality may work well in authoritarian contexts, where the institutions need to consult fewer stakeholders, which facilitates consensus building (Killick 1998, 114). This is somewhat similar to the argument by Evangelista (1995) that, in a somewhat paradoxical way, state strength may facilitate external influence. While authoritarian regimes thus overall may be less receptive to external actors, those actors who do manage to gain access often hold a privileged status and see a higher implementation rate. Conversely, as societies become more open, external actors have easier access but also have to compete with other societal actors and ideas.

On the issue of ethnic policies, however, authoritarian leaders and authoritarian governing styles *decrease* the effectiveness of the use of membership incentives because political requirements, such as those on ethnic minority issues and the democracy requirements advanced alongside them, are often a threat to the political survival of authoritarian leaders (Burnell 1994; Vachudová and Snyder 1997). Thus, authoritarian leaders are unlikely to provide any institutional access at all. This is one of the reasons that the HCNM was less active in Slovakia and Romania during the Meciar and Iliescu regimes than in the Baltic States. Thus, Brown (1997a; 1997b) argues that one of the sources of ethnic conflict is "bad leaders." Similarly, Pridham notes that the scope for EU influence on regimes with authoritarian tendencies, which he calls "hybrid regimes" or "pariah regimes," "is probably very limited" (1999, 1224). Specifically, membership incentives may be particularly prone to failure if leaders can protect their personal interests better by not following the institutions' recommendations. Thus, for example, if leaders maintain power via corrupt or undemocratic practices, joining European structures that demand more democratic behavior would undermine their personal power. Similarly, if leaders rally power and popularity by using ethnic issues to provoke fear, conforming to international standards on ethnic minorities could threaten their personal power base. Thus, while the cost-benefit analysis on behalf of the country may favor following international recommendations, the leader's personal cost-benefit calculation comes out in the red. Consequently, Hawkins argues, authoritarian leaders will follow international norms to placate international opponents only when it "allows the regime to shore up its authority and legitimacy and to deflect international pressures" (1997, 407–8). Generally, authoritarian leaders interpret norms to their advantage—that is, to justify violations (Shannon 2000).

Hypotheses Derived from Theory of Domestic Factors

In summary, policies will be less akin to institutional and international preferences when domestic opposition, in particular nationalist influence, in parliament increases; parliament in general holds nationalist or strict preferences on an issue; or domestic leadership relies on corruption or prefers to maintain personal power at the expense of democracy. Conversely, institutionally preferred outcomes are more likely when the influence of ethnic minorities in parliament increases. The latter may be the result of the efforts of the institutions but of the bargaining power of the ethnic minorities in the coalition.

SUMMARY OF HYPOTHESES

In countries facing ethnic tensions, I offer these hypotheses.

A. The Engagement Hypothesis

Institutional engagement improves policy outcomes. International institutions can produce policy outcomes compatible with international norms. Without institutional involvement, policy outcomes are seldom compatible with international norms.

B. The Strategy Hypotheses

B1. *Alone, normative pressure tends to fail.* Normative pressure alone is rarely sufficient to bring about the institutions' preferred policy outcomes.

B2. *Conditionality combined with normative pressure enhances the likelihood of success.* International institutions can significantly increase their ability to produce their preferred policy outcomes in a target state if they link membership incentives to changes in behavior.

B2i. *The effectiveness of conditionality depends on its credibility.* The linkage to membership incentives may fail if conditionality is not credible either because the state believes that the institution will admit it even if the state does not make the specified policy change (overconfidence) or because the state believes that the institution will withhold or stall admission even if the state does make the specific policy change (lack of confidence).

B2ii. *Gradual incentives and mechanisms for admission build credibility, add levers, and subsequently increase the effectiveness of membership incentives.*

C. The Domestic Hypothesis

Increased domestic opposition decreases the probability of compatible outcomes and may even hinder institutional efforts. Basically, policy outcomes are less likely to be compatible with international standards and institutional requirements, when

Ci. Domestic opposition by a political group in parliament increases,

Cii. Parliament has strong nationalist tendencies or strict preferences on an issue, and

Ciii. The domestic leadership relies on corruption or prefers to maintain personal power at the expense of the general democratic norms of the international institutions.

Civ. Conversely, compatible outcomes are more likely when the influence of ethnic minorities in parliament or in government increases. This may not be because of the efforts of the institutions, however, but rather because of the bargaining power of the ethnic minorities in the coalition.

CHAPTER 3

Quantifying and Exploring the Data

To ANALYZE the legislative issues related to ethnic minorities from 1990 through 1999 in the four countries, I traced each issue over time and observed how international institutions were or were not involved in the issue, how the legislature addressed the issue, and how the issue in general fit into such larger events as parliamentary changes, elections, institutional developments, and so on. The first step in the analysis was to write systematic timelines putting all domestic and European events into a larger context. Next, I wrote domestic case studies detailing the issue area, the initial preferences of parliament, the preferences and actions of the institutions, and so on. Each case lent itself to a set of standard questions about observable implications of institutional actions, including sequencing and timing as well as the content of policies in comparison with international preferences. I then assessed the degree of domestic opposition, the type of institutional involvement—if any—and the government's policy behavior. I found it preferable not to lag the dependent variable.[1] To address the potential discrepancy between policy and implementation, I also considered implementation in cases where it cast further light over an outcome. Thus, for example, cases such Baltic citizenship policy as well as the treaties with Hungary specifically discuss implementation failures. This allows the study to focus on legislation, gaining the benefits of a consistent measure, while not being fooled by paper compliance. Generally, however, as I readdress in the conclusion implementation of the policies on ethnic minorities is lagging, which actually can be both good and bad for ethnic minorities, depending on the character of the legislation.

UNDERSTANDING THE VARIABLES

The Outcome Variable: Minority-related Policy

The qualitative analysis seeks a full description of the outcome variable. If the institutions made recommendations, what were they and were they met? Was an outcome that worsened the situation prevented? This effect is important to consider; otherwise one could falsely interpret the status quo as a failure of institutional engagement. While progress is clearly preferable to the status quo, preventing regression is also a valuable achievement. How large were the domestic compromises made considering the initially expected outcome? If the institutions did not make any recommendations, how did the outcome compare with international standards?[2] Thus, regardless of whether the institutions were involved, the study examines each case individually and compares the outcome with the various efforts to alter it.

For the quantitative analysis, the study evaluates if the outcomes were "not compatible with institutional goals or international standards," "partly compatible with institutional goals or international standards," or "compatible with institutional goals or international standards." For convenience, I refer to these outcomes as "not compatible," "partly compatible," and "compatible." While some cases defy rigid classification—which is why the qualitative analysis is invaluable—the classification scheme is shown in appendix II.

The Explanatory Variables: Normative Pressure and Conditionality

I operationalize "normative pressure" as an instance in which an institution expresses a concern about a policy and makes recommendations on the direction of the policy. For the qualitative analysis I ask, Who applied the pressure? How frequent was it? What was its content? Was the language clear? How much institutional authority did the messenger or the communication have? For the quantitative analysis I primarily determine whether any institution made specific comments on the policy issue or not. If such efforts were present in any significant form *and if no attempts to use incentives were present*, I label normative pressure only as present, and if not, I label it as absent.

Conditionality is operationalized as an instance when an institution links admission to the fulfillment of a recommendation. For the quantitative analysis, I primarily ask whether any institution made a direct linkage between membership and the country's behavior on a certain policy issue or not. I label conditionality as I label normative pressure: present or absent. Note that normative pressure is always present with conditionality. If pressure equals 1, regardless of whether incentives were used, then the conditionality variable will only capture the marginal effect of using incentives.

The qualitative variable consists of a thicker description of the linkage. Aside from examining whether any institution make explicit linkage between behavior and membership, I ask if the institution behaved in such a way that the country had good reason to believe that the institution would reward the benefit if the requirements were met. Or, did the country have good reasons to believe that it could obtain the benefits without meeting the requirements? That is, I consider the credibility of the conditionality.

Domestic Control Variables

On the domestic political preferences, the study is mostly concerned with a parliament's degree of opposition to a change in policy. I refer to this as the normative gap between the preferences of the institutions and those of the state actors. Where institutions are not involved, the gap refers to the difference between the preferences of the government and international standards in general.[3] As I discussed in chapter 2, several factors influence the overall parliamentary disposition. The normative gap increases if nationalists (or other strong opponents) to the particular policy in parliament hold key positions in parliament. Are they part of a majority or minority government coalition, or are they in the opposition during a minority or majority government? If nationalist parties, or parties strongly opposed to the institutional goals on ethnic minority policy, control the government and the government has a firm majority, then policy incompatible with the institutions or international standards should follow. Also, if the nationalists form a strong opposition, then they may also be able to push their policies through or block improvements. This would be more likely when there is a minority government that depends on the opposition. Also, the stronger the views of the nationalists or politicians opposed to the institutional or international norms, the stronger their influence may be if they are in positions to bargain with the government or coalition partners. This can vary across issues within one government.[4] The normative gap also increases if the parliament in general holds strict nationalist-like preferences on a particular issue or if a strong leader opposes the policy. But the normative gap decreases if ethnic minority politicians are part of a government coalition and can bargain for favorable outcomes.

Thus, to make a quantitative assessment of the influence of domestic opposition, the study considers all these factors and codes the influence of domestic opposition quantitatively as being weak, moderate, or strong.[5] The quantitative data also assesses separately whether minorities are part of the government coalition, and whether authoritarian leadership was present or absent. Table 3.1 provides an overview of the quantitative variables. I have also included an a variable called involvement, which is equal to one if institutions are involved, regardless of whether they are using normative pressure only or membership conditionality, and zero otherwise.

Data Sources and Limitations

Given that the study is not concerned with who was persuaded but rather with ultimate behavior, the most important data for the dependent variable is the initial policy on a given issue and the final policy. While the dependent variable does include considerations of implementation, for parsi-

TABLE 3.1
Coding of variables

Variables	Coding
Normative pressure *only*	Yes/no
Membership conditionality	Yes/no
Involvement	Yes/no
Domestic opposition	Weak/moderate/strong
Authoritarian leadership	Yes/no
Ethnic minorities in government	Yes/no
Policy outcome	Not compatible/partly compatible/compatible

mony and consistency I use legislation as the primarily measurement. I do consider implementation issues to the extent that they cast further light over an outcome. Generally, implementation of the policies on ethnic minorities is always lagging. This has both good and bad results. In education policy, where the parliament may vote to enforce the state language as the only language of instruction, a protracted lag benefits minorities, as this prolongs the use of their native language. Likewise, in language policy in which an individual would be required to know the state language to hold certain positions, it benefits the ethnic minority if the state does not have the capacity to enforce that policy for some years. On the other hand, lagging implementation of legislation on right to travel documents will harm minorities who depend on such documentation. Similarly, lagging capacity building of public officials to speak the language of ethnic minorities impairs any rights they may have to address officials in their native tongue. Thus, the implementation lag can go both ways. The solution is to use legislation as the primary measurement, and then to make adjustments based on observed implementation consequences.

On the independent variable, the most important data is a record of the frequency, content, and character of international involvement. Regarding causation, the most crucial data is the ability to link the above data via an observed process of interaction, action, and reaction. In assessing the domestic opposition, the most important data is party documentation, parliamentary discussion, news media, and interviews. Most of the above data is available, except the informal records. Also, in many cases policy makers do not state their direct motivations, although this information can to some extent be obtained through interviews.

Several sources contributed to tracking the ethnic minority-related legislation and events in Slovakia, Romania, Latvia, and Estonia from 1991 to 1999. First, I interviewed seventy-six persons at the EU in Brussels, the HCNM in The Hague, and government and other experts in the countries.[6] Second, I used primary documents from national parliaments and parties, and institutional records. Third, I used media reports, including translation of national media in the FBIS, World New Connection, and the Lexis-Nexis database. To counter biases introduced by such translation services, I made it a standard practice to use interviews to check my version of the story against the perceptions of different policy makers. I also balanced my input by reading such sources from the countries as TASS, CTK, and MTI. Finally, I used secondary scholarly analysis, including work by national scholars, publications from various advocacy groups, and so on.

Selection Bias

Two possible kinds of selection biases may cause particular problems. First, do institutions choose to become involved more frequently when the domestic opposition is weaker? Second, do institutions only make recommendations they think states will accommodate? In either case the effectiveness of international institutions would not be very surprising. Appendix I shows the data on involvement. Rather than the first bias, a selection bias points in the opposite direction. That is, institutions are more involved in cases when the domestic opposition is strong. Such selection bias only strengthens any conclusions as it makes it harder, not easier, for institutions to be effective. Regression analysis confirms that a stronger nationalist influence increases the likelihood of involvement. This may result from higher pressure within the institutions to become involved in the case of high-profile issues. This selection bias may pose a statistical problem: domestic opposition may wrongly be attributed with some positive effect because it is a predictor of involvement. Regression analysis does not, however, show nationalism as a significant predictor of whether institutions will use membership incentives or normative pressure.

Qualitative analysis also shows that institutions do not only make recommendations that are easily accommodated. Their recommendations are often controversial in the domestic arena, and they are often quite narrowly delineated, as demonstrated in the precise language of the letters of the HCNM or requests for Latvia and Estonia to amend their citizenship laws to allow stateless children to become citizens at birth. It has sometimes been the case, however, that the institutions' requests were so demanding that the institutions had to be satisfied with compromise solutions because they realized that further insistence could backfire. In such instances one has to evaluate how considerable the concession to the institution was, and if it would have occurred without the institution's original demand. This is also why the coding of the outcome variable has three levels, not just two, to allow for such intermediate outcomes.

As with any quasi-experimental design, systematic differences in involvement in different countries could also be a concern, because other unknown factors could then explain the outcomes. As table I.c in appendix I shows, both in absolute and relative terms, institutions used membership incentives most in Slovakia and least in Romania. Many cases in Latvia and Estonia never received international attention, which was never the case in Slovakia. While these country differences should be kept in mind during the analysis, however, the distribution of involvement type is better than if there had been a clear distinction between Latvia and Estonia versus Romania and Slovakia, which is not the case. All in all, the cases provide good grounds for gaining analytical leverage on the hypotheses.

Testing Interactive Relationships

With sixty-four observations, the quantitative data allows for testing additive models about the role of normative pressure, conditionality, and domestic opposition. The number of observations leads to problems of identification, however, when one moves to test interactive effects between domestic opposition and institutional efforts. The selection bias discussed above further complicates quantitative testing of interactive relationship, because domestic opposition, as a predictor of institutional involvement, may indirectly have some positive effect on outcome. Thus, the study's inferences about interactive relationships rely on descriptive statistics and draw their main support from the qualitative case studies.

STATISTICAL RESULTS AND INSIGHTS

I first provide simple tabular overviews of the relationships between variables and then, when possible, apply ordered logit analysis, which is particularly useful with more than two ordered, discrete outcomes. At the end of this analysis, I summarize the quantitative findings in a discussion of predicted probabilities and discuss the relationships suggested by the data.

The Engagement Hypothesis

The engagement hypotheses proposes that regardless of what approach the institutions take, the domestic policy choices are more likely to be compatible with international standards when international institutions are en-

TABLE 3.2
Distribution of outcomes by institutional involvement

	Compatible outcome	Partly compatible outcome	Not compatible	Total
Institutions involved	16	7	21	44
Institutions not involved	2	2	16	20
Total	18	9	37	64

Pearson Chi^2(2) = 6.2165 Pr = 0.045

TABLE 3.3
The role of institutional involvement in determining policy

Independent variable	Coefficient
Involvement	3.2120***
Domestic opposition	-0.9350**
Minorities in government	1.3478
Authoritarian leader	0.1521

*** p < 0.001 ** p < 0.01
n = 64
log likelihood+ -47.318917
Pseudo R^2 = 0.2213
Model + ordered logit

gaged. Quantitative analysis confirms this. Table 3.2 gives a simple comparison of the outcomes of the cases in which the institutions were involved with the cases in which they were not. Without institutional involvement, 20 percent of cases show a compatible or partly compatible outcome. But with institutional involvement, 52 percent of cases (an additional 32 percent) show compatible or partly compatible outcomes—this even though, as the discussion of selection bias addressed, institutions tend to become more involved in harder cases.

The relationship holds even when controlling for the influence of domestic opposition. Ordered logit analysis, shown in table 3.3, suggests that a binary factor of institutional involvement is significant in explaining the outcomes, even when the logit includes the domestic opposition.[7] This lends strong support to the hypotheses that in comparison with cases where international institutions do not become involved, engagement by international institutions is more likely to produce policy outcomes that are compatible with international standards.

TABLE 3.4

Distribution of outcomes by type of institutional involvement

	Compatible outcome	Partly compatible outcome	Not compatible	Total
Membership conditionality	14	2	3	19
Normative pressure only	2	5	18	25
Institutions not involved	2	2	16	20
Total	18	9	37	64

Pearson Chi^2(4) = 29.3660 Pr = 0.000

The Strategy Hypotheses: Type of Institutional Involvement

While institutional engagement overall improves policy compatibility with international standards, what does the analysis reveal about the individual institutional strategies? What happens when the cases in which institutions only use normative pressure are isolated from the cases in which they also use incentives? To analyze this, it is necessary to create a dummy variable for cases in which institutions used normative pressure alone and another dummy variable for the cases in which they combined incentives with normative pressure. Since there are many cases that do not involve the institutions at all, these dummy variables are not perfectly negatively correlated.

The quantitative analysis supports the initial hypothesis: institutional involvement is more often associated with positive change when institutions combine incentives with normative pressure rather than when they use normative pressure alone. Indeed, although both factors are significant, the difference in magnitude is quite large.

Table 3.4 shows that "compatible" outcomes occurred in almost three-quarters of cases combining membership conditionality with normative pressure, but it only occurred twice when institutions used the nonincentive-based techniques alone, or in 8 percent of the cases. This suggests that incentives are essential in bringing about the policy change. Normative pressure alone is only partially effective; actually, in the tabular overview, the outcomes for using pressure alone hardly differ from those in which institutions were uninvolved. This overview of course does not control for domestic opposition, which is very important. Ordered logit analysis, however, which does control for the degree of domestic opposition, also supports the conclusion that incentives are extremely significant in determining the outcome. Normative pressure alone, while also statistically significant, carries less explanatory power.

TABLE 3.5
The role of institutional involvement in determining policy

	Regression I	Regression II	Regression III	Regression IV
Involvement	3.2120***	—	—	—
Normative Pressure only	—	2.4181*	2.4740*	2.6143*
Membership conditionality	—	6.0704 ***	6.1812***	6.3506***
Domestic opposition	−0.9350**	−1.3670 ***	−1.2433**	−1.3929**
Minorities in government	1.3478	—	1.5461	1.5222
Authoritarian leader	0.1521	—	—	0.5792
Log likelihood	−47.318917	−36.885034	−35.843168	−35.687695
Pseudo R²	0.2213	0.3930	0.4101	0.4127

Based on 64 observations.
Model: Ordered logit
* $p < 0.05$; ** $p < 0.01$; ***$p < 0.001$

Note in table 3.5 that the coefficient on membership conditionality is an expression of the combined effect of using normative pressure and incentives. That is, whenever membership conditionality is set equal to 1, normative pressure is always present. Another way of looking at the data is to define "normative pressure" as equal to 1 whenever normative pressure is present and to allow this to figure separately in a regression. This results in identical logit results, but one where the coefficient on "membership conditionality" in regression II is reduced to 3.65, which is then a pure expression of the marginal effect of using membership incentives. The coefficient on the normative pressure variable is then equal to 2.42, confirming that it is exactly picking up the difference between the coefficient for conditionality and the original 6.07 coefficient for the combined use of normative pressure and conditionality. Thus, one can say that 2.42 is the independent effect of using normative pressure alone, and 3.65 is the marginal effect of using conditionality as well.

Examining whether the effect of using normative pressure is somehow skewed because conditionality only appears together with normative pressure is also important. Even if one examines just cases in which institutions were either not involved or in which they used normative pressure only, however, the results confirm the findings (see table 3.6). Here, the coefficient on using pressure is similar to that of the above regressions, only slightly lower. Even the coefficient on domestic opposition also remains almost the same. These results confirm the robustness of the findings.

TABLE 3.6
Determinants of outcome for subset of cases without incentive use

	Regression V
Normative Pressure	2.333462*
Domestic Opposition	−1.333028***
n	45
log likelihood	−25.257833
Pseudo R²	0.2165
Model	ologit

*p < 0.05
***p < 0.001

So how important is normative pressure when used alone? Despite the minor variation in outcomes in table 3.3 between cases with no involvement and cases with normative pressure only, normative pressure does have some effect. The key, however, is that, the significance of normative pressure only appears when also considering domestic opposition.[8] This occurs precisely because normative pressure alone tends to be most effective when the opposition is low. In conclusion, the original coefficients seem consistent, whether the data are divided or not. This increases the confidence in the results. Normative pressure is not a negligible factor in explaining policy behavior, and it deserves discussion and attention, but membership incentives add much more explanatory leverage.

Predicted Probabilities

Converting the regression analysis results from table 3.4 to predicted probabilities makes it easier to grasp the magnitudes of each factor, although one should be quite cautious when interpreting results where some scores are predicted from very few cases.[9] Table 3.7 shows the predicted probabilities based on an ordered logit including the significant factors of "domestic opposition," "pressure only," and "membership incentives." (For a complete table, see appendix III). If

$$S_j = X_{1j}\beta_1 + X_{2j}\beta_2$$

is the predicted score, and k_1 and k_2 are the cut points, and u_j is the error term, which is assumed to be logistically distributed in ordered logit, then the probability that $S_j + u_j$ lies between a the two cut points is

$$\Pr(k_1 < S_j + u_j < k_2) = 1 / (1 + eS_j - k_2) - 1 / (1 + eS_j - k_1)$$

Table 3.7
Predicted probabilities of a compatible outcome

	Institutions not involved (percent)	Normative pressure only (percent)	Normative pressure and conditionality (percent)
Strong domestic opposition	0	3	57
Moderate domestic opposition	3	23	93*
Weak domestic opposition	24	74*	99

* These calculations are based on less than five observations and should be interpreted with caution.

Table 3.7 shows the predicted scores for obtaining a compatible outcome for each of the types of institutional involvement, while holding the degree of domestic opposition constant. Thus, for example, given a strong domestic opposition, the predicted score of a compatible outcome increases from 3 percent when institutions use normative pressure alone to 57 percent when institutions also link membership incentives to the behavior.

Domestic Opposition: How Large a Role?

As expected, the regressions consistently show that the degree of domestic opposition is a statistically significant factor in predicting the policy outcome. Domestic opposition, however, appears to be significant partly because it explains the cases without institutional involvement. Table 3.7 also suggests that the influence of normative pressure alone may gain some of its significance from its ability to influence cases in which the domestic opposition is weak. Thus, when the domestic opposition is weak, the predicted score for a compatible outcome rises by 20 when international institutions use normative pressure alone, as opposed to only a 3 percent effect at high levels of domestic opposition. When the domestic opposition is weak, the effect is even greater, though the small number of cases here suggest caution in interpreting the results. In general, both methods appear to work better the lower the domestic opposition. As discussed above, under data limitations, this can only be taken as a suggestion of some interactive effect and not as evidence, since the predicted scores are based on an additive model that does not include factors that allow domestic opposition to interact with institutional involvement. Table 3.6 does suggest, however, that the stronger the domestic opposition, the less likely are compatible outcomes, which is consistent with the hypothesized effect of domestic opposition. Surprising, however, is the fact that *the added effect of incentive use is large even when the domestic opposition is high*.

TABLE 3.8

Outcome for subset of cases with strong domestic opposition

	Compatible outcome	Partly compatible outcome	Not compatible	Total
No involvement	0	0	6	6
Normative pressure only	0	3	12	15
Membership conditionality	7	2	3	12
Total	7	5	21	34

Pearson Chi^2(4) = 18.9936 Pr = 0.001

Thus, using incentives seem to have remarkably good results despite the degree of nationalism. Table 3.8 shows the outcomes of the cases of strong domestic opposition broken down by institutional involvement. Incentives largely worked in these cases, while normative pressure alone did not. Thus, while some evidence in general favors the hypothesis that the greater the domestic opposition, the less institutions can bring about their desired policy outcomes, it nevertheless appears that institutions can overcome quite high levels of domestic opposition when they combine membership incentives with normative pressure.

Other Domestic Factors

Authoritarian leadership, as in the cases of Meciar and Iliescu, or the presence of minority parties in the government coalition, understandably does influence outcomes. Thus, seventy-one percent of cases of authoritarian leadership had outcomes that were not compatible with international standards, compared to only 53 percent of cases with no authoritarian leadership. Even more notably, while 75 percent of cases with *minorities in government* had compatible outcomes, this was only the case in only 21 percent of cases with no minority representation. Caution is necessary here, however, as the cases with authoritarian leadership or minorities in government are quite low. Also, these variables are correlated with the level of domestic opposition, which is why the inclusion of authoritarian leadership in regression IV of table 2.1, is somewhat spurious. The inclusion of minorities in government does in regressions II and IV does show the expected direction of effect, although it is not statistically significant. Indeed, descriptive quantitative analysis indicates that these factors simply are not exhaustive explanations because these factors are lacking from many cases. Thus, saying that these factors explain the outcomes is probably an oversimplifica-

TABLE 3.9
Outcome by presence or absence of authoritarian leader

	Not compatible	Partly compatible	Compatible	Total
No authoritarian leader	25	7	15	47
Authoritarian leader	12	2	3	17

Based on 64 cases.
Pearson $Chi^2(2) = 1.6441$
Pr = 0.440

tion. Noticeably, however, even when controlling for authoritarian leaders or ethnic minorities in government and the size and significance of the other explanatory variables, normative pressure only, incentives and pressure, and domestic opposition remain consistent. This suggests that the findings about these variables are robust. (See tables 3.9 and 3.10.)

SUMMARY

The quantitative analysis of the data supports the hypotheses that institutional engagement leads to more compatible policies, and that institutions achieve the greatest impact if they use membership conditionality rather than normative pressure alone. On the influence of domestic opposition, the quantitative data finds that domestic opposition is indeed significant in predicting the outcome of policies. The predictive power of domestic opposition, however, may not be consistent. The descriptive data indicate that domestic opposition may be most influential when international institutions are not involved at all, and, further, that domestic opposition may be better able to thwart normative pressure efforts than conditionality use. Thus, the quantitative data finds domestic opposition to be a significant factor that may also interact with the institutional efforts to decrease their effectiveness.

Authoritarian leadership or the presence of ethnic minorities in government does show predictable relationships with policy outcomes. Given that these factors are often completely absent from cases, however, they naturally represent an incomplete explanation. That is, policies are not merely shaped by the domestic opposition or by the presence or absence of authoritarian leadership or ethnic representation in government.

INTRODUCTION TO THE QUALITATIVE ANALYSIS

To improve understanding of the causal relationship between domestic opposition, the different institutional types of involvement, and policy out-

TABLE 3.10
Outcome by presence or absence of minorities in government

	Not compatible	Partly compatible	Compatible	Total
No minorities	35	9	12	56
Minorities	2	0	6	8

Pearson Chi^2(2) = 10.1313 Pr = 0.006

comes, qualitative analysis becomes crucial. The case study analysis in the following chapters relies on structured, focused comparison and process tracing. Structured focus comparison "defines and standardizes the data requirements of the case studies . . . by formulating theoretically relevant general questions to guide the examination of each case" (George and McKeown 1985, 41). Process tracing examines causation by using interviews, secondary sources, and written statements to understand the thinking of the main actors and the connection between events. Thus, the main goal of the case studies is to discover if the chain of events or decision-making process unfold in the manner predicted by the theory, and whether actors speak and behave as the theory predicts (Van Evera 1997, 64). The systematization of the historical data and the attention to how events unfold complemented by quantitative analysis makes inferences sounder. Thus, case studies go beyond correlation arguments and allow more understanding of the motives and attitudes of decision makers. It also permits further study of observable implications about timing and action-reactions (Chayes and Chayes 1993; Underdal 1998).

The study includes sixty-four case studies of various issues that governments in different countries have addressed over time. Rather than dividing these cases into types of involvement and discussing them accordingly, however, I discuss the cases by country. This provides the reader with better insights into the situation in each country and makes the accounts much more narrative. The disadvantage, of course, is that the overview of the argument can get lost. Thus, in the conclusion I pay extra attention to summing up the cases in the light of the arguments of the book. The next four chapters discuss Estonia, Latvia, Slovakia, and Romania in turn. Each chapter proceeds by discussing the ethnic situation in each country and providing a brief overview of the political context over the course of the decade. Next I discuss individual cases by issue. Thus, how three different governments dealt with a single issue, which in the quantitative analysis is broken into three different cases, will appear as one long case, in which I draw comparisons over time.

Table 3.11
Case study overview

		Domestic opposition	Involvement	Outcome
	Latvia			
1991	Initial citizenship legislation	S	P	I
1992	Law on foreigners and stateless persons	M-S	N	I
1993–4	Citizenship law	M-S	I	C
1994–5	Language requirements for naturalization	M	P	I
1994–5	Law on Status of Former Citizens of the USSR	M	I	C
1995–7	Attempt to amend citizenship law	S	P	I
1998–9	Easing naturalization tests	M	P	S
1998	Citizenship law: stateless children and quotas	S	I	C
1991	Education law	M-S	N	I
1995	Education law amendments	M	N	I
1996	Attempt to amend education law	M-S	N	I
1998	New education law	S	P	I
1992	Language law amendment	M-S	P	I
1995	Attempt to amend language law	M	N	I
1997–8	Attempts to amend language law	S	I	S
1999	New language law	M-S	I	C
1994–5	Local and national election laws	M	N	I
1996	Attempt to tighten election laws	M-S	N	I
1991	Cultural autonomy	W	N	S
1996	Unemployment benefits	M-S	N	I
1997	Labor Law	S	P	S
	Estonia			
1991–2	Citizenship legislation	M	N	I
1991–2	Amendments to simplify naturalization for loyal citizens	W	N	C
1992–4	Language requirements for naturalization	M	P	I
1993	Residence: initial law on Aliens	M-S	I	S
1994	Policy to speed implementation of law on aliens	M	P	I
1994–5	New citizenship law	M	P	I
1995–6	Testing requirements for naturalization	M	P	S
1995–7	Law on residency and its implementation	M	N	I
1997	Law on residency: permanent residents	W-M	I	C
1998	Citizenship for stateless children	M-S	I	C
1992–5	Language legislation	M	P	I
1995–6	Attempt to amend language law	M	N	I
1997–9	Amendments to amend language law	M	N	I
1999	New language law	M	I	C
1993	Education: law on public schools	M	N	I
1998	Education law	W	I	C
1993	Local election law	W	N	S
1996–8	Local elections law	M	P	I

TABLE 3.11
Case study overview (*cont'd*)

		Slovakia		
		Domestic opposition	Involvement	Outcome
1992–3	Laws on the use of personal and place names	S	P	I
1994	Laws on the use of personal and place names	W-M	P	C
1994–8	Education issues	S	P	S
1994–8	Bilingual school certificates	S	I	I
1998	School certificates	W	I	C
1995–6	Language law	S	P	I
1996–8	Minority language law	S	I	I
1998	Minority language law	W	I	C
1994–8	Cultural subsidies	S	P	I
1994–8	Election laws	S	I	I
1995	Treaty with Hungary	S	I	C
1994–5	Round table	S	P	I
1995–7	Penalty code	S	I	C
1995–8	Local administrative reform	S	P	I
		Romania		
1992–6	Bilingual road signs	S	P	I
1997–9	Bilingual road signs	W-M	N	I
1990–1	Law on national minorities	W-M	N	I
1996–7	Law on national minorities	S	P	I
1992–6	Language in official contacts	S	P	I
1997–9	Language in official contacts	W-M	I	C
1994–6	Reform on school language	S	P	S
1996–9	Education law	M	P (mild I)*	C
1992–6	Appointment of ethnic prefects	S	N	I
1996	Appointment of ethnic prefects	W	N	C
1994–6	Treaty with Hungary	S	I	C

* Although Agenda 2000 mentioned the expectation of educational reform, the use of incentives in this case was very mild. In the quantitative data this case is coded as pressure only, perhaps favorably biasing the explanatory power of normative pressure

N = No involvement   W = Weak
P = Normative pressure only   I = Incompatible
I = Membership Incentives   S = Somewhat compatible
S = Strong   C = Compatible
M = Moderate

CASE STUDY OVERVIEW

Table 3.11 provides an overview of the cases by country and issue, with a breakdown of the domestic opposition, the type of involvement, and the outcome. While I do not discuss all the cases in detail in this book, table 3.11 provides a good link between the quantitative analysis and the case studies. It shows how the cases derive from systematically dividing country studies into issues and government periods. It also facilitates an analytical overview of each issue, demonstrating in many cases how the legislative outcomes were incompatible or only somewhat compatible when the institutions were not involved or relied only on normative pressure, and how the use of incentives frequently brought about compatible outcomes in terms of favorable legislation.

PART II

Case Studies

CHAPTER 4

Lativia: Overcoming Opposition

LATVIA'S POST–World War II history is similar to that of Estonia. Because of Soviet population policies, by 1989 the Latvian share of Latvia's population had declined to levels even lower than the Estonian share of Estonia's population.[1] (See figure 4.1.)

The non-Latvian population was generally not concentrated in any one geographic area and did not live in border areas with Russia. According to the 1989 census, however, Latvians had become a minority in the eight largest cities. For example, in Latvia's capital, Riga, in 1994, ethnic Latvians only accounted for 37.7 percent, while ethnic Russians, Belarussians, and Ukrainians were 57.3 percent. Thus, the dominant language in Riga was Russian.[2] In all of Latvia, 60.4 percent of Latvians knew Russian, while only 18.3 percent among non-Latvians knew the Latvian language.[3] Thus, if anything, Latvians had accommodated to the needs of the Russians, rather than visa versa. While some assimilation naturally occurred, intermarriage, for example, was only at about 20 percent.[4]

As the independence movement grew, the USSR tried to assert itself militarily.[5] After attacks on the parliament and on the ministry of the interior in Riga, however, the failure of Moscow's attempt at a military solution was clear, and 1991 continued with political confrontation only, until Latvia regained independence.[6]

After independence, at least a third of the population was effectively stateless.[7] Thus, Latvia needed to pass a citizenship law and to provide a legal status for noncitizens. Issues related to language, legislation, and employment also needed to be resolved. The noncitizens faced several practical restrictions on their rights, including limitations on travel, and the inability to hold several jobs, including firefighter and airline pilot, and to receive certain benefits from the state. Tensions mounted. Many noncitizens had voted for independence and felt cheated when they were denied citizenship and voting rights in the newly independent country. On the other hand, Latvian politicians overall were patriotic in the sense that they were eager to reestablish and protect the Latvian state. Thus, even more so than in Estonia, many parties advocated a strict ethnic policy.[8]

As table 4.1 shows, numerous parties competed in this Latvian political environment. Several were rather short lived, merging with other parties or playing only minor roles. The most vocal opposition on ethnic political

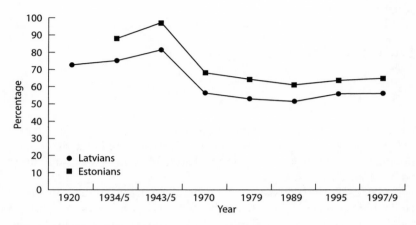

Figure 4.1. Latvian/Estonian population, 1923–99.

issues came from the Fatherland and Freedom party (FF) and the Latvian National Independence Movement (LNNK). While operating within a democratic framework and with their eyes looking toward integration with Europe, however, these parties did not combine corrupt practices with nationalist rhetoric, as is often associated with hard-line nationalism in such places as for example the former Yugoslavia. Nevertheless, they had considerable electoral support and represented legislative views that often conflicted with international institutions' advice on ethnic issues. Indeed, even more moderate parties often sided with the FF and the LNNK to pass legislation that restricted the rights of the noncitizens and non-Latvians. And although the nationalist-leaning parties were not part of the government from the fall of 1993 until the end of 1995, they still wielded considerable influence. The minority governments in power had to make compromises with the opposition, including the FF and LNNK. After December 1995 the FF and the LNNK became part of the government. During these years, however, the coalition was also often very broad, which demanded compromises to maintain the government. The FF/LNNK had the greatest influence during 1997–1998, when a member actually occupied the post of prime minister. While the FF/LNNK maintained considerable influence in Latvian politics, more extreme parties, for instance, the Siegerists, did not.[9]

CASE STUDIES

This chapter discusses four high profile ethnic minority issues that surfaced in Latvia during the 1990s. Each of the cases illustrates an argument in this

TABLE 4.1
Latvian governments, 1990–99

Government	Parties	Total seats
Ivars Godmanis (LPF) May 1990 to Summer 1993	LPF members and non-members backing the front	about 3/4 of total
Valdis Birkavs (LW) August 3, 1993 to July 14, 1994	LW LZS (LZS quit on July 14, 1994.)	48/100
Maris Gailis (LW) September 15, 1994 to December 22, 1995	LW NEPU plus independents	
Andris Skele (independent) December 22, 1995 to January 20, 1997	LW LZS (LZS quit on February 26, 1996) LNNK FF DPS LVP	73/100
Andris Skele (independent) February 13, 1997 to July 28, 1997	LW LNNK FF DPS others	65/100
Guntars Krasts (FF/LNIM) August 7, 1997 to April 29, 1998	LW FF/LNNK DPS (quit on April 8, 1998) LKDS/LZS + others	65/100
Guntars Krasts (FF/LNIM) April 29, 1998 to November 26, 1998	LW FF/LNNK LKDS others	48/100
Vilis Kristopans (LW) November 26, 1998 to July 1999	LW FF/LNNK JP	46/100
Andres Skele (People's Party) July 16, 1999–	LW FF/LNNK TP	62/100

Acronyms: LW: Latvian Way; LZS: Latvian Farmers Union; TPA: Political Union of Economists; LNNK: Latvian National Independence Party; FF: For the Fatherland and Freedom; DPS: Democratic Party Saimnieks; LVP: Latvian Unity Party; LKDS: Latvian Christian Democratic Union; LZP: Latvian Green Party; LNRP: Latvian National Reform Party; LPF: Latvian Popular Front; JP: New Party; TP: People's Party; NEPU: National Economics Political Union.

book. First, election laws illustrate how lack of institutional involvement often leads to policies that do not meet the needs of ethnic minorities. Next, education law demonstrates how a singular strategy of persuasive efforts fell short in achieving the desired policy changes. The language law, on the other hand, is an excellent example of how institutions can overcome even strong domestic opposition. Finally, issues of residency and citizenship underscore the necessity and effectiveness of combining normative efforts with conditionality.

ELECTION LAWS

In terms of research design, the case of election laws in Latvia provides a useful control case in that it illustrates the domestic behavior in the absence of the international engagement that this study emphasizes. It is not enough to show that international institutions are associated with outcomes compatible with international behavior. To demonstrate a cause-and-effect relationship, one must also show that outcomes in the absence of institutional engagement were not equally compatible with international standards. The case of Latvian election laws is particularly well suited for this comparison, as it is a case in which institutions were not involved at any time. Thus, there cannot be any spillover effects over time.

Three different Latvian governments had the national and local election legislation on their agenda. In 1994 many deputies emphasized language as a proof of loyalty and as a tool to minimize the influence of noncitizens and non-Latvians. The parliament passed a law on local elections that effectively limited the participation of almost half of Latvia's population from voting or standing in local elections.[10] The law, which limited voting and standing in elections to citizens, did not legally contradict international norms. Because of Latvia's large noncitizen population, however, the consequences were quite undemocratic: vast numbers of people were barred from any form of political participation, and Latvians governed many areas without any ethnic Russian representatives in local government, although the Russian-speaking population had a vast majority there. Even more questionable was the law's barring anyone from running who was not "proficient in the state language in accordance to the highest (third) level."[11] Candidates who had not graduated from a school with instruction in Latvian had to certify the highest knowledge level of the state language.[12] This barred many ethnic non-Latvians, even those Russian-speakers who were citizens, from running for local office. The international community did not react, and ethnic Russian attempts to soften the law failed.[13]

In the spring of 1995 the parliament began work on a national election law to bar Communist Party members and non-Latvian speakers from running for national office. The final version of this law also required candidates to have the highest level of language proficiency.[14] If the candidate had not completed the necessary education in a school with Latvian as the language of instruction, then the candidate had to submit a notarized document indicating the highest level of Latvian language skills.[15] As with the local election law, this barred many ethnic non-Latvians who were citizens from running for national office. Thus, Latvia had curbed the ethnic Russian political representation on both the local and the national level. In sum, the Latvian government unsatisfactorily solved the issues at hand in the absence of involvement by international institutions. Indeed, the election legislation was poor both from the perspective of the national minorities and from the viewpoint of democratic standards of representation.

Not until May 2002, outside the timeframe of this study, did Latvia finally abolish the language proficiency requirements for elections following private citizen action, which resulted in a judgment of the European Court of Human Rights on *Ingrida Podkolzina vs. Latvia*.[16] First, however, a month earlier, lawmakers approved constitutional amendments enshrining Latvian as the language of the parliament and local elected bodies. Further, the election law amendments were actually seen as catering to warnings voiced by NATO Secretary General George Robertson during a visit that the language requirements could hurt Latvia's chances of a NATO invitation.[17] Thus, even the better outcome in the end could be attributed to some form of conditionality.

EDUCATION LAW

Latvia's treatment of the education law is interesting because it is a case in which the HCNM engaged, sometimes in great detail, while the EU never did display much concern or interest in the matter. Thus, it provides a good test of the independent effect of purely normative-based efforts to engage governments in dialogue to urge them to conform to international standards. Unfortunately, however, cases like this are often overlooked because of the low level of engagement and the relatively poor results.[18]

Indeed, for years no institutions were concerned with education in Latvia, and the governments passed laws with questionable implications for minorities. Initially, in 1991, the Supreme Council adopted an education law[19] that fully guaranteed the right of education in Latvia for Latvians, but the rights of other nationalities were ambiguous.[20] The law provided for Latvian as the main language in Latvia's higher educational establishments from the second year onward.[21] This could make teaching in higher educational establishments in Russian highly problematic.[22] In March 1992 amendments to the language law[23] provided that as of July 1, 1993, all state-financed higher education institutions had to teach in Latvian beginning with the second year of studies.[24] By 1995, because of the logistical challenges of converting to Latvian instruction when so many children did not speak Latvian, however, the vast majority of the Latvian school system was still Russian-speaking. Certain politicians, in particularly those on the committee in charge of writing a new education law, preferred a strict plan for transition to Latvian education. In fact, the education law became an issue in the election campaign in 1995, with some parties arguing that the state should only finance education in Latvian. In August 1995 the parliament amended the education law so that as of September 1996, at least two subjects had to be taught in Latvian in all minority schools from the first to the ninth grade, and three humanitarian or exact subjects in grades 10 through 12.[25] A new and stricter law on education got bogged down by an overwhelming number of amendments.[26] Despite the numerous difficulties with the education system, the OSCE and the CE remained aloof from the debate.

The new FF/LNNK[27] candidate, Guntar Krasts, became prime minister in August 1997 after the Skele government's collapse. With seventeen parliamentary seats, FF/LNNK was the second-largest block in the legislature. The new party had just reaffirmed its nationalistic agenda on the occasion of its merger two months prior. In the joint congress in June, FF leader Maris Grinblats said that the new party's program would be based on national values, passage of a tough citizenship law, the promotion of the repatriation of aliens, and the preservation of the "purity of the Latvian language." Further, the program stated that the "the State shall support integration and assimilation of those nationals who are not ethnic Latvians. It is necessary to enhance a voluntary repatriation of persons arrived in Latvia during times of occupation and of their descendants."[28]

By 1997, as the education issue heated up, European institutions began to criticize the new language law, which now incorporated the education provisions. While the CE and the OSCE criticized the language law, however, they focused mainly on the law's provisions regarding the private sector, and not on the education provisions. The education provisions remained in the draft state language law when it was considered in the second reading in the spring of 1998.[29] The second-reading draft law envisaged a complete transfer to Latvian as the only study language in professional education institutions, while in general schools where Latvian was not the language of instruction, at least half of the courses should be taught in Latvian.[30] The provisions were to take effect starting September 1, 2005.

Not until 1998 did the HCNM really engage the educational provisions. In the fall of 1998 he met with politicians on the education issue to persuade the politicians that the law was incompatible with international standards. He voiced concerns about conflicts with international norms and potential practical difficulties, and offered extensive written comments on the language law, in which the educational provisions were still embedded. In particular, he recommended replacing the requirement of least half the subjects be in Latvian with the phrase, "Ethnic minorities have the right to be educated in the mother tongue in primary schools, in addition to learning the state language." He added, "While I fully support the necessity of transitional provisions relating to the implementation of the provisions on education, I propose that the specified dates for implementation be reviewed."[31] Soon afterward the HCNM sent another letter. His efforts were clear attempts to persuade policy makers of the morally optimal educational arrangements. He noted that the international documents dealing with education of national minorities envisaged that children must be ensured opportunities to study in their native language in primary school. He argued that primary schools should teach students mainly in their native language, and that only toward the end of the primary education could the schools introduce a few nontheoretical subjects in the state language. He also noted that if students had to take exams in the state language, then the state had a responsibility to ensure adequate teaching of the state language, so as not to disadvantage those students.[32]

These efforts did not work, however, illustrating the difficulties of getting the attention and cooperation of policy makers in the absence of linkage to tangible payoffs such as institutional membership. In spite of the fact that the HCNM's recommendations were detailed and specific to international standards, his efforts fell on deaf ears. A separate education law reemerged, and just after the October 1998 elections, parliament approved the second reading of the education bill, which would gradually shift instruction in all state secondary schools into Latvian by 2004. In late October, the outgoing parliament adopted the education law in the final reading, without incorporating many of the OSCE recommendations, which had indeed made it into earlier drafts. The measures were to be phased in over the next decade, while some institutions of higher education planned to switch to Latvian-only instruction as early as 1999, and others planned on following in 2004. Primary and the secondary education certificates could only be issued to children having passed a state language exam. Professional qualification exams and theses for academic degrees would only be accepted in the state language, except in special cases. The law also had a provision that state-financed continuing or adult education should be in the state language.[33] The law did allow special education programs for national minorities in languages other than the state language. Thus, Russian would continue to be allowed as the language of instruction in private schools and in some special-education institutions.[34] The downside was that the law did not define the parameters of those programs but left that function to the ministry of education. An expert in Latvian-language training issues later commented, "The education law has no implementation mechanisms and it is not flexible."[35] The Russian faction in the Latvian parliament tried in vein both in 2001 and 2002 to have the education law amended to accommodate more teaching in the native language for minorities.

Latvia's education law thus shows a parliament passing a law without incorporating the recommendations of the HCNM, despite efforts on his part to persuade policy makers. It exemplifies the argument that persuasion alone rarely leads to behavior change. The case also points out the difficulties faced by external actors in the absence of support from other external actors. Government officials may take this lack of involvement as a signal of tacit endorsement, or at least officials understand that external actors are willing to overlook the policy.

But the education law is also an example of how lagging implementation can have some benefits for minorities. Thus, by April 2003 the transition to the mandatory Latvian system has been poorly prepared and it appeared that the 2004 deadline would pass with instruction continuing in Russian in many minority schools.[36] Some, however, might decry this as damaging integration efforts.

LATVIA'S LANGUAGE LAW

The language law is an excellent example of how institutions can overcome even strong domestic opposition. Like education policy, language policy in Latvia has been a remarkably contentious issue. The main difference, however, is that while only the OSCE cared about the details of the education law, even the EU was concerned about the language law, as the same provisions directed against Russian speakers also could interfere with labor and trade issues with the rest of Europe.

Attempts to revise the language law had been ongoing since 1995, but the law had vanished amid the elections. By 1997–1998 the nationalist-leaning parties were in the majority government and, as discussed above, Krasts held the seat of prime minister. The language law held pride of place for the government parties, who had tried to push a strict law for years.[37] Thus, the first draft of he language law completely ignored any of the international recommendations from earlier years.

After European ambassadors to Latvia criticized the new draft, however, the drafting committee decided to send the draft to the European institutions for examination before the parliament's debate for the second reading.[38] While the second draft made some improvements, it nevertheless failed to address the key issue of the language use in the private sector.[39]

The European institutions responded with a coordinated effort. The HCNM visited Latvia at least four times, and the CE sent a team of experts.

Both institutions commented in detail on the draft laws. The CE made a detailed report, and the HCNM made several communications specific to the law.[40] The OSCE and the CE agreed on the major points; thus, the message was unambiguous. The EU also stated that it fully supports the "work of the [OSCE] Mission. . . . We note the improvements to the draft language law, but note that further changes are needed to bring the text fully into line with international instruments."[41]

Underscoring the strong domestic opposition to the recommendations from European institutions, the parliamentary education, science, and culture committee rejected all attempts to soften norms for the use of the Latvian language.[42] The nationalists became even more eager to pass a strict language law after some controversial citizenship law amendments passed. They saw the language law as a way to correct the leniency of the citizenship amendments.[43] HCNM van der Stoel continued to write letters and comment.[44] The commission's draft for the third reading did incorporate more of his advice, but so much controversy surrounded the law that the parliament returned it once again for further revisions.[45] Because of parliamentary procedural rules, the next government, formed in the end of 1998, had to pass the language law in the second reading once again. With the FF/LNNK again a member of the government, the agenda was still to pass a stricter language law.

The pressure from the international organizations increased steadily from the time preceding the second reading and climaxed around the time of the third reading. The EU-Latvia Joint Parliamentary Committee "called on the Latvian Parliament to ensure that the draft law on the state language is in conformity with international conventions; [and] noted the need to have a balanced approach regarding language restrictions also in the private sector."[46] The HCNM visited in January 1999 to discuss the law. When parliament passed the draft in the second reading, however, it still contained controversial references to enterprises and self-employed persons, which in many cases would place difficult or impossible language burdens on Russian-speakers.[47] Again, the international institutions worked in unison. The HCNM visited at least three times, during which he held news conferences and met with the foreign minister, and sent letters of detailed recommendations. He criticized the lack of distinction between the private and the public sphere, and argued that the law gave the executive branch too much leeway in deciding implementation.[48] The CE also sent expert visits and criticized the law in a report.[49] The EU expressed concern in meetings, and the foreign ministers of several EU member states lambasted the Latvian prime minister at an economic meeting in Salzburg.[50] EU officials commented in the international press.[51] Warnings from EU and OSCE officials and member states flooded in as the final reading approached.[52] Most importantly, the EU made the link to EU admission clear, and even the Latvian prime minister emphasized that EU membership was at stake.[53] Both the EU's van den Broek and HCNM van der Stoel telephoned Foreign Minister Valdis Birkavs and warned that the state language bill could hurt the EU progress report on Latvia.[54]

After the coalition government fell apart,[55] former Prime Minister Andris Skele, now the leader of the new center-right People's Party, formed a majority coalition government between the People's Party, the FF/LNNK, and the Latvian Way. The coalition had a majority and supported a nationalist position on the language issue, which was then the only current issue. The coalition's new policy agreement placed a high priority on "protecting Latvia's language and culture," listing that priority above strengthening relations with the EU.[56] Thus, the coalition's policy agreement put it on a collision course with the Latvian president over the country's controversial language law.

Demonstrating the degree of domestic opposition to outside interference, the government went against all international recommendations. Although the EU avidly protested the new government's plan to pass to the language law in the proposed version,[57] the parliament nevertheless passed the law in the third reading, possible based on some deal making surrounding the formation of a new government.[58] Most of the criticized provisions remained intact.

After the legislation passed, the EU, the CE, and the OSCE all appealed to the president with letters and personal visits to return the law to parliament.[59] The OSCE mission criticized the law. CE Secretary General Daniel Tarschys urged the parliament to reconsider the law.[60] The EU representative in Latvia discussed the law with the president and warned that the law would create problems for Latvia's bid to open membership talks with the EU.[61] Even Tarja Halonen, the foreign minister of Finland, who held the EU presidency, visited Latvia and said that the language law would hurt Latvia's chance to join the EU. Referring to amending the law, she said, "For an outside observer, on behalf of the European Union presidency, good timing would be to do it now."[62] As a result, the president returned the law to parliament, leaving the government with practically no progress on the issue since the start of the government, or even since before elections. The international institutions had averted the implementation of this version of the law, which they disliked, but the final outcome was still uncertain.

The fact that the parliament actually passed the controversial law was a testimony to the strength of the nationalists in the government. That the president vetoed the bill in her first weeks on the job was a testimony to the influence of the international institutions. The president specified when she returned the law that the parliament had to eliminate all ambiguities connected with possible corruption, inaccuracies, and objections from the European community.[63]

Given that all the members of the new government had voted for the language law, the situation in August 1999 did not look promising. Urging the new government to amend the law, the OSCE, the CE, the EU, Britain's Prime Minister Tony Blair, and others praised the president's decision and urged conformance to international standards.[64] The EU reassured policy makers that Latvia's chance of opening negotiations was good—pending passage of a favorable language law.[65] Showing the lack of consensus, however, the three ruling coalition parties even disagreed over when parliament should reconsider the vetoed state language law.[66]

Demonstrating the strategic considerations of the international efforts, the government finally decided to consider the law on the day before the upcoming EU summit, where the EU would make new decisions about Latvia's progress in the accession process. Despite the decision to discuss the law on this key date, however, the outcome was unpredictable. Fully realizing the high level of domestic contention about the issue, the EU made sure that the linkage to EU admission was clear. In October, when the EU commission recommended that the EU start negotiations with six more countries, including Latvia, the commission's annual report specifically noted the language law as a potential obstacle. The head of the EU delegation in Latvia and officials of EU member states reiterated the link.[67] As the final reading approached, OSCE experts also visited Latvia several times to discuss the language law with different parliamentary factions.[68] Meanwhile, the coalition was arguing intensely over how to vote on the language law. In the debate, Latvia's Way Party Chairman Andrejs Pantelejevs stressed that the language law would be a "serious trial" for the People's Party, and said that the party must understand that the language law might influence Latvia's EU talks.[69] On the other hand, FF deputy Juris Dobelis argued that "taking into account the reality of the situation in Latvia, it is impossible to implement all of the demands made by international organizations."[70] Underscoring the dynamics between the international institutions and the domestic actors, the debate constantly focused on "both strengthening positions of the Latvian language and legally more or less meeting requirements of Europe's experts."[71] Given that the Latvian parliament had planned to discuss the law in its final reading the day before the Helsinki Summit, Latvia had placing itself in a precarious position. The question was if the policy makers dared bring it to a test of wills with the EU, or if politicians with nationalist preferences on the language law would finally compromise.

On December 9, 1999, as the EU was meeting in Helsinki, the Latvian parliament finally approved an amended version of the controversial language law, which satisfied the EU and the OSCE.[72] Despite strong opposition to the institutions' demands, the incentive to join the EU prevailed. The case demonstrates international institutions' ability to overcome even very strong domestic opposition when they combine persuasion with conditionality and coordinate their approaches. The case also illustrates the value of a gradual admission process, during which the institutions can use meetings and decision points as leverage for further steps toward compliance.

THE CITIZENSHIP LAW

The developments around the issues of residency and citizenship in Latvia underscore the necessity and effectiveness of combining normative efforts with conditionality. Of all the policy issues in Latvia, citizenship has been the most controversial. The varying degrees and types of institutional involvement in the issue over time provide an excellent opportunity to understand the dynamics behind the policy decisions. The beginning of the citizenship issue demonstrates that early outside pressure was rather ineffective. The next steps on the issue, however, show that when the CE used membership conditionality, the policy changes were more obtainable. The next years provide a good example of how persuasion and social influence efforts alone yielded few results for international institutions, which were still trying to improve the citizenship law and implementation. Finally, the last part of the citizenship saga illustrates the effect of combining persuasion with conditionality.

Latvia's politicians began to discuss the citizenship law in the summer of 1990, when the supreme council established a special working group on citizenship and the constitution.[73] In October 1991 the supreme council issued an extremely strict resolution on citizenship.[74] The resolution restored citizenship only to those who were citizens of Latvia before 1940, and their descendants, leaving about seven-hundred thousand inhabitants without Latvian citizenship. The resolution set down the requirements for those wishing to become citizens of the Republic of Latvia: knowledge of the Latvian language, knowledge of Latvian laws and legal structure, sixteen years residence in Latvia, an oath of allegiance, and the renunciation of citizenship of another state. Military personnel and several other categories of persons were completely ineligible for citizenship, and the resolution also barred persons without a "legal source of income."[75] Naturalization could begin no sooner than July 1, 1992. The Equal Rights deputies representing ethnic Russians strongly protested the resolution, but in mid-November the supreme council nevertheless affirmed the draft law on citizenship.[76]

European institutions offered little guidance before the decision and little criticism afterward. CE experts visited Latvia several times after Latvia had applied for CE membership in September 1991, but the CE did not use Latvia's application to push the citizenship issue at this time. The visiting experts concluded that "there remained outstanding the question of a law on citizenship and the definition by law of the rights and status of non-citizens."[77] The full assembly approved a resolution expressing concern about the "proliferation of ethnic friction" in the Baltic States and elsewhere in Eastern Europe and called for "high standards of minority protection safeguarding the rights of all residents."[78] Nevertheless, Latvia received encouragement and special guest status with the CE. When Catherine Lalumiere, secretary-general of the CE visited Riga in early 1992, she said that Latvia had made much progress toward democratization, implementation of human rights, and economic reforms.[79]

The OSCE also voiced some concerns. Given the timing creating the HCNM, however, these did not come until early April 1993, when the HCNM sent his first recommendations. The HCNM recommended that a new citizenship law should be adopted soon, children born in Latvia who would otherwise be stateless should be granted Latvian citizenship, residence requirement should not exceed five years from day of arrival, any constitutional test should be straightforward, language requirements should not exceed the level of "conversational knowledge" and should exempt people over sixty years of age, there should be no income requirement for unemployed persons, and exclusion from citizenship should only occur based on evidence of a court. With elections approaching, however, the HCNM's recommendations did not gain much attention, let alone create debate.[80] Diplomatic pressure thus failed during this period, because of the intense nationalist forces combined with the late and only tentative institutional pressure.

CE Conditionality

After the new government took office, however, the linkage to CE membership became absolutely clear. Shortly after elections, Heinrich Klebes, deputy general of the CE parliamentary assembly, visited Latvia and stressed the link between CE admission and the citizenship law. He emphasized that Latvia could enter the CE if Latvia would consider the recommendations of the CE when making its citizenship law. A delegation of experts from the CE also visited Latvia to discuss the citizenship law in September 1993. They held consultations with three parliamentary commissions in which they stressed that the principles of human rights should be taken into account in drafting the citizenship law.[81] At this at least some Latvian policy makers observed that the main reason the CE would not be able to admit Latvia in 1993 was concern about the citizenship law.[82] Since Estonia had already been admitted, this was a blow to Latvia. Meanwhile, the OSCE also became more involved. Having visited several times since

April 1993, in September HCNM van der Stoel visited Latvia again and urged a quick adoption of "as liberal as possible a citizenship law."[83] The OSCE also decided to send a mission to Latvia.

Nevertheless, extreme opposition to a liberal citizenship bill continued. The board of the LNNK declared that a mass naturalization of colonists threatened the right of Latvians to be real masters in their fatherland.[84] An opinion poll published in the Riga newspaper the *Diena Daily* showed that 39 percent of Latvians agreed with the establishment of annual quotas in granting Latvian citizenship in such level that citizens would form 75 percent of the population—which meant little to no naturalization for years to come.[85]

In late September five parties or factions presented draft laws ranging from the so-called zero-option (or automatic citizenship) advocated by the mostly Russian Equal Rights faction to a rigid exclusionary policy called for by the right-wing nationalist FF faction. In the middle were proposals by the LNNK, the moderate Latvia's Way faction, and the liberal-leaning Harmony faction. Surprisingly the draft proposed by the Latvian Way–Farmers Union faction gained a majority, and thus became the basis for a draft law. Nevertheless, both the Russian politicians and the nationalists criticized the draft law.

Meanwhile, after reviewing the draft citizenship law, HCNM van der Stoel sent his comments in December 1993. He recommended that parliament amend article 9, mandating quotas, to instead set forth a system of naturalization giving priority to certain categories of noncitizens and eventually opening up naturalization to everyone within few years. He also reiterated recommendations on limiting residence requirements to five years, easier language and constitutional tests, waiving the language requirements for the disabled and elderly, and making clear that unemployment does not disqualify a person from applying for citizenship. Further, he advocated addressing the issue of stateless children and clarifying the categories concerning restrictions for naturalization.[86] The letter was clearly an attempt to persuade the Latvian government of both the moral uprightness and the sensibility of following his advice. He came to Latvia in January to discuss his recommendations.

The CE also commented extensively on the draft of the citizenship law, criticizing the quota system and instead supporting a system similar to the OSCE's. The CE also recommended exempting the old and disabled from the test, and to clarify several legal terms. Further, the CE, like the HCNM, advocated giving citizenship to stateless children. The CE also argued that it was wrong to arbitrarily exclude retired army personnel from applying for Latvian citizenship, but that there should be a more flexible provision allowing for individual scrutiny of cases.[87]

Opposition to the international comments mounted. By early 1994 the stricter LNNK proposal was setting the main terms of the debate, including a key requirement limiting the future rate of naturalization of noncitizens to 1 percent of the total number of citizens or about two thousand per year, effectively barring tens of thousands from ever receiving citizenship before their death. At the end of January the LNNK and the FF factions announced they would collect signatures from 10 percent of eligible voters to submit their own bill on citizenship to the president. The CE and the OSCE reiterated their reservations about quotas on granting citizenship and about the notion of granting citizenship on a very restrictive basis.

In May 1994 the government began to redraft the citizenship law to incorporate the CE and OSCE recommendations. After the nationalists scored a victory in local elections,[88] however, the parliament passed the second of three readings a law on citizenship that included very strict quotas.[89] Even so, the FF faction and the LNNK thought the bill was too liberal. The law stipulated preferential naturalization of persons of whom at least 1 parent was an ethnic Latvian, persons who came to Latvia and lived there before June 17, 1940, Lithuanian and Estonian ethnic minorities, and spouses of Latvian citizens who had been married for at least ten years. All these groups should know the Latvian language. Citizenship would not be given to persons whom a court had recognized as having propagated the ideas of chauvinism, nationalism, and fascism as well as working against Latvian independence, as well as Soviet military retirees if they were not ethnic Latvians or spouses of Latvian citizens. Other people would be able to apply for naturalization from January 1, 1996, with preference given to those born in Latvia. From the year 2000 persons in other categories could be naturalized with a naturalization quota of 0.1 percent of Latvia's citizens per year.

The reaction from the OSCE and the CE to the quotas that remained in the law was strong and clear. A Latvian delegation met with the HCNM in Prague and with representatives of the CE parliamentary assembly in Strasbourg. They were told that if the parliament did not change the quota system in the law on citizenship, then the door to the CE would be closed.[90] Nevertheless, on June 21, 1994, the parliament approved the law on citizenship without changes from the second reading.

The CE, the OSCE, and diplomats from various embassies in Riga immediately condemned the law. The European countries and institutions were united in their insistence. The ambassadors of Italy and Sweden and the head of the OSCE mission met with President Guntis Ulmanis to warn that CE admission depended on removing the quotas from the law.[91] Britain also urged revision of the law.[92] Thomas Markett of the CE said that "with the adopted provisions of the law, it will be impossible to admit Latvia into the Council of Europe."[93] The EU fully backed the CE and OSCE recommendations. EU ambassadors gave the head of the Latvian CE delegation, Alekandrs Kirsteins, a note from the EU urging Latvia to consider follow recommendations of the HCNM and the CE.[94] The EU summit in Corfu also urged Latvia to change the law.[95]

This time Latvia responded to the criticisms, and the CE conditionality was the clear motivating factor. Prime Minister Birkavs asked the president to return the law to parliament, stating specifically that the current law had to be changed because it jeopardized both CE admission and associate membership with the EU. The prime minister's statement read, in part,

> By keeping this principle in the law, Latvia cannot expect the Council of Europe to change the aforementioned attitude, which will practically result in delay in Latvia's admission to that organization. And Latvia has already expressed the wish to join it as early as September 1991. The beginning of the talks with the European Union on the granting of the status of associate member, and thus also further integration into the European Union, is endangered.[96]

President Guntis Ulmanis returned the law to the parliament with a request for revisions to meet the standards of the OSCE and CE.[97]

In the midst of a government crisis,[98] Latvia nevertheless responded well. The parliament approved an amended aw on citizenship in late July.[99] The amendments replaced the quotas with a "window system," which the European institutions had helped devise. Various categories of people could be nationalized in stages up to the year 2003. The first group to be processed would be those married to Latvian citizens and ethnic Estonians and Lithuanians. The next group would be immigrants in specific age groups. After 2003, all groups would be handled equally. The amendments did not, however, address all the recommendations by the international community. The law did not grant mandatory citizenship to individuals meeting all requirements, exempt the elderly from language tests,[100] base naturalization on the actual time of residence in Latvia, or grant automatic citizenship to children born in Latvia to stateless parents after the passage of the law. Applicants had to know the language, the constitution, the national anthem, and the history of Latvia, and to have lived in Latvia for five years after May 4, 1990. They had to have a legal source of income, and take an oath of loyalty. Naturalization by this law could not occur until May 4, 1995.[101]

Despite the law's remaining inadequacies, international praise abounded because the main concern, the quotas, were gone. The EU president lauded the amendments.[102] The CE parliamentary assembly rapporteurs to Latvia recommended its entry into the CE and rejected accusations from Russia that Latvia had not met the CE recommendations. They noted that "we must recognize that the Latvians have good reasons and the right to protect their own identity as well as they can. Seen in this light we much consider the new act is as generous as it could be and that in due course it will do justice to all those whose presence, originally, has been forced upon the Latvian people."[103] To remedy some of the inadequacies, the government also adopted a law on the status of noncitizens in April 1995.

In conclusion, although the OSCE and the CE did not seem to make any progress until the very last minute, after the law had actually been passed, the European institutions eventually motivated the revision of the amendments. Prime Minister Birkavs perhaps most pointedly confirmed this when President Guntis Ulmanis returned the law to parliament: "We shall not allow the Latvian people to perish because of the citizenship law. "We shall not allow this law to bar our way to Europe, the only place where Latvia can survive."[104] The parliamentary debates also showed increasing concern with the possibility of being excluded from the CE.[105] Showing the value of combining conditionality with persuasion and engagement, the window system itself was developed together with the OSCE and the CE, giving them additional influence over the actual outcome. One member of parliament from the nationalist LNNK noted, "In 1994 the CE was very important. . . . At that time I was chairman for the Foreign Affairs committee and the Latvian delegation to the CE. The CE pressured us. If we want membership we must have citizenship for all—so we found the windows compromise. We had lots of discussions within the political committee. The CE was very much part of this process."[106] It is also evident, however, that the nationalists were able to restrain the changes. Latvia kept the language requirement for all ages, stateless children born in Latvia gained no privileges, and Latvia slowed naturalization. One member of parliament said, "The international institutions wisely understood not to ask for too much."[107]

A Period of Ineffective Involvement

The next years illustrate how persuasion and social influence efforts alone yielded few results for international institutions, which were still trying to improve the citizenship law and implementation. Nationalism and citizenship issues had dominated the 1995 election campaign. The FF campaigned partly on its alternative citizenship law, which was notably harsher, and governmental support for the repatriation of "colonists."[108] The parliament was splintered. No party gained more than 18 seats in the 100-seat chamber, and left- and right-wing populist parties outperformed more mainstream movements. The FF and LNNK became part of the government coalition, and the coalition agreement explicitly barred changes in the citizenship law.[109]

Between 1995 and 1997 the HCNM repeatedly visited Latvia and sent letters with recommendations. He reiterated the need to waive language requirement for those over 65 years of age, to ease the tests in specific ways, to allow stateless children to gain citizenship, and to reduce the application fee.[110] Eventually, as it became apparent that this tactic was not working, he also suggested that Latvia abolish the window system.[111] The minister of foreign affairs replied politely that most of the recommendations were not possible at the time.[112] In a test of the willingness to ease the law, in February 1997 the parliament rejected a proposal to amend the citizenship law to automatically naturalize the twenty-five thousand Poles living in Latvia without Latvian citizenship. The following month the parliament rejected a proposal to end the windows system and grant citizenship to Latvian-born children of permanent residents and spouses of Latvian citizens after five years of marriage.[113] In sum, during this period the government responded only to minor parts of the OSCE recommendations. Latvia eased some of the requirements for the citizenship tests and lowered the naturalization fees, but changed little regarding the window system, the stateless children, the tests, and the fee system.

The Effects of EU Membership Incentives

In 1997–1998, however, the institutions once again successfully combined persuasion and incentives to change the citizenship law. Dissatisfied with the slow pace of naturalization, the international institutions wanted Latvia to abolish the window system entirely and grant stateless children citizenship at birth. The government, though, had a strict nationalist stand on the citizenship issue and had publicly committed to no further facilitation of naturalization. In fact, the government preferred that the citizenship law be tightened further. In a public rally in August 1997 Grinblats promised that the process of naturalization would not be accelerated as long as his party was in the government.[114] Prime Minister Krasts publicly defended the controversial window system.[115] Subsequently, the parliament again twice rejected proposals to ease the citizenship law.[116]

But the EU kept pushing the issues. The EU Agenda 2000, published in 1997, had already called for changes to the citizenship law, and in early 1998 the EU association partnerships for Latvia urged "the review of the "window policy" and facilitation of naturalization of stateless children." The EU also stepped up its support of the OSCE. As the head of the EU delegation in Latvia phrased it, "In March 1998 we really began to stress this issue of the citizenship law. And we came out and supported van der Stoel and said that he is the bottom line."[117]

In response to the international pressure, the more nationalist-leaning faction worked still harder against change. In March 1998 the FF/LNNK

faction, to whom the prime minister belonged, proposed a draft with naturalization quotas that translated into about two thousand persons a year.[118]
Then in March and April 1998 events in Latvia sharply focused attention
on the citizenship law. Protests in Riga brought renewed pressure from the
institutions as tensions with Russia rose.[119] The question of language and
citizenship carved a deep rift in the cabinet, and the government narrowly
averted a crisis when the coalition factions agreed to establish a working
group to examine amendments to the citizenship law.

In a strong example of domestic political calculations driving policy, to
maintain power Prime Minister Krasts and his fellow nationalists began to
compromise. Speaking to his party's congress, Krasts said the EU provided
the final push. "There was no other way to get a positive progress report
from the EU in October," he said. "We were forced to go ahead—well,
forced wouldn't be the right word. It was reasonable from our side to go
ahead with changes. . . . Not to get a positive report would be more negative than current instability or current pressure from Russia. In that case,
we would be out of the game entirely."[120]

In early May parliament approved the amendments to the citizenship
law in a first reading, but not without a fight. And the text was not fully in
accordance with the recommendations.[121] Meanwhile the permanent council of the EU urged that all coalition parties support the changes, which
they hoped would be adopted without delay, specifically noting, "That includes the amendment to the laws related to stateless children."[122] The
57–16 vote that pushed the amendments through a second reading, while
decisive, was glaringly partisan, and once again failed to meet the institutions' demands.[123] The EU responded with a presidency declaration stating
that "the EU hopes that the parliament will complete work on the legislation abolishing the windows system and granting citizenship to stateless
children without delay,"[124] adding that reform of the citizenship law was a
"key criterion" for beginning EU entry talks. Finally, the parliament
adopted the amendments, which abolished the window system and gave
citizenship to stateless children without a language exam.[125]

One more bump marked the road. The domestic opposition was still
strong. The enraged nationalists immediately called for a referendum on
the amendments, and a bitter campaign followed. EU commissioner van
den Broek used a visit to urge the Latvian people to keep the amendments,
noting that they were necessary for Latvia to keep moving towards the EU.
He said that if the amendments were voted down in a referendum, it would
be "a bitter morsel for the EU to swallow."[126] For most of the time leading
up to the referendum, however, the international institutions tried to keep
a low profile, leaving the Latvian people to debate the normative aspect of
the issue among them. Meanwhile, the nationalists tried to combat the
international pressure. After an intense debate during which arguments

ranged from concerns about what was morally right to what was "Latvian" and to what the future of Latvia in Europe should be, 53 percent approved the amendments to the law in the October 3, 1998, referendum.

Thus, these four periods of citizenship legislation in Latvia provide strong examples of the effect of persuasion combined with incentives. At the same time they show how mere persuasion and social influence alone was insufficient to produce change. They also provide a good example of the benefits of policy coordination between the international institutions. Finally, the last amendments to the citizenship law illustrate the element of political cost-benefit calculations by policy makers, in this case of Prime Minister Krasts in particular.

Conclusion

Four main issues have dominated ethnic politics in Latvia, namely, citizenship, language, education, and voting rights. Many issues have been associated with citizenship in one form or another, such as residency rights, naturalization requirements, and the status of children born without citizenship. The degree of variation in the governments' willingness to accommodate ethnic minorities has co-varied remarkably with the involvement of the international institutions, ranging from a willingness to recall and reverse policies when the international actors put sufficient incentives on the line, to neglect or even political exploitation of the issues when international institutions appeared uninterested. This variation supports the argument that the engagement of international institutions is a strong explanatory factor in understanding domestic policy on ethnic minorities. Further, the timing of several cases underscores the causal connection between incentives and policy behavior, in that it is possible to see a pattern of issue-linkage by the institutions and response by policy makers within a short period of time. In particular, statements by politicians involved in making the changes also tend to confirm that institutional membership incentives have driven the changes in citizenship law.

On the other hand, the issue of education illustrates how politicians may listen politely to diplomatic efforts to persuade or otherwise convince them of their failure to meet international standards. Such efforts, however, are sufficient to get policy makers to change the policies when they otherwise stand to gain politically from them.

Latvia also provides good examples of the influence of domestic opposition. The case of the language law is a particularly good illustration because the issue was one of the core missions of the more nationalist-leaning parties in the mid and late 1990s, when they partly saw it as a remedy for other concessions they had been unable to block. Their often fierce determination to introduce language proficiency requirements into a vast field of jobs and official activities significantly slowed the speed with which the EU and other actors could bring the law into alignment with their standards. This tendency to introduce language proficiency levels also surfaced in the election law, where the European institutions remained largely uninvolved in the 1990s.[127] In sum, the Latvian cases support the hypotheses about institutional involvement, membership incentives, and domestic opposition very well.

CHAPTER 5

Estonia: Reluctant Cooperation

As IN LATVIA, the root of the ethnic issues in Estonia can be found in the fifty years of Soviet control after World War II. In the 1930s Estonia was a largely homogenous society with only about 12 percent ethnic minorities, only a few percent of those being Russian. As a result of mass deportations (1940–41), war and mobilization (1941–45), and mass emigration, the population of Estonia decreased from 1,136,000 in October 1939 to 854,000 in January 1945. By 1945 Estonians formed approximately 94 percent of the population.[1] After the war, however, Moscow encouraged large-scale immigration to Estonia from other parts of the Soviet Union, while also deporting many Estonians to Siberia. By 1959 the Estonians share of the population had declined to 75 percent, and by 1989 Estonians comprised only 62 percent of the population. Meanwhile, the proportion of Russian speaking groups had grown from just a few percent in 1945 to 30 percent in 1989. The number of towns where non-Estonians were an ethnic majority grew from two in 1934 to twelve in 1990, including the capital, Tallinn. (See figure 4.1.)

The ethnic division was exacerbated by the fact that Moscow did little to encourage the new Russian immigrants to integrate into Estonian society. Most of the immigrants lived in new, isolated housing districts in Tallinn or in the industrialized northeast of the country, where the Soviets controlled the factories, producing outputs largely for Soviet markets. Few of these immigrants spoke Estonian. As a result, when Estonia regained independence from the Soviet Union in 1991, about 30 percent of Estonia's 1.4 million, or as many as 400,000, had no citizenship in Estonia or elsewhere and most were Russian-speakers with no Estonian.[2]

Ethnic issues were acute throughout the transitional period to independence. Only a third or less of the Russian-speaking population had favored independence, while another third had categorically opposed it. Seeing the writing on the wall, even as early as 1989, pro-Soviet forces had established the Intermovement to protect the rights of Russians and other minorities against what they viewed as Estonian nationalism. Tensions had grown in May 1990, when the Intermovement tried to storm the Estonian parliament building, and the January 1991 Soviet military crackdowns in Lithuania and Latvia refueled fears.

Reemerging as an independent country after decades of Soviet rule, Estonians and Estonian politicians thus wanted to reestablish the Estonian nation and ensure the survival of the Estonian identity. Patriotic sentiments made politicians urge a more nationalistic policy of caution regarding language and other rights for noncitizens and ethnic non-Estonians. Reluctance to accommodate noncitizens was pervasive, and both ethnic Estonians and Russians were skeptical about ethnic relations throughout the 1990s.[3]

The web of politics in Estonia after independence was complicated. Estonia's economic reform was quite successful, and Estonia's position vis-à-vis the EU received particularly strong support from Finland. Like Latvia, however, Estonia suffered from unstable government coalitions and subsequent frequent changes in government, even between elections. Thus, Estonia has had seven prime ministers, some presiding over different coalitions. As table 5.1 shows, the National Fatherland Party (NFP) and Estonian National Independence Party (ENIP) were part of the majority government coalitions between 1992 and 1994. Even at the end of the Vahi government and during the Siimann government, however, they were important opposition parties, as these governments lacked a majority and needed the cooperation of the opposition.

The most extreme parties, however, such as the Estonian Citizen, the Right-wingers, and the Estonian Home, never achieved great electoral influence. The more popular parties that opposed extending rights to non-Estonians included the ENIP and the NFP. These parties favored restrictive legislation, but they did not advocate nondemocratic means or use racist statements against non-Estonians. Realizing the need to solve the issues regardless of the past, the rest of the parties reflected the general Estonian population's apprehension, which came from decades of occupation. Thus, while ethnic Russians did not face extremist nationalist and racist parties and tendencies, the general attitude toward them was not at all accommodating. During most of the 1990s the more nationalist-leaning parties had significant input into the policymaking process. While Russian speakers gained representation in parliament, not only was it vastly out of proportion with their large demographic share, but they were also consistently marginalized in the policy-making process.

CASE STUDIES

As in Latvia, the main issues in Estonia have been citizenship, language, education and elections. While the issues were quite similar, in some cases Estonia took a less restrictive approach; for instance, Estonia never had the issue of quotas in its citizenship law. In addition, the European institutions were in some ways more open to Estonia. Thus, the CE did not make use of the incentive of membership in the same way as it did in the case of

TABLE 5.1
Estonian Governments

Government period	Government coalition parties	Majority?
Edgar Savisaar (Aug. 21, 1991–Jan. 23, 1992)	EPF other affiliations	*
Tiit Vahi, Interim PM (Jan. 27, 1992–Sept. 1992)	EPF other affiliations	Same
Mart Laar (Oct. 19, 1992–Sept. 26, 1994)	NFP M ENIP	Yes (53/101)
Andres Tarand (Oct. 27, 1994–March 1995)	Same	Same
Tiit Vahi (April 17, 1995–October 9, 1995)	KE KMU ECP	Yes (57/101)
(Nov. 3, 1995–Nov. 22, 1996)	KE KMU ER	Yes (60/101)
(Nov. 22, 1996–Feb. 25, 1997)	KE KMU	No (41/101)
Mart Siimann (March, 16, 1997–March 1999)	KE KMU	No (37/101)
Mart Laar (March 1999–)	ER IL M	Yes (53/101)

* Difficult to speak of majorities within this government as party affiliation were unclear.

Acronyms: M: Moderate; EPF: Estonia Popular Front; ECP: Estonian Center Party; KE: Estonian Coalition Party; KMU: Rural Union bloc; ER: Estonian Reform Party–Liberals; NFP: National Fatherland Party; IL: Pro Patria or Fatherland Union (merged ENIP and NFP).

Latvia's citizenship law, and the EU also included Estonia in the so-called first wave of candidates, while Latvia remained in the second wave for some time thereafter. The similarity in issues, coupled with the differences in the domestic approach and international approach, makes it particularly interesting to compare the two countries.

The rest of this chapter will discuss some of the cases from Estonia, starting with the issue of language requirements for local and national candidates, followed by the language law, and finally by the citizenship law with particular attention to the issue of stateless children.

Language Requirements for Local and National Candidates

As in Latvia, the issue of language requirements for local and national candidates provides a good example of how domestic calculations of political survival figured into the policy choices of governments that were otherwise fairly moderate on ethnic minority issues. Whereas institutions remained completely uninvolved in Latvia, in Estonia they did use persuasion in the mid-1990s. The case is a good illustration, however, of how the international efforts of persuasion fell mostly on deaf ears.

According to the constitution adopted in June 1992, Article 156.2, noncitizens had the right to vote in local elections. Nevertheless, an intense debate evolved in early 1993 over the right of the noncitizens to vote and stand in local elections. Since noncitizens comprised vast majorities in some local communities, this became controversial. On May 19, 1993, the parliament finally passed the law on local elections that gave the right to vote to all permanent residents of Estonia who had lived in Estonia for at least five years. But an amendment passed together with the law denied non-Estonian citizens the right to stand in elections. Despite domestic and Russian protests, President Meri signed the law shortly thereafter. This in itself, however, was not in contraction with international standards, as such; few other countries gave the right to vote to noncitizens, though, of course, few other countries found themselves in a similar situation. Given the extremely high percentage of non-Estonians in Estonia, however, which in some regions, like Narva, was close to 80–90 percent, the basis of democracy was a stake. Thus, the representatives of the OSCE[4] mission in Estonia warned that the law on local elections would create tensions in northeast Estonia, where very few of the residents would be allowed to run for office. Nevertheless, the years following saw little international reaction.

The issue of the local election law resurfaced in 1996 as new local elections approached. At that time the government was relatively moderate on ethnic issues. The rightist bloc, which had been in power, had flopped in the 1995 national election, and two hard-right nationalist parties, Estonian Citizens and the Independent Royalists, which had been moderately successful in 1992, failed to win any seats. Surprisingly, the Russians election coalition managed to gain six seats in the 101-seat parliament. Nevertheless, the coalitions that formed under Prime Minister Tiit Vahi were unstable majorities. The first lasted only six months. For the coalition to hang together, the government program stated, "The principles of the laws on Citizenship, Aliens and Language will not be changed."[5] Thus, the government was committed to the status quo on minority issues, even though the new government parties were less nationalist than their predecessors.

Driven primarily by the practical necessity of the local election coming up in October 1996, the government began in January 1996 to discuss some changes to the law on local elections. Initially the changes were mostly legal corrections to the law and some minor adjustment to facilitate implementation.[6] The chairman of the parliament's constitutional law committee, Tiit Kabin, said the new bill was needed because of irregularities in the text of the present law and also because the section regulating aliens' participation in voting no longer fit the current situation.[7]

By April, however, when the parliament passed the amendments, they included controversial articles about language proficiency. The initiative to include the language proficiency requirements came from the more nationalist opposition, which had a basic interest in hindering Russian-speakers' participation in the local elections. Although the government was not nationalist, it was volatile and had begun to cooperate with the nationalist-leaning Pro Patria (the Estonian Freedom and Fatherland Party) to survive. Thus, the new articles stipulated that candidates who had not graduated from an Estonian-language elementary school, high school, or university would have to take a special language exam to prove their proficiency in Estonian. The law left several areas up to the government to define later.

The OSCE as well as domestic actors protested the law. Domestically, leaders of the Russian-speaking community in Estonia and the official Minorities Roundtable appealed to President Meri to veto the law. Justice Chancellor Eerik-Juhan Truuvali criticized the parliament's decision to delegate to the government authority to establish by decree what could be defined in laws.[8] International actors also tried to persuade the government to leave the language requirements out of the law. On May 7 the HCNM traveled to Tallinn. In meetings with policy makes, he argued that the law failed to correspond to international civil rights agreements. Some foreign embassies also expressed their concern over new articles.

Although President Meri returned the law to parliament, about a week later the parliament nevertheless passed a version that retained the language requirements. While not required to take a test, as initially envisioned, candidates still had to certify over their signatures that they met the requirements established by the language law. The law stipulated that knowingly giving false information constituted a basis for the annulment of a candidate's election mandate. Thus, it would be quite easy to oust any candidate elected on a false claim of language proficiency. Showing the lack of response to the HCNM's appeal, the majority of the parliament supported the decision. Seventy-three members of parliament voted in favor of adopting the amended law, with seven abstaining and five not taking part in the voting. The Russian faction abstained. Viktor Andreyev of the parliament's Russian faction said that because of overly tough language requirements, the local councils in northwestern Estonia in particular could become Estonian-speakers' clubs rather than elected bodies of local power. "The political aim of the law," Andreyev said, "was to create obstacles for minority candidates to run."[9]

Stressing the minimal impact of the OSCE efforts, Mart Nutt, an opposition member who was involved in the law, commented that the reason for the partial change was the domestic protest, most notably from the chancellor.[10]

There are several reasons why international persuasion efforts did not have much effect on Estonia's election law. First, Estonian politicians had no reason to believe that most of Europe was taking notice of their policy. Aside from the fairly quiet OSCE effort, local embassies did not direct Europe's attention to the issue. Second, policy makers correctly calculated that few consequences would result from not following the advice of HCNM van der Stoel. In March and April 1996 European institutions' were focused on EU accession, and several European states were sending Estonia all the right signs. Quite indicative of the enthusiasm of the times, French President Jacques Chirac expressed his support for Estonia's accession to the EU in an April 4 letter to Meri.[11] Likewise, Dutch Prime Minister Wim Kok and German Foreign Minister Klaus Kinkel were among others who reassured Estonia of swift admission.[12]

Eventually Prime Minister Vahi's government became too weak and he resigned. In March 1997 Mart Siimann became the premier-designate of a minority government with only 37 deputies. While quite open to reform on ethnic issues, the minority government could not function without cooperating with the opposition, which increased the influence of the nationalists. The time was ripe for nationalists to take a new stab at the election laws. Thus, the fall of 1997 brought a new controversial attempt to introduce language requirements for candidates running in national elections. While the initial attempts failed because of legalities, by the end of 1998 the nationalist-leaning opposition parties had gained considerable influence over the weak minority government, and the language issue became very hot.[13] The nationalists made language a campaign issue, and considerable public pressure favored passing the amendments. By November the opposition party, Pro Patria, introduced amendments to both the local and national election laws. While the local election law already had a provision on language proficiency, discussed above, the new amendments were significantly more detailed.[14] The amendments passed in mid-December 1998, and required members of parliament and local governments to have sufficient knowledge of Estonian to take part in the work of those bodies.[15]

Again, the OSCE tried to persuade the politicians to reverse the decision. The HCNM sent a formal letter to Estonian President Meri urging him not to promulgate the amendments. Van der Stoel argued that the amendments did not accord with either the Estonian constitution or Estonia's international obligations and commitments, and that they would not contribute to the national integration process.[16] Nevertheless, Meri signed the legislation because "[t]here was a lot of pressure within the country to accept this language legislation, and a lot of media against Van der Stoel," an OSCE mission member explained.[17] A proponent of the amendments commented, "There is a demand for candidates to know the language. Otherwise we could have a situation where local boards started operating in Russian. That is what we fear. Still in some parts of Estonia, it is difficult to get by in Estonian. That is not right. Because of this fact, parliament demands that candidates know Estonian."[18]

Thus, the cases of the local and national election laws in Estonia show that OSCE pressure was mostly ineffective at persuading politicians to abandon language requirements for candidates. Politicians strongly favoring strict language requirements did not dominate the government, yet nevertheless politicians calculated that not passing strict language legislation would almost certainly lead to domestic disapproval in upcoming elections, and that this was too high a cost for the mere benefit of the approval of the OSCE. Thus, persuasion made little headway, and the results were ultimately similar to those in Latvia, where no international actors were involved.

As a footnote, developments on the election law after the conclusion of this study support that actual changes required more staunch methods from the international community. Thus, Estonia did abandon the language requirements in November 2001, but only after NATO admission was on the line.[19]

Language Law

In contrast to the election laws, where the use of persuasion alone was rather ineffective, the case of the language law shows how different the domestic response can be when international institutions also use membership incentives.

Concurrent with the changes to the election law, politicians restarted efforts to tighten the language law in December 1998. The amendments initiated by the Pro Patria party passed in February 1999, just weeks before the election. They made mandatory for private sector employees, nongovernmental organizations, and even self-employed entrepreneurs the use of Estonian at a level of proficiency established by the government.[20]

The HCNM had not been explicitly involved in the language law leading up to the 1999 amendments. On April 6, 1993, many years before the passage of the law, however, HCNM van der Stoel had cautioned the government on language issues in his first letter of recommendations to the

Estonian government. Among other things, he recommended that "the use of the Estonian language in the internal affairs of private enterprises and organizations should not be made mandatory." As the discussion of credibility in chapter 2 argues, however, institutions increase their influence when they present a joint front, but they badly damage any response when they send contradictory signals. Such was the case in 1993. Although the CE was in the process admitting Estonia in 1993, there is no record of the CE raising the language issue, and nothing much happened on the issue at all for years, except fairly constant attempts by Pro Patria to tighten the law. After the 1999 bill passed, however, the international protest suddenly became loud, coordinated, and clear. What happened in the next year and a half is an excellent example of how the combination of conditionality with extensive persuasion efforts can eventually bring national law into line with international standards.

First, van der Stoel wrote a letter to Estonian Foreign Minister Toomas Hendrik Ilves,[21] and visited Estonia in June 1999. The EU also raised the issue in association council and joint parliamentary committee meetings. One member of the governing party acknowledged the high profile of the international effort: "Our faction has discussed this issue of the language legislation several times since the law was passed, including the concerns of the international community and the practical implications."[22] Extensive exchanges of drafts and comments circulated between the OSCE, the EU, and the Estonian government in the summer and fall 1999. As the implementation regulations were still controversial, the EU appealed to Estonia to postpone the regulations. In a compromise under the pressure to publish some regulations, Estonian did adopt the regulations on the public sector, which were of course less controversial. An Estonian delegation went to Brussels shortly thereafter to discuss the regulations on the private sector. It was then agreed that some modifications and clarifications should be made and that the regulations would then again be sent to the EU for comment. Around this time, one Estonian official said, "There has been fierce consultation between us and the EU on the law and the regulations. Just last week we had a meeting on the upcoming progress report—which will come out October 13 this year. The new report will most certainly touch on the language law issue."[23] He added, "Just today, we sent the regulations on the private sector to the EU. We have followed all van der Stoel recommendations on the law. We worked closely with him in drafting the regulations/decree. We discussed every single word with him."

The EU credibility was strengthened when the EU commission report that came out a few weeks later did indeed pass a harsh public criticism on the still unfinished language legislation: "The Language law, . . . restricts access of non-Estonian speakers in political and economic life constitutes a step backwards and should be amended."[24] Initially, the prime minister called the European Commission experts' criticism "not quite grounded,"[25] but in a speech to parliament a few days later he said that the Estonian government agreed to most of the shortcomings pointed out by the commission.[26] A few days later, the president of the OSCE's parliamentary assembly, Helle Degn, was in Estonia, and she also pressed officials to liberalize the language law.[27] The president of Finland, which then held the EU presidency, also emphasized the importance for Estonia of a language law harmonized with EU norms.[28]

Stressing the considerable domestic opposition to the issue, Prime Minister Mart Laar said in October 1999 that that the European Commission's criticism of the Estonian language law was not fully justified and that the government had no plans to send a new amendment to parliament.[29] Nevertheless, by February 2000 the foreign ministry acknowledged that Estonia must ease the requirements of the language law to enter the EU, even though the move was likely to meet strong opposition in parliament. "As in the case of other laws, also the Estonian language law must not contradict the rules of the European Union, and to ensure this certain contestable issues have to be eliminated," foreign ministry press secretary Taavi Toom said, generating immediate criticism from Pro Patria.[30]

Work to modify the law to meet the EU demands proceeded, with the EU combining the conditionality with efforts to persuade. At the EU–Estonia Association Council on Monday February 14, 2000, the council noted the EU's readiness to continue providing Estonia with expert help on the issue.[31] Estonia also sent its proposals for amendments to the language law to the EU and asked for an opinion of the law from a European Commission's expert working group.[32] At the end of March Estonia received a positive reply from the EU.[33]

On May 16, 2000, the chairman of the Estonian parliamentary committee for culture, Mart Meri, submitted amendments to the language law for consideration by parliament. He told deputies that the amendments were meant to harmonize the law with the demands of the EU, other European organizations, and international conventions.[34] In a June 6 speech to the Estonian parliament, German Chancellor Gerhard Schroeder pointed out the need to meet respective recommendations of the European institutions. "I very much welcome the application of recommendations by the Organization for Security and Cooperation in Europe (OSCE) and the European Union and I firmly hope that the last obstacle, the language law, will be overcome in agreement with these recommendations," Schroeder said.[35] On June 8 Foreign Minister Toomas Hendrik told the parliament that amending the language law, which the commission had sharply criticized the previous fall, was imperative for accession to EU.[36] A few days later, on June 14, 2000—just days before the start of a meeting of EU leaders and candidate countries' foreign ministers in Feira, Portugal, which gave new impetus to their internal debate on preparing for enlargement—the parliament finally passed amendments to the language law by a vote of 50–1, removing the controversial provisions.[37] EU and OSCE praise was immediate.[38]

This case is thus a good illustration of the effectiveness of intense and prolonged cooperation between the OSCE and the EU, and the combination of persuasion with conditionality. The EU use of conditionality was credible and clear. Showing evidence of the causality, policy makers at several times during the process made clear statements explaining that the desire to join the EU was driving the policy changes. The timing of several steps in the amendment process could also be directly linked to interactive steps with the OSCE and the EU.

CITIZENSHIP AND STATELESS CHILDREN

The issue of stateless children provides a good example of a three-phase development of institutional involvement. First, international institutions were not involved and the outcome was not compatible with international standards. Next, international institutions used persuasion without notable result. Finally, international institutions linked their recommendations with membership, provoking policy change.

The issue of stateless children had its origins in the days of Estonia's newfound independence, when citizenship was most crucial. The problem of stateless children arose when former Soviet citizens, ineligible for Estonia citizen, or subject to various tests and waiting periods, did not get Estonian citizenship. Their children were by definition stateless and did not even hold the old Soviet identity cards.

The Laar government coalition that emerged from the 1992 elections had a strict attitude toward the citizenship issue. The government included ENIP, which had voted for more a restrictive citizenship law. Pro Patria itself stressed that it saw re-migration as necessary, since, in its view, the massive Soviet-era immigration to Estonia had been illegal. The Pro Patria slogan was "cleaning house," represented on election posters by a man with a broom (Lieven 1993, 285). Parliament also included eight members of the Estonian Citizen Party, which rejected the 1938 citizenship law as too liberal, and called for it to be amended to restrict naturalization still further. The Ministry of Ethnic Relation was abolished, and there was little relief in sight for the noncitizens. One expert has described the government's policy toward the non-Estonian population as mostly one of "strategic benign ignorance." That is, the government position was that there were no problems that needed to be addressed on a national level and that any problems were mostly individual and thus up to the individuals themselves to solve.[39] The Laar government thus was content to stall the naturalization process by dragging its feet on the definition of language requirements.[40]

The HCNM was the first to raise the issue of stateless children in Estonia. A CSCE mission visited Estonia in the end of 1992, and HCNM van der Stoel visited Estonia in early 1993, expressing the hope that "the future solution of the citizenship issue in Latvia and Estonia would be such that the Russian-speaking minority would get the right to citizenship."[41] The OSCE mission opened in Estonia soon thereafter to work on, among other things, citizenship and migration issues. In April 1993, after yet another visit to Estonia, the HCNM sent his first letter to the Estonian government with specific recommendations. Among other things, he recommended that children born in Estonia who would otherwise become stateless should be granted Estonian citizenship.[42]

The Estonian government did not reply to van der Stoel's letter for three months. A member of that government gave two explanations. "Van der Stoel made many suggestions for changes and we did consider his input, but we also did not want to touch the law after it had first and finally been passed. Also, we believed that van der Stoel took the side of the Russians and we did not want to listen to that."[43]

The OSCE persuasion effort also suffered from lack of coordination. Apart from the strength of government opposition to addressing the issue of stateless children issue, the HCNM may also not have received much response because the CE failed to support the OSCE recommendations. A month later, in an opinion on the application of Estonia for membership of the Council of Europe, the rapporteur actually praised Estonia, stating that "the law on citizenship is extremely liberal."[44] Completely failing to utilize its potential leverage in a more conditional manner, the CE admitted Estonia shortly thereafter without any mention of changes in the citizenship legislation.

In July 1993 Prime Minister Laar finally responded to the HCNM. In his letter, he said, "As far as the requirements for citizenship are concerned, the Government intends to take concrete steps in the near future to ensure that the recommendations made on this subject by the High Commissioner on National Minorities last April will be put into effect." But still nothing happened on the issue of stateless children.

The inaction on the domestic front was matched by inaction from the institutions. For a year and a half the CE, OSCE, and EU made no further comments on the citizenship law or the regulations. As the Mart Laar government failed and Andreas Tarand took over for the remaining months before the 1995 elections, the government parties were already supporting a new draft of the citizenship law, the gist of which would be to extend the residency requirements to five years and to add a test on the Estonian constitution to the naturalization tests.

Reawakening, the HCNM alone urged care in the passage of a new citizenship law. Van der Stoel sent another letter to Minister of Foreign Affairs Jüri Luik on the occasion of the second reading of the draft law on citizenship, reminding the minister of his letter of April 6, 1993, which contained comments and recommendations on the legislation on citizenship, including his remarks about stateless children. Several CE experts also reviewed the law, but they again provided differing opinions and little direction. The EU was silent on the issue, plowing ahead with economic cooperation and a Europe agreement, and in no way implying concern.

In January 1995, as the upcoming elections promised changes in party support, the outgoing parliament approved a new citizenship law.[45] Although this had been a chance to incorporate them, the law largely ignored van der Stoel's recommendations. Mart Nutt, a deputy from the more nationalist Fatherland Party, author of Estonia's citizenship policy, and a member of the parliament's constitutional law committee, commented on van der Stoel's involvement. "Did we consider his other proposals then about stateless children or making language tests easier?—No we didn't. We felt he was acting for the Russians. And we didn't want to examine the questions only because we felt van der Stoel acted only after the Russians would raise the issues."[46] This comment, while offered by a more nationalist-leaning politician, nevertheless suggests another reason why international attempts at persuasion may fail, namely, the issue of legitimacy. If domestic politicians and others perceive the actor presenting the normative arguments as biased, this will naturally decrease the effectiveness of the normative pressure.

In April 1997 van der Stoel again visited Estonia and reiterated his old and so far unheeded recommendation that Estonian should grant citizenship to stateless children, perhaps hoping that the new government would be more responsive. Like the previous government, however, this even weaker 37-member minority government supported the status quo on citizenship policy. While the parties in the coalition themselves were perhaps open to some liberalization, their adherence to the status quo was seen as necessary for survival in light of the government's weak power base and the presence of nationalist opposition. This same parliament eventually passed the language requirements for election candidates despite OSCE appeals, discussed above.

Pointing out the domestic opposition, Prime Minister Siimann emphasized to the HCNM that the present government would not change the principles of Estonia's law on citizenship.[47] After van der Stoel left, Nutt, now acting frequently as spokesperson for the more nationalist opinions, branded the recommendation by the HCNM as potentially dangerous. Nutt commented to the media that it was dangerous for Estonian independence in the long term to grant automatic Estonian citizenship to former

Soviet citizens' Estonian-born children. "This would directly cut back non-Estonians' integration into the Estonian society, because it would eliminate an important stimulus to keep in touch with the country's domestic policy life and to learn Estonian," said Nutt.[48]

The situation thus looked rather impossible when the EU entered the game. The pressure to liberalize the law heated up considerably as the EU made membership part of the citizenship legislation equation. In a visit to Tallinn a week after the HCNM visit, the EU commissioner on external relations, Hans van den Broek, commented that the work of the OSCE was of great importance. In a letter a month later, the HCNM followed up on this issue and argued extensively for the granting of citizenship to stateless children.

In a rather revealing move, the Estonian government formed a commission of experts chaired by Andra Veidemann, the minister for ethnic affairs, just a month before the scheduled appearance of the EU Agenda 2000 opinion on the readiness of EU candidate states for advancement in the accession negotiation process. The task was to discuss and make proposals to the government concerning the integration of non-Estonians into Estonian society. It had become clear that as the EU commission was preparing its Agenda 2000 report, it was cooperating with the HCNM on the assessment of the political criteria regarding the treatment of minorities. Thus, when the report came out in July 1997, the EU commission opinion stated, "The Estonian authorities should consider means to enable stateless children born in Estonia to be naturalized more easily." This, combined with more general comments about the need to facilitate and speed up naturalization, presented a strong and clear message to Estonia. Bolstering EU credibility, some member states, such as Denmark, reemphasized this message, as did the first meeting of the Joint European Union–Estonia Parliamentary Committee in Tallinn[49]

The Estonian parliament got the EU message. The then minister of ethnic affairs said in response to the Agenda 2000 criticism that "The minister of foreign affairs, I and the minister of justice discussed this and proposed an amendment [regarding stateless children]."[50] She added that, "Right from the beginning the right wing said that they won't vote for the amendment. They said it betrayed the interest of the Estonian nation. . . . Anyhow, different ministers defended this legislation in parliament. The EU argument was a very strong one." The EU was not only using conditionality but was also making an effort at persuading Estonian politicians of the issue's normative dimensions. A Russian political activist said that "this amendment was made only after strong pressure from abroad. The EU made it very clear on paper—about the contradictions with the conventions of the child."[51]

Perhaps taking advantage of the potential impact of the upcoming EU summit in December 1997, HCNM van der Stoel visited Tallinn again in November 1997 and met with the Prime Minister Siimann. They discussed among other things naturalization problems of noncitizens' children born in Estonia.[52] A few days later the EU parliament reiterated the commission opinion.[53]

On December 9, 1997, just a few days before the EU summit that would decide which countries would be invited to open negotiations with the EU, the government decided to discuss amendments to the citizenship law, which would allow children of noncitizens born in Estonia after February 26, 1992, to become citizens. The draft said that parents must have lived in Estonia for at least five years and the child must not have the citizenship of some other country.

The reaction from abroad was immediate. Within a week the HCNM and the EU each issued statements praising the move.[54] In addition, the heads of state of the EU at the Luxembourg summit approved the European Commission's Agenda 2000 opinion, thus inviting Estonia to open membership negotiations with the EU.

Demonstrating the strength of the political disagreements in Estonia, however, the domestic opposition immediately balked at the government's draft. Pro Patria, one of the leading forces in the United Opposition group, with eight seats, vowed to fight the amendment, declaring it contradictory to the principle of restoration of the Estonian State on the basis of legal succession. Parliamentarians from the Reform Party, the largest opposition group, with nineteen seats, said they would most likely vote against the bill. "Generally it doesn't seem to be acceptable," Reform Party MP Ignar Fjuk said. The Moderates, also of the United Opposition, said they had not yet adopted a stance on the issue yet.[55] Thus, a flurry of activity on the issue began.

In January 1998 the parliament rejected a bill submitted by Russian politicians on improvements and amendments to the citizenship law. This repeated itself in March, when Pro Patria was actually able to call off the discussion altogether. As the EU negotiations were about to start in March, however, the government introduced its draft on the stateless children to the parliament, and the bill passed in the first reading.

Soon, the EU asserted itself again in the Estonian accession partnership, where it noted as a short-term (1998) objective under the political criteria that Estonia should "take measures to facilitate the naturalization process and to better integrate noncitizens including Stateless children." The second meeting of the EU–Estonian Joint Parliamentary Committee also appealed to the government of Estonia to increase its effort to integrate non-Estonians into Estonian society and to finalize the legislative changes launched to facilitate and speed up the naturalization of non-Estonians, in particular as regard to children of stateless parents.[56]

Slowly, Estonian politicians began to come around, realizing that the cost of failing to pass the citizenship law amendment could indeed be to gain EU membership. The EU conditionality was clearly changing the payoff calculations of key decision makers. The head of the human rights department in the ministry of foreign affairs worked extensively on the law with the OSCE and the EU. He said that while Estonian politicians disagreed with the recommendations from abroad, they eventually had to give in: "About the stateless children issue we argued for a long time about how to interpret this. . . . Anyway, van der Stoel visited Estonia again and reopened this issue. . . . Many governments and the EU started to back him up. The EU was our first priority and this was well understood by [EU Foreign Affairs Commissioner Hans] van den Brook, and van der Stoel—who obviously talked together. We had lots of contact and meetings with ambassadors of the EU countries."[57] Nevertheless, the domestic opposition was hindering progress.

The EU once again pushed for change. On November 4, 1998, the European Commission issued its first regular report on Estonia. The commission noted, "[I]t is regrettable that the Parliament has not adopted amendments to the citizenship law to allow stateless children to become citizens." The day after, van den Broek met with Estonian President Lennart Meri and discussed the need to adapt Estonian legislation concerning stateless children. The HCNM staff also went to Tallinn to talk further with opponents of the amendments.[58]

This time, the combined OSCE and EU efforts moved things along. Two weeks later parliament concluded the second reading of the bill on amendments to the citizenship act, and on December 8, 1998, lawmakers voted 55–20 to pass the amendments. Votes against the amendments came from the right-leaning Fatherland Union, the People's Party, and some deputies from the Reform and Country People's Parties. Those opposed to the bill had argued unsuccessfully in favor of applicants' having to pass a language proficiency test.

A few days after the law passed, the EU presidency issued a statement praising Estonia for this "important step" and acknowledging "that Estonia has now fulfilled the OSCE recommendations with regard to citizenship." Further, it said the amendment was "consistent with the principles and aims of the European Union."[59] The HCNM also praised the decision.

The conditionality hypothesis argues that the clear addition of incentives causes policy makers to vote for a policy change, even if they may not believe in the change. How clear is the evidence that the change was brought about by the EU membership conditionality? Members of parliament as well as international experts and NGO workers all said that international pressure was pivotal on the issue of granting citizenship to stateless children. One well-positioned observer said, "There was a lot of debate about the citizenship issue even in the public. External pressure was really important in making Estonia in some way sell out on the issue. The EU focused strongly on the issue of stateless children."[60] One of the more nationalist opposition politicians who himself had authored much relevant legislation and who voted against the amendment said that the van der Stoel recommendation on stateless children only gained weight because of the EU: "The Ministry of Foreign Affairs wanted to make a gesture to the EU. They had said to the EU that all the recommendation of Max van der Stoel would be fulfilled. But there was no [domestic political] consensus on the issue."[61] Another member of the opposition, who actually changed her vote, also acknowledged that the EU pressure helped change the minds of some parliamentarians: "The government amendment to the citizenship law approved in December 1997 . . . had high priority for EU progress report and we knew it was a political obstacle [to EU integration]. . . . Some of my colleagues said in their speeches that they were voting for the law because of international pressure and because we [could] lose our nice position and relationship with the EU."[62] Thus, this case brings both evidence of policymakers strategically changing their vote, and of conditionality having an effect even in spite of strong domestic opposition.

The case also supports the argument made in the chapter 2 that institutions can maximize their leverage and eventual impact by using a gradual admission process. Gradualism stimulates policy change by providing several intermediate levers as well as mechanisms for partial reward for partial progress. The case of stateless children in Estonia is particularly good for showing the usefulness of the gradual accession process executed by the EU. The timing of these changes were linked to EU summits and upcoming decisions. Attention to the issue increased visibly after the EU entered the debate and connected the issue to membership. The government's decision to discuss the amendments came just a few days before the EU summit that would decide which countries would be invited to open negotiations with the EU. The pressure and incentive, and their linkage, were reinforced several times throughout the legislative process.

RESIDENCY ISSUES

A discussion of ethnic minority issues in Estonia would be amiss without including the "Aliens' Law," which has often been touted as an example of the influence of international actors on domestic norms. While I argue that the accomplishments were moderate, when actually compared with the recommendations of the OSCE, the case is nevertheless a remarkable example of international institutions as domestic policy actors. Indeed, Estonia responded to a very tight package of international pressure and persuasion combined with significant domestic protest. With the exception of economic threats from Russia, however, no direct link was made to membership in any institution or any other material payoff. Thus, this case is an example of the effectiveness of a high level of coordination and intensive persuasion efforts by international actors.

After the initial resolution on citizenship was passed, the status of noncitizens constituted a legal void in Estonian legislation. This void was made particularly problematic by the passing of the local election law, which gave voting rights to noncitizens. Thus, with upcoming local elections in the fall, Estonia needed to pass a law to define the status of noncitizens. In his speech to parliament, Prime Minister Laar promised a draft law setting out the rights and duties of noncitizens, who should be issued special identification documents in lieu of passports. With the Laar government's campaign slogan to clean house and its advocacy of assisting Russians to resettle in Russia, noncitizens had no reason to expect a break from this government.

In June 1993, after Estonia was safely in the fold of the CE, the alien's law came before the parliament. It required all noncitizens to apply for residency status if they wanted to remain in Estonia. Naturally, many people thought it was demeaning that they had to apply for a residency permit, even though they had been born in or had been living for years in Estonia. There were protests in Tallinn and Narva against the anticipated passage of the law; seven thousand people in a meeting in Narva threatened to close down the power station, block the roads, and take up weapons if the parliament passed the law.[63]

Seemingly blind to domestic Russian upheaval, however, on June 21, 1993, the parliament passed the law in the final reading, requiring non-Estonians to obtain a residency permit or apply for citizenship if they wished to remain in the country for more than two years. All initial permits would be temporary, and only after three years could temporary permit holders obtain a permanent residence permit.

Ethnic Russians were anxious for several reasons. The law provided for deportation for those who failed to obtain a permit. Some of the bases for denial of permits appeared susceptible to arbitrary interpretation. For example, provisions denied permits to an alien "who does not respect the constitutional system and does not observe the laws of Estonia" or "whose actions have been directed against the Estonian State and its security" (Visek1997, 333). Former Soviet military officers and their families who had remained in Estonia would not be given residency permits. Also, aliens who had lost their legitimate source of income could have their permits revoked. Lastly, aliens were required to inform the authorities of any changes in their residency, employment, family standing, and so on.

Moscow immediately said it planned a series of political and economic sanctions, and international protests mounted. Van der Stoel met with the Estonian ambassador in Moscow and asked the president of Estonia not to promulgate the Law on Aliens before it had passed international expert examination. Swedish Prime Minister Carl Bildt expressed dissatisfaction with the law. Meanwhile, Russian President Boris Yeltsin declared, "The Estonian government has misjudged Russia's goodwill and, giving way to the pressure of nationalism, has 'forgotten' about certain geopolitical and demographic realities," further he contended that "the Russian side has means at its disposal to remind Estonia about these [realities]."[64] Coincidentally, Russia then halted deliveries of natural gas to Estonia, supposedly because of a backlog of unpaid debts.

Only after the Estonian president requested international expertise, after Russia cut off the natural gas supply and threatened sanctions, and after the Narva town council on June 28, 1993, decided to hold a municipal referendum on national-territorial autonomy, did some EU member states react. Even so, the response was rather low-key; some ambassadors of European Commission countries gave Active Premier Liia Hänni a message from the European Commission countries expressing the hope that the Estonian government would achieve mutual understanding with opponents of the Law on Aliens.[65]

Meanwhile, the OSCE and the CE presented their recommendations. The OSCE mission had already made recommendations in a letter to Nutt, the law's author. Now, the HCNM presented President Meri with his proposals for giving more legal rights to applicants. The biggest recommendation, however, concerned the restriction of not issuing residence permits to former foreign military personnel. Van der Stoel recommended that this restriction only be applied to those officers and their families who had been demobilized in Estonia after 1991. Joining with the OSCE, soon thereafter the CE released a report that criticized the law for not providing sufficient judicial control, for lacking legal certainty, and for not recognizing acquired rights. The CE experts added that the language of the law vague and need to be revised.[66]

Finally, Swedish Prime Minister Bildt, a strong ally of Estonia, visited Tallinn twice in two weeks to mediate the crisis. He issued a statement criticizing Russia's harsh reaction, but also calling the law's serious deficiencies "regrettable." He added, "It is extremely necessary now to use international mechanisms, which might help to break the vicious circle [of Estonian-Russian accusations] and relieve tensions. This concerns above all the [resources] of the Council of Europe and the CSCE" (Pettai 1993).

The international efforts had their desired effect. President Meri and the parliament held extensive consultations, and Meri returned the law to parliament, citing international experts. According to the president's televised address to the nation, it was the opinions of the CE and CSCE that led his to return the law.

Two days later, an extraordinary session of the parliament reexamined the Law on Aliens and made several changes. A new article in the law guaranteed residency permits to any alien who had settled in Estonia before July 1 , 1990, and had been registered as a permanent resident in the former Estonian SSR, as long as the alien's status was in accord with all the other requirements of the law. Also, the stipulation that permanent residency permits had to be renewed every five years was dropped. The amendments also clarified the definition of "lawful income" as recommended by HCNM van der Stoel, expanded the rights of applicants for residence permits to the protection of the courts, and restricted the opportunities to refuse to issue residency permits to persons who had been sentenced by a court of law. In a statement outlining the changes, Prime Minister Laar admitted that the changes had been made to meet European standards: "By adopting the Law on Aliens amendments, the parliament has shown its readiness to observe European legal principles."[67] The government soon issued the basic implementation.[68]

But how significant were the changes? Certainly, the parliament adopted some of the suggestions made by the CE and OSCE. But the main essence of the law remained unchanged: the law defined Russian-speakers as noncitizens and gave them two years to decide whether to opt for Estonian nationality or only resident status. The government said it had incorporated "all the changes suggested by the Council of Europe" and by the OSCE, but one major recommendations of the OSCE, regarding retired military personnel, remained essentially unchanged. This meant that the many thousands of former Soviet Army officers who have retired in Estonia would face expulsion. The law, however, did give the right to the government to make exceptions but did not establish any guidelines. Thus, in reality the changes were not major, and the deepening crisis in northeastern Estonia facilitated the fact that the government was willing to involve the OSCE and the CE at all.

Nationalists later expressed satisfaction that the changes "did not seriously alter the Estonian position." "There has been no major change in the conception of the law," said Mart Nutt, the formulator of the original bill. The main changes were "in the legal terminology and in the legal guarantees."[69] Klara Hallik, the former minister of ethnic affairs, agreed: "The 1993 aliens act was very critical because it recognized the noncitizens as illegal residents. In fact, the amendments didn't change the basic act. Everyone was still forced to apply for residency permits—which meant that otherwise they were here illegally."[70]

Regardless of how substantial the changes truly were, praise from Europe was forthcoming. Since the essence of the law, based on a Swedish model, did not violate human rights, the international organizations had difficulties further protesting. The EU issued a political cooperation statement saying that the EU member states were pleased that the changes to the law on aliens were in line with the recommendations of the CE, the CSCE, and EU. The statement said the amendments were "a clear indication of the attachment of Estonia to democratic principles and its commitment to political dialogue and compromise and non-confrontation with its communities and its neighboring countries." Van der Stoel also said that Estonia had taken a "major step" forward by revising the law on aliens. As a sign that he was not at ease with the outcome and the upcoming referendum in the northeast, however, he also issued a press statement on the "assurances" of continued cooperation, that he had received both from Prime Minister Laar and from representatives of the Russian community, and noted that "many difficult questions still have to be solved."[71]

This case is frequently cited as an example of international pressure's averting a crisis in Estonia, and the international attention probably did calm the situation somewhat. The actual effect of the changes, however, was debatable. Whether this can be classified as a case of pure persuasion is also doubtful, as Russian threats and their cutting off the gas supply may have altered the payoff calculations of some policymakers. In any case, this is certainly an example of a homeland (Russia) effectively placing an issue onto the agendas of the international institutions.

The case also teaches about lost opportunities. According to Nutt, one of the authors of the law on aliens, the CE had not offered any input into either the issue of residency or the law on aliens before its passage, even though the CE had recently admitted Estonia. "On the aliens law in 1993, we did not receive any input from the CE prior to the first passage of the law. We had been working on the law since 1991, but since we were not a member of the CE, they did not give us any advice on this," he said.[72] Thus, it was not until the first passage of the law that the international community reacted, Nutt said.

The point, of course, is not that individual countries never produce positive legislative developments without international involvement. But governments only pass pro-ethnic legislation unsolicited when the purposes align with their own goals. For example, Prime Minister Laar argued in 1992 that the particularly loyal forty thousand Russians who applied for citizenship before the election of the Estonian Congress in February 1990 should receive citizenship without the language test. During his government, the parliament did amend the Resolution on the Application of the law on citizenship to allow simplified naturalization for the "permanent residents of Estonia, who registered as applicants for Estonian citizenship prior to the elections for the Congress of Estonia."[73] This allowed several tens of thousands of noncitizens who were considered loyal to become naturalized without taking the language exam. In so doing Laar was making good on an earlier promise to the "green card" holders,[74] which Laar and the Fatherland coalition together with the ENIP had made when they needed support for the Congress.

CONCLUSION

As in Latvia, the issue of language requirements for local and national election candidates surfaced on the domestic agenda. Whereas institutions remained uninvolved in Latvia, the OSCE did attempt to influence Estonian policy makers in the mid-1990s. Nevertheless, international efforts of persuasion fell mostly on deaf ears. Estonian politicians had no reason to believe that most of Europe noticed their policy. Aside from the fairly quiet OSCE effort, the local embassies did not direct attention to the issue in Europe. Second, policy makers correctly calculated that few consequences would follow ignoring the advice of HCNM van der Stoel. In March and April of 1996 Estonia's main focus was on EU accession, and several European states were sending Estonia all the right signs.

In contrast to the election law case, the case of the language law shows how different the domestic response can be when international institutions also use material incentives together with persuasion. Note, too, how Estonia, which in 1998 was already in the "first wave" of EU candidates, was somewhat slower to respond to the EU criticism of the language policy, given that Estonia could take its position in the admission queue to the EU somewhat more for granted. Nevertheless, both cases illustrate that when the true conditional nature of the EU membership became apparent, both countries adjusted their policy in response to the admission requirements.

Finally, the issues of citizenship and stateless children illustrate a three phase development of institutional involvement. At first, international institutions were not involved and the law contained several weak points relative to international standards for residency and citizenship—especially given the large proportion of ethnic minorities without citizenship in the country. Next, international institutions used persuasion but without notable result. Finally, when international institutions linked the recommendations with membership, policy changed. Clearly, the early efforts also suffered from lack of coordination between the OSCE and the CE, which failed to support the OSCE recommendations. As in Latvia, however, when the institutions finally did link the citizenship issue and in particular the issue of stateless children with EU membership, key policy makers frankly stated that this change in payoffs largely drove the domestic policy changes.

Finally is the issue of the language of instruction in the education system, a case not discussed in this chapter but included in the larger data set. This, too, was an example of how the government modified the law quite quickly after EU's Agenda 2000 report, issued in 1997, mentioned the issue . Thus, in all, the Estonian cases provide solid support for the decisive role of the international institutions in the formulation of ethnic minority policy, and in particular for the usefulness of membership incentives above persuasive techniques alone.

CHAPTER 6

Slovakia: The Meciar Hurdle and Beyond

SLOVAKIA HAD BEEN primarily under Hungarian rule for centuries when the Slovaks joined with their neighbors to form a new state, Czechoslovakia, in 1918. During and after World War II the government confiscated Hungarians' property, expelled between seventy thousand and ninety thousand persons to Hungary, and resettled about forty-four thousand Hungarians in Bohemia and Moravia. Following World War II Czechoslovakia became a Communist state. Minority rights were constitutionally guaranteed beginning in1969, but minority problems persisted under the surface (Vachudova and Snyder 1997). Several policies indirectly targeted the Hungarian minority.[1]

After the collapse of the USSR in 1989 ended Soviet influence, the Czechoslovak Federal Assembly adopted a charter of fundamental rights and freedoms in January 1991, prohibiting all forms of discrimination and reaffirming the right to higher education in the mother tongue. The 1992 elections secured overwhelming support for the Movement for a Democratic Slovakia (HZDS), however, which soon began to use nationalist rhetoric for political gain and to cooperate with the nationalist Slovak National Party (SNS). In July 1992 the Slovak National parliament proclaimed Slovakia's sovereignty, and adopted the Slovak Constitution on September 3, 1992.[2] The new state of Slovakia officially came into existence on January 1, 1993.

The immediate consequence of the dissolution of Czechoslovakia was that the Hungarians became a much more visible minority group. In Czechoslovakia, Hungarians constituted only about 3 percent of the overall population. With the independence of Slovakia, however, the roughly 570,000 Hungarians living in southern Slovakia constituted about 10.6 percent of the population, according to the 1991 census. In some southern districts, Hungarians made up 42.9 percent of the regional population (Strhan and Daniel 1994, 268). The Hungarians were fairly concentrated geographically; the thirteen mixed Slovak-Hungarian districts had proportions of Hungarians varying from 4.1 percent in Kosice to 87 percent in Dunajska Streda. Seventy percent of Hungarians lived in relatively homogenous areas where they accounted for about 60 percent of the population.[3]

Slovak Politics after Independence[4]

Even before Slovakia gained independence, Slovak political leaders, in particular Vladimir Meciar, exploited nationalist rhetoric as an electoral tactic (Mego 1999). Meciar was prime minister until November 1998, with only a brief interlude from March to November 1994. His HZDS-led government cooperated primarily with the nationalist SNS, and although the Hungarian minority parties had some representation in parliament throughout the 1990s, they were seldom part of a coherent opposition block. Thus, between 1993 and 1998 nationalists had a strong influence in Slovakia (Pridham 1999, 1226). In 1997 Meciar even went so far as to propose a "population exchange" to Hungarian Prime Minister Gyula Horn to "facilitate the voluntary migration of ethnic Hungarians from Slovakia to Hungary and Hungary's Slovak minority to Slovakia."[5]

After the 1998 elections, Meciar's HZDS was still the largest party in parliament, but its number of seats shrank from 61 to 43. SDK, the largest opposition party, won 42 seats. Although the difference was small, the other political parties quickly refused to form a coalition with the HZDS, excluding Meciar from the government. The new government parties, however, were reluctant to include the Hungarian party in the government coalition. The Hungarian representatives only joined the new 1998 government because of combined domestic and European pressure. This, however, did not mean the end of nationalist voices in Slovak politics. Although the HZDS lacked sufficient votes to form a government, former Prime Minister Meciar's party remained the single most popular party, and Meciar retained hopes of returning to power. (See table 6.1.)[6]

Case Studies

This chapter discusses six issues in Slovak ethnic politics, examining conditionality and normative pressure in contexts of domestic opposition different than those in the Baltic States. Whereas the Baltic States had broader, though less extreme domestic opposition in the sense of the oppositions' being less xenophobic, Slovakia and Romania provide cases of narrower but more exploitative nationalist opposition. There is also considerable variation in governments over time, as discussed above.

The first issue concerns the use of personal and place names. This issue, which plays out over two different Slovak governments, shows an international institution, in this case the CE, losing considerable leverage by not having a gradual admission process that allowed it to secure some compliance before moving on to full membership. The rest of the cases illustrate

TABLE 6.1.
Slovak Governments

Government	Parties	Seats	Total seats
Vladimir Meciar June 1992–June 1993	HZDS	74	74/150
October 1993–March 1994	HZDS	66	80/150
	SNS	14	
Jozef Moravcik	SDL	29	60?/150
March 1994–November 1994	KDH	18	
	DU and other HZDS defectors	?	
	SMK (not officially in coalition)	(14)	
Vladimir Meciar	HZDS	61	83/150
December 1994–November 1998	SNS	9	
	ZRS	13	
Mikulas Dzurinda	SDK	42	93/150
December 1998–present	SDL	23	
	SMK	15	
	SOP	13	

Acronyms: HZDS: Movement for a Democratic Slovakia; SNS: Slovak National Party; ZRS: Association of Workers of Slovakia; SDL: The Party of the Democratic Left; SDK: Slovak Democratic Coalition; KDH: Christian Democratic Movement; DU: Democratic Union; SOP: The party of Civic Understanding; SMK: The Party of Hungarian Coalition.

both conditionality successes and failures, even within the period of the same government. Thus, for example, Meciar's government eventually responded to demands to sign a treaty with Hungary, and the Slovak government finally relented when the institutions linked its penalty code with EU membership. On election law, school certificates, and language law, however, Meciar did not budge. This suggests that narrow but extreme opposition may be more resilient to external pressure than broad-based but milder opposition. The cases of the language law and the school certificates also provide a good opportunity to examine how a change of government facilitated the effectiveness of conditionality.

THE LAW ON NAMES

In chapter 2, I argued that credibility and subsequently the effectiveness of membership incentives increases when institutions use gradual commitment mechanisms for integration. Indeed, several cases discussed in other chapters, such as the Latvian language law, illustrate how the EU made effective use of the many steps it invented in the admission process. Various annual summits, the 1997 Agenda 2000 and the 1998 and 1999 update reports, accession partnerships, decisions to open negotiations, and so on, all functioned as individual levers. The issue of the laws on personal names and town and village names shows how the lack of a gradual admission procedure left the CE with much less influence after already admitting a country. Most importantly, failure to secure compliance before awarding full membership depleted institutional influence.

When Slovakia vied for CE membership soon after gaining independence, the CE asked Slovakia to adopt two laws: one to allow persons who were not ethnic Slovaks to use their own forms of their names, and the other to allow the use of bilingual signs in towns and villages. Slovak politicians widely discussed the CE concerns, and Prime Minister Meciar's government said it was prepared to meet the CE conditions.[7] A June 1993 CE report on Slovakia's application for membership noted, "The authorities resolved to make every effort to find solutions to the problems which might arise for minorities."[8] The rapporteurs recommended Slovakia for admission, and the CE admitted Slovakia before the passage of the laws. As part of the admission commitments, however, the CE stressed that it was admitting Slovakia with the understanding that Slovakia would pass the two laws on names within six months.[9] But a week after CE admission, and after actually passing an acceptable draft law about the use of personal names,[10] the government backed out of that version of the bill and nothing much came of it in the summer of 1993.[11] In September, despite a visit by the HCNM to discuss the issue, the parliament passed a less favorable version of the law, which applied only to the naming of newborns.[12] The parliament declared the issue closed.[13]

As the CE had already granted membership, the international institutions were left with only persuasive options. The CE sent a mission to Slovakia, and the director of the CE political department, Hans-Peter Fuerrer, met with Meciar and Vice Premier Roman Kovac. He publicly criticized the law on names and the issue of town and village names, and said that he had been assured that the CE demands would be met.[14] HCNM van der Stoel also discussed the law with Meciar. When Slovakia had still not rectified the issue at the end of the initial six-month monitoring period, the CE decided to continue monitoring of Slovakia. Such monitoring, however, was a standard practice shortly after admission, and thus this decision did not put particular pressure on the Slovak government. Walter Schwimmer, a CE deputy later to become CE secretary-general, who had visited Slovakia on a mission, criticized the law on names as well as the government's draft law on the bilingual road signs.[15] The normative pressure led nowhere. President Kovac signed the controversial law on names on the basis of Meciar's assurances that the government would soon submit an amendment to the law on registries to parliament to solve the remaining contentious issues.[16] The government did not do this.

The other CE concern, the issue of the town and village names, did not fare any better. The Slovak government's strategy seemed to be one of supposed ignorance. The issue of place name signs fell under the jurisdiction of the minister of transport and communication, Roman Hofbauer. Just before the CE admitted Slovakia, he was asked if he had decided yet on the restoration of bilingual signs, since this issue was one of the conditions of Slovakia's membership in the CE. He replied that he did not know about such a condition and that he did not intend to restore bilingual signs.[17]

Subsequently, after CE admission the government made no effort to restore bilingual signs and did not respond to CE and OSCE advice. In August 1993 many towns in southern Slovakia populated by the Hungarian minority removed bilingual signs, apparently in response to a new transportation ministry directive. Meciar refused to respond to complaints, calling it a local problem.[18] The HCNM wrote in October supporting the CE conditions: "It is also my understanding that your Government will take legislative measures in the near future on the basis of which the bilingual naming of towns and villages in minority areas can take place."[19] October brought only more sign removals in southern Slovakia. Criticism by the CE fact-finding missions and the statements of CE Political Director Hans-Peter Fuerrer, and rapporteur Walter Schwimmer had little effect. In January 1994 the parliament finally discussed a law on town and village names. But the parliament—including the Hungarian deputies—rejected it because only towns and villages with a 30 percent minority population would have had the right to use bilingual signs.[20]

Thus, the law on names and the law on town and village names demonstrate how, once the CE had already admitted Slovakia, persuasive efforts failed at bringing about the promised policy change. The CE membership was a clear incentive for adopting favorable laws on names and on town and village names. The CE wasted this leverage, however, because it did not make use of additional intermediary steps before admission but instead admitted Slovakia based on a promise to pass the laws. Politicians and experts agreed that Meciar had little concern for the commitments to the CE: "Meciar saw those laws a requests from the Hungarians. He said, if those are the requests, then we don't need the CE."[21]

It was not until the summer of 1994 that Slovakia adjusted the laws to meet the commitments. By that time other factors had contributed to the changes. Most notably, a government more eager to please the West had replaced Meciar, and this weak government relied indirectly on ethnic minority politicians for support.

SLOVAKIA'S TREATY WITH HUNGARY

The treaty between Slovakia and Hungary is an example of a response to international pressure and incentives despite strong nationalist opposition. The EU, NATO, the United States, the HCNM, and individual EU member states, in particular France, urged the singing of the treaty via letters and personal contacts. Although Slovak Prime Minister Meciar tended to shrug off international critics, the social influence and incentives worked in this case. They worked because Meciar saw it in his own personal interest to improve his image with the West and to improve his legitimacy as a statesman. The success of the signing, however, was marred significantly by the implementation failure.

Work on a bilateral treaty to settle relations between Slovakia and Hungary had begun in 1991 but made little progress primarily because of ethnic politics in both countries. By 1994 it became clear that the EU considered the resolution of bilateral ethnic issues and border disputes an important preaccession criteria. At the Brussels European Council meeting in October 1993 the EU approved the Balladur Plan, or so-called Stability Pact, to stem instability from minority issues.[22] Indirectly, this made the signing of bilateral treaties a requirement for admission.

As they approached the culmination of the Stability Pact in March 1995 with a conference on European stability in Paris, the EU, and especially France, pressured Meciar to sign the treaty. In Hungary, however, Viktor Orban, chairman of the opposition Federation of Young Democrats–Hungarian Civic Party made provocative calls for autonomy and lobbied actively against a treaty. Meanwhile, Meciar refused to address the Benes decrees, which provided for the expulsion of Germans and Hungarians after the World War II. Thus, the outcome of Meciar's visit of January 25 to Budapest surprised even the Slovak opposition media. Within a single day the prime ministers achieved progress on most issues, which until then had been deadlocked, and agreed that the two countries would conclude a treaty before the March 20 conference. Since disagreements were still threatening their ability to reach a mutually acceptable text, however, the international institutions maintained their pressure. HCNM van der Stoel visited Bratislava in February to urge Meciar to sign the treaty. Other international leaders also stressed the importance of the treaty,[23] and pressured both premier ministers.

Cooperation grew more difficult, however, as each country put their text on the table and in a series of meeting experts began to hammer out the differences. The greatest point of contention was the issue of the inclusion of CE Recommendation 1201 and any possible references to "autonomy."[24] On March 5, 1995, the talks at the level of state secretaries collapsed. The

Slovak foreign ministry stated that "until Budapest gives up the illusion of a protectorate over Slovak Republic's citizens of Hungarian nationality an insurmountable obstacle would stand in the path of Slovak-Hungarian settlement."[25] Hungarian diplomatic sources said that the document was unlikely to be signed.[26]

At this point French Prime Minister Edouard Balladur wrote a letter on behalf of the EU to encourage progress on the treaty.[27] Both countries stuck to their conditions. Meciar said that demands for autonomy and "above-standard" rights for the half-million Hungarians in Slovakia prevented agreement.[28] The Hungarian state secretary said that the minority rights had to be appropriately guaranteed.[29] Talks thus continued to falter but were propelled and reignited continuously by the Stability Pact Conference deadline. The negotiations went to the level of the foreign ministers. Both EU and NATO pressure continued. Even U.S. President Bill Clinton urged Meciar to seek a conclusion to the treaty.[30] Demonstrating the power of the international pressure, the talks went to the level of prime ministers just days before the EU conference deadline.

Domestic opposition remained considerable. Slovak Foreign Minister Juraj Schenk said that six "open questions" remained. "These are problems on which Slovakia cannot yield," he stressed.[31] The leader of the coalition-member SNS, Jan Slota, stressed that inclusion of CE Recommendation 1201 in the treaty would lead to rifts in the coalition.[32] Laszlo Kovacs, the Hungarian foreign minister, said that the Hungarian government "did not want a treaty with Slovakia at any cost," and that no treaty could be concluded based the latest Slovak draft proposal.[33]

The EU membership conditionality helped overcome the difficulties on both sides of the border. To everyone's astonishment, the two prime ministers reached an agreement after seven hours of nonstop discussion.[34] Acknowledging that EU membership incentives had driven the talks, Meciar said, "We are aware, as one of the [EU] associated countries, that the Stability Pact, through its course and actual results, will speed up our bona-fide participation in the European Union."[35] Democratic Union (DU) representative Roman Kovac, a former deputy premier, said that "the agreement forms a certain element of stability . . . [and] the expectation of completing the agreement for Associate Membership of the European Union."[36] French Premier Edouard Balladur reinforced their remarks, saying, "The agreement is a marked step toward drawing these two countries closer into the structures of Western Europe and the EU continent."[37] Later, Slovak and Hungarian experts also acknowledged that Horn and Meciar had signed a treaty mostly because of direct Western—and especially the French—pressure.[38] A week later, Meciar again stressed that the treaty "puts both countries on the road to European integration,"[39] and that in concluding the treaty, Slovakia had "gained political support" in the West.[40]

If the account of the treaty ended here it would stand as a strong achievement of the EU and other international actors, given the earlier high degree of contention about the issue. But Meciar's government not only failed to ratify the treaty for a year but also blocked its implementation for years. Although the government coalition had 83 seats in the 150-seat parliament, without nine deputies from the SNS, Meciar's HZDS, and the Slovak Workers' Party, it lacked two votes to ratify the treaty. SNS leader Jan Slota said that CE Recommendation 1201 on national minorities "negated" the treaty, and further commented, "The rejection of the basic Slovak-Hungarian treaty is a cardinal question for us. None of the SNS deputies will vote for it, if it, God forbid, appears on the parliamentary agenda."[41]

The OSCE and the EU urged ratification of the treaty in several ways during the next year.[42] As it turned out, Meciar had to make a bargain with his minor coalition partner, the SNS, and promised the SNS to vote for several controversial pieces of legislation. Thus, Slovakia finally ratified the treaty in March 1996 but simultaneously passed other legislation against the spirit of the treaty, such as the language law and the penal code (discussed below). Slovakia also adopted an "interpretive statement" that revoked substantial rights that the treaty accorded to the Hungarian minority.[43] The government then spent the next two years dodging the implementation of the treaty.

Despite the delayed ratification and the poor implementation, the signing of the treaty must be labeled a success, at least from the perspective of the European institutions' managing to bring about their stated objective. Whether the EU objective was right is outside the scope of this study. Whether it was well conceived is a subject of debate, since it backfired domestically in other policies. Nevertheless, at the time the EU did achieve what it wanted and indeed hailed the Slovak-Hungarian treaty as the success of the Stability Pact Conference. Thus, even in a case of strong domestic opposition, where the leadership faced noncooperative coalition partners, external pressure from international organizations worked because the international prestige from cooperation increased domestic political capital in terms of image improvement and other factors.

THE PENALTY CODE

The penalty code is remarkable in that the Slovak government tried to pass it three times, showing their strength of preferences, yet eventually abandoned the law because of criticism from the EU and other European institutions.

When the nationalist SNS formally entered the coalition in 1995, the party primarily focused on the Hungarian minority.[44] To criminally prosecute members of the opposition, and in particular Hungarian deputies who spoke about Slovakia abroad, the SNS thus argued for a penal code amendment. In April 1995 in connection with a campaign of civil disobedience to be launched in mid-May by ethnic Hungarians, SNS chairman Jan Slota said, "If anyone wants to question Slovak sovereignty, he must be punished accordingly. We want to pass the 'law on the protection of the republic'. . . . And then we shall apply it."[45] In January 1996 the HZDS promised the SNS to pass the law in exchange for SNS votes to ratify the Slovak-Hungarian Treaty.

The HCNM and the EU reacted strongly to the draft bill. In a letter the HCNM tried to persuade the government that the amendment contradicted international standards. "[I]t would be undesirable to amend the penal code . . . the danger would be great that new formulations of the law would go beyond the restrictions on the freedom of expression permitted under article 10 of the European Convention for the Protection of Human Rights and Fundamental Freedoms."[46] The day after, EU Foreign Affairs Commissioner van den Broek called on Slovakia "to further develop and strengthen democratic institutions and to respect ethnic minority rights and freedom of speech."[47]

Nevertheless, a month later Prime Minister Meciar's three-party coalition government rammed amendments to the penal code through parliament after cutting short a fierce debate.[48] The proposed amendment read, "Anyone who with the intention of harming the constitutional order, the integrity of the territory or the defense of the Republic or undermining its independence organizes public meetings will be liable to a term of imprisonment of between 6 months and 3 years or a fine."[49] People could be jailed for "disseminating false information abroad damaging to the interests of the republic," or organizing public rallies judged to be "subversive." Most importantly, however, the amendment gave no clear definition of the "interests of the republic" or "subversion," and critics said the law would lead to political trials, or at least to a new atmosphere of fear and self-censorship.[50]

A week later the EU clearly linked the issue to EU membership. In a presidency declaration, the EU welcomed the ratification of the treaty with Hungary, but also said,

> The European Union is concerned about certain provisions in the [criminal code] amendments, which appear to affect freedom of expression and other democratic rights and expresses the expectation that these provisions will be carefully considered with a view to finding solutions in accordance with democratic

principles and in a way which is compatible with the conclusions of the Copenhagen Summit of the European Union and with the EU membership for which Slovakia has applied.[51]

The EU conditionality had some effect, but the battle continued. Days later, President Michal Kovac, already at political and personal war with Prime Minister Meciar, returned the amendments to the parliament.[52] The government coalition parties nevertheless continued to work on passing the law. In May 1996 HCNM van der Stoel visited Slovakia. In June EU Foreign Affairs Commissioner van den Broek warned Slovakia not to assume that enlargement would proceed even if Slovakia ignored EU concerns. "Amendments to the penal code on subversion and the dissemination of information are hard to reconcile with the principles of freedom of assembly and the freedom of expression, which are fundamental to any democracy," he said.[53] The French and German European affairs ministers also warned Slovak officials that the penal code had "stirred emotions in the EU."[54]

Hungary played right into the hand of the SNS, when the conference held in Budapest, "Hungarians and Hungarians Living Abroad," issued a declaration reading that "the formation of an autonomy is a basic condition for the maintenance of the identity of Hungarians living abroad."[55] The SNS warned that Hungary was supporting minorities' hazardous tendencies toward autonomy, and promised to re-debate the penal code in the parliament.[56]

Concerned with the turn of events, the HCNM wrote another letter with a series of concerns and recommendations, and the CE and the OSCE remained involved in the drafting of the law.[57] The European Parliament passed a resolution asking Slovakia to respect human rights, ethnic rights, democracy, and the rule of law as pledged under the association agreement. This only angered nationalists further, and just days later they again placed the criminal code on the agenda.

The parliament soon adopted a second and supposedly milder version of the amendment to the penal code. The clauses on treason and calls for mass disturbances remained. During the debate, SNS chairman Jan Slota said that "with the help of this law, people who want to break up the republic will be where they belong."[58] Using a technicality, however, the president returned the law again at the end of December.[59] In a final attempt, the SNS pushed the amendment on the agenda once more in February 1997. This time a united opposition, with the help from HZDS and ZRS defections, defeated the amendment. The next day EU External Affairs Commissioner Hans van den Broek welcomed the Slovak parliament's decision not to accept "controversial" amendments to its penal code.[60]

Was the final rejection the result of international efforts? Bela Bugar, a prominent Hungarian deputy, stressed that the international denouncement was indeed important.[61] Others agreed that "[o]n the penal code, the International community had a very clear and absolute role."[62] An opposition deputy underscored the point: "The penal code amendment was not a game. The law was aimed at making it possible to punish people like myself."[63] That the amendment actually appeared on the agenda three times also suggests that the government was indeed serious about the bill. Had it been just a piece of political propaganda, passing the amendment once or even twice should have been sufficient. Thus, this is a case in which the European institutions contributed to overcoming repeated attempts by nationalists to pass legislation opposed by the institutions.

THE ELECTION LAW

The issue of the election law, which Meciar fixed along ethnic lines, is an example of how the interests of an authoritarian leader conflicted with the goal of joining the EU, which required adhering to Western democratic standards. Soon after the Meciar government pushed through a new territorial administrative division in 1996, the HZDS began to discuss various electoral reforms, which, given the new division, would favor the HZDS. In March 1998, as elections approached, the parliament finally passed the amendments with some controversy. Miklos Duray of the Hungarian Coalition (MK), noted, "By itself, [the law] is not a problem, but what is a problem is that it is serves a momentary purpose."[64]

After the national election law passed, the European institutions became involved as Slovakia set about passing the local election law. The OSCE sent representatives from the Office for Democratic Institutions and Human Rights. Later, in a letter to Zdenka Kramplova, minister of foreign affairs, HCNM van der Stoel wrote that "with regard to the draft Law on Local Elections ... I have serious concerns about its essential thrust and effects. As I understand the bill, its main aim is to fix the electoral representation along ethnic lines. I believe this is generally undesirable and would in its effects violate the fundamental principle of democracy."[65] Finally, the EU joined the criticism during an EU-Slovak joint parliamentary committee meeting.[66] The EU linked the election law changes directly to EU membership. Commenting on a visit to Slovakia in May, EU Foreign Affairs Commissioner van den Broek said, "I am concerned about ... recent changes to the electoral law. I therefore called on the Slovak authorities to take steps to address these issues. Together with free and fair elections, improvements in this area are instrumental to bringing Slovakia closer to the EU."[67]

The parliament nevertheless passed the amendments including the rules for ethnic quotas in local governments.[68] In a completely illogical reply to van der Stoel's letter criticizing the draft electoral law, Minister of Foreign Affairs Zdenka Kramplová wrote to the HCNM that "In connection with the draft Law on Local Elections I have the honour to inform you that this draft law has already been adopted in the National Council of the Slovak Republic."[69] Thus, the government passed the local election law against the preferences of international institutions.

Underscoring his authoritarian style, Meciar and his government became increasingly indifferent or even hostile toward Western international organization and countries as the election neared. Meciar attributed all the responsibility for Slovakia's image and integration difficulties to the opposition and to President Kovac. Thus, despite the strong criticism of the European institutions, and the EU's explicit linkage of the issue to admission, the Meciar government ignored all advice. By this time Meciar's only concern was reelection by any means. There was simply no room in his utility function for the approval of European institutions. Everything else was subservient to this goal. Thus, this case illustrates how an authoritarian leader can indeed completely block the efforts of international institutions when his personal power hangs in the balance.

SCHOOL CERTIFICATES

The issue of the withdrawal of bilingual school certificates in Slovakia is another examples of how both institutional persuasion and incentives failed to sway a nationalist government for whom the issue became symbolic of its authority and political profile. After the 1995 government-promoted language law came into effect on January 1, 1997, different ramifications of the law began to manifest themselves. Thus, soon thereafter the education ministry issued a statement requiring school reports to be in Slovak only.[70]

While the domestic response from the Hungarian population was strong,[71] the initial international reaction was weak. The first international reaction came from HCNM van der Stoel, who discussed the law in his April 1997 visit in. When EU Commissioner for Foreign Affairs van den Broek visited Slovakia in late May, he said that Slovakia needed to send "positive signals" and take "practical steps" toward redressing political shortcomings, but he did not mention the school certificates and he also assured the government that there was no danger of the EU's canceling Slovakia's association agreement.

Meanwhile, the ethnic Hungarians continued to mobilize mass protests and actually placed the issue on the international agenda. After the government fired an elementary school teacher for issuing bilingual school-leaving reports to ethnic Hungarian students, the Hungarian Coalition sent letter to the top officials in the OSCE, the CE, and the EU.[72]

The timing was good, because the EU was just about to issue its Agenda 2000 report and thus had a powerful gradual tool at its disposal. The July 1997 EU Agenda 2000 opinion, which was a tool for EU decision making about accession, noted, "This ambiguous situation is further aggravated by certain government decisions concerning the Hungarian minority such as . . . the cessation of bilingual school reports in Hungarian schools (a teacher not respecting this rule can be dismissed)."

EU conditionality still failed. Miffed by the EU in general and excluded from the EU's first wave of candidate countries chosen for admission, the Slovak government chose to ignore the EU for the moment. Perhaps provoked by the lack of response, the European institutions upped their engagement. In March 1998 the European Commission released a press statement pointing to problem areas, such as the abolition of bilingual school-leaving certificates in schools with high minority percentages. Days later a senior delegation led by HCNM van der Stoel, CE Political Director Hans-Peter Fuerrer, and EC Central Europe Director Catherine Day arrived in Bratislava to discuss the protection of minority languages.

Now on the campaign trail, and in a battle with the European institutions as well as with the Hungarian minority, the government responded a week later by firing the headmasters of two schools because they failed to report to the ministry that the pupils refused to accept the school reports written only in Slovak. The EU fired back at the EU-Slovakia parliamentary committee in May 1998. EC Director-General for External Relations Guenther Burghardt underscored that the treatment of minorities must be fully regulated before the EU would negotiate with Slovakia. He specifically said that the decision to abolish bilingual Slovak-Hungarian school-leaving certificates was unnecessary.[73] Yet, although the reinstatement of bilingual school reports technically would be a very simple legislative adjustment, the government continued its policy.

Thus, this example reveals the stubbornness of the Slovak government in the face of pressure from all three institutions, a united institutional approach, and a clear link between the issue and the incentive of EU membership. Why didn't the incentives and the pressure work? The stubbornness may be explained by several factors. The most obvious is that the EU was already criticizing Meciar on many other issues on which he would not comply because they would weaken his power. Thus, although the issue of bilingual reports was linked to opening negotiations, Meciar knew that unless he actually conformed on all the other issues as well, the school report issue would have little independent effect on opening negotiations. Thus, the benefit he achieved from his constituency outweighed any potential benefit from the institutions.

Language Legislation

The language law under Meciar is another example of how external efforts were unable to change behavior, even over an extensive period of time. It also demonstrates the calculations of the Meciar government and how those favored the status quo.

Slovakia's first post-Communist language law was approved in 1990, when Slovakia was part of the Czechoslovak republic and when the issue of minorities was somewhat different. The law was quite liberal, allowing for the use of minority languages in official dealings in communities with an ethic minority of at least 20 percent. Later, when Slovakia joined the CE in 1993, it committed to continue to allow minority languages to be used in official contact.[74]

After Meciar formed his government with the SNS and ZRS after the 1994 elections, however, the January 1995 government program revealed plans for a new law to "protect" the state language.[75] Despite extensive efforts by the OSCE and the CE to persuade the Slovak government to abandon the bill or at least ensure ethnic minorities of their continued language rights,[76] the parliament passed the law on the state language without incorporating the 20 percent clause.[77] This left the minority language issues in a legal vacuum. Slovakia's foreign minister promised in a letter to van der Stoel that "The use of the national minority languages will be set down by a special law. The introductory work on it has already started in the Ministry of Culture."[78]

Encouraged by this, in the spring of 1996 the HCNM , the CE, and the EU continued pushing for the passage of a law on minority languages. The HCNM visited in January and followed up with another letter.[79] The CE released a report arguing that the law left a legal gap on the issue of the right of minorities to use their mother tongue in official contacts.[80] At a session of the Slovak-EU Association Council, EU Foreign Affairs Commissioner van den Broek urged Slovakia to pass a law on minority languages.[81]

Despite these combined social influences and conditionality efforts, by April 1996 the government completely retracted its promise to draft a law on minority languages. In a letter to HCNM van der Stoel, the foreign minister wrote that the rights of minorities were already guaranteed by several parts of existing laws and thus did not need a separate law.[82] The European institutions were not convinced by this argument, however, and persisted in their demand for a law on minority languages. Warnings from the EU and member states continued.[83] In November 1996, when the HCNM visited Slovakia for the seventh time, Meciar told him there was "no need" for a minority language law.[84] The ministry of culture then issued a report arguing once again that existing provisions eliminated the need for a separate law.[85]

The CE, the OSCE, and others increased their efforts. Van den Broek stressed that the issue remained a major EU concern,[86] and the EU reiterated the link to membership negotiations.[87] The CE said that it would continue to watch the situation of ethnic minorities in Slovakia and to focus on their language rights and relevant legislation. In July 1997 the EU dropped its diplomatic bomb on Slovakia with the Agenda 2000 opinion, excluding Slovakia from the first wave of candidate countries and judging it the only country to still not fulfill the political admission criteria. The criticism of the missing minority language law was loud and clear. Besides noting several deficiencies of Slovak democracy, the opinion stated,

> The first problem arises from the law on the national language of November 1995, which repealed the earlier provisions allowing the use of a minority language for official communications in any town or village where the minority represented more than 20% of the population. The Slovak authorities had given commitments to the European Union and the OSCE's High Commissioner for national minorities that it would adopt a new law on the use of minority languages. It should also be noted that Article 34(2) of the Slovak Constitution expressly states that minorities may use their own language for official communications and that the arrangements for exercising that right should be laid down by law. Nevertheless, Slovakia has not yet passed comprehensive legislation on this point and has gone back on the commitments it gave earlier. It is true that other texts govern the use of minority languages in specific fields (public life, courts, radio and television, public schools and road signs) but these do not cover all situations and there is still no overall text.

The Slovak government responded by calling the report unbalanced, and a few days later Meciar implied that passing a minority language law would not change the EU treatment of Slovakia. "Let us say openly what could possibly happen by the end of the year. If we were to meet all the demands that have been made of us, do you think that the position will change and that talks with Slovakia will begin? I can tell you that they will not."[88] Thus, Meciar tried to disconnect EU membership as an incentive by suggesting that the EU conditionality lacked credibility, because the EU could not be counted on to admit Slovakia, even if the government replied with this specific request.

In November, after rejecting a minority language law proposed by the Hungarian coalition, the government issued a memorandum claiming that minority rights in Slovakia were already protected under existing legislation.[89] The EU commission disagreed and reiterated its point. "The protection of ethnic minority languages is an essential part of the criteria for Slovakia to have any possibility of entry into the EU."[90]

Thus, the attitude of the Slovak government accounted for Slovakia's relegation to the second wave of EU applicants. The November meeting of the EU-Slovak Joint Parliamentary Committee concluded that progress had been insufficient: "There has been no legislative proposal to back up a memorandum the Slovak Government has submitted to the EU on minority languages."[91]

By March 1998 Meciar was juggling the upcoming elections and pressure by the CE, the OSCE, and the EU for Slovakia to adopt a law on minority languages. Keen to once again use the Hungarian card in this election campaign, adopting the law was not in his plans. Attempting nevertheless to appease the institutions, the government invited them to discuss the law. At first the Slovak government had thought to meet with the institutions individually, so as to perhaps play them against one another. The institutions, however, insisted on a joint effort. Even so, the meetings were rather fruitless.[92]

The institutions continued to push the issue, and the EU continued to clearly connect it with membership. The March 1998 accession partnership with the EU listed as short-term (1998) political criteria "the adoption of legislative provisions on minority language use and related implementing measures." Van den Broek said, "I am concerned about . . . provisions concerning the use of minority languages. I therefore called on the Slovak authorities to take steps to address these issues. Together with free and fair elections, improvements in this area are instrumental to bringing Slovakia closer to the EU."[93] Further, a June 1998 CE report noted that Slovakia's ethnic Hungarians faced discrimination, particularly in restrictions imposed on the use of their mother tongue.[94] In an interview for the Slovak opposition daily *Sme* just weeks before elections, German Foreign Minister Klaus Kinkel said that "the EU will not admit any new members who have not solved their policy towards ethnic minorities" and that "in the Slovak case there are points which still have to be made clear," such as the missing law on the use of ethnic minority languages.[95]

In summary, the case of the minority language law issue during this Meciar government illustrates how even strong persuasion efforts combined with incentives can fail. The failure may be explained by several factors. First, domestic preferences: the minor coalition partner, the SNS, was strongly opposed to the law, and most of the HZDS felt likewise. Thus, the payoff calculation included a potential cost of loss of power. Second, lack of credibility of the direct link between the actions and the reward: because Slovakia was having so many problems with the EU—enumerated in the Agenda 2000 opinion and several démarches—Meciar did not believe that conformance on this one issue would make a difference in the EU decision to negotiate with Slovakia. Third, lack of attraction to the membership award: before 1997, Meciar had been overconfident that the EU would not actually exclude Slovakia from membership. After 1997, however, he was so insulted that he perhaps did not care that much for EU membership after all. All his energy was focused on winning the upcoming election, and for that the ethnic card was more instrumental for him than weak EU promises.

NEW GOVERNMENT RESOLVE: THE LANGUAGE LAW AND SCHOOL CERTIFICATE ISSUES AFTER MECIAR

The language law and the school certificate issue are good opportunities to examine how a change of government facilitated the effectiveness of conditionality. They also show that the change of government itself was not sufficient to bring about the change, which is crucial to consider when studying the effect of external actors.

The 1998 elections brought the Hungarian minority parties into the coalition government and put passage of a minority language law on the government agenda. Driven by EU incentives, the government soon began to prepare a draft law. Specifying the minority language issue, Foreign Affairs Minister Eduard Kukan said, "In the first months of 1999 the government wants to fulfill the short-term political criteria which should have been fulfilled in 1998."[96] Slovak and EU deputies alike praised the post-election developments in Slovakia and urged the parliament to quickly pass a minority language law.

Demonstrating that passage could not be taken for granted and thus could not be ascribed solely to the change of government, considerable domestic disagreement about the law still existed. Slovak Prime Minister Mikulas Dzurinda drew fire for making concessions to Hungarians. Returning from a working meeting in Brussels, EU chief negotiator Jan Figel said that Slovakia had a chance of "approaching the table at which EU membership is under negotiation," but if a law on ethnic languages was not adopted, a "big question mark" would hover over the issue.[97] Nevertheless, infighting in the government coalition encumbered progress. HCNM van der Stoel and representatives of the CE and the EU held talks in Bratislava for two days. Most contention focused on the threshold percentage that would be required for minorities to obtain the rights of the law. The Hungarians wanted the threshold at 10 percent, while the rest of the coalition argued that the threshold should be 20 percent in accordance with tradition.

As contention about the law grew, so did the role of the EU incentive. Foreign Minister Kukan said, "If Slovakia avoids fulfilling this last political criterion, it will not be accepted in the first group of EU candidates.... Slovakia cannot rely on EU understanding if it fails to meet this requirement."[98] The EU ambassador to Slovakia said the EU considered it "very important" for Slovakia to pass the law and that this was the "only political criterion" that Bratislava had failed to fulfill in order to be invited to accession talks.[99] Slovak Democratic Coalition deputy Ivan Simko also said it was necessary to approve the law because it was one of the EU requirements.[100] Similarly, the new Slovak president, Rudolf Schuster, urged the government to ignore opposition protests and stressed that Slovakia should pass the law on minority languages because it has been promised to the EU.[101]

Further, demonstrating that the passage of the law would not be automatic just because the minorities were now part of the government coalition, the government had to approve the draft without the support of the Hungarian Coalition Party, which found the law not liberal enough.[102] Indeed, the ethnic Hungarians accused the government of working to please Brussels, rather than to meet the needs of the minorities. A few days later, about a thousand Slovaks protested in front of the government. "They want to Magyarize all Slovaks," and "Hungarians across the Danube" supporters of the nationalist SNS party shouted.[103] While continuing to collect signatures for a referendum, Meciar's HZDS tried to postpone the parliamentary debate on the bill, saying it must be "widely debated" by the public before the parliament votes on it, and warning that its passage now could lead to a "polarization of society."[104] In the days before the parliamentary debate, EU embassies strongly encouraged passage. As the vivid debate began in parliament, however, the SNS and HZDS announced that they had collected the necessary 350,000 signatures for a referendum.

Nevertheless, after a three day debate the parliament approved the bill in the first reading. One hundred thirty of the 150 deputies had taken the floor and delivered over four hundred factual remarks before the final bill passed a few days later. The bill guaranteed the use of minority languages in official contacts with state bodies only in those cases in which the minority group made up 20 percent of a particular municipality. The Hungarian Coalition Party (SMK), which had hoped for a 10 percent threshold, voted against the bill, but their tacit consent was expressed in their presence in the chamber, which allowed the needed quorum. The European institutions expressed satisfaction with the law, and the president denied a referendum on the grounds that the Slovak constitution prohibited plebiscites on human rights issues.

This case shows an issue in which the linkage of membership incentives to behavior clearly was not enough, as demonstrated by the failure of the European institutions, including the EU, to get Meciar's government to pass the law during his government. It further shows that a change of government was not sufficient to bring about the changes: only the continued involvement by the European institutions maintained the momentum for change. Even with the new government, the issue was highly controversial. Indeed, in this case, as several officials noted, it was truly a combination of the change in government and the linkage to EU membership that drove

the legislative solution.[105] Illustrating the influence of the Brussels enlargement process, the Slovak parliament was eager to pass the bill in time for
a review by EU officials of a Slovak petition requesting inclusion in the
December EC, where the EU would decide on what countries to include
in what was then called the "first round" of EU entry talks.

The issue of school certificates tells a story similar to that of the language
law, though the new government was much more accommodating on the
school certificate issue. After elections, the institutions kept up the criticism
of the report issue. The CE published a report criticizing the withdrawal of
bilingual school reports.[106] The EU update report once again mentioned the
problem. On the day of the critical EU report, in which Slovakia had hoped
for a better assessment given the recent change of government, Deputy Premier Pal Csaky, responsible for minority issues, said that Slovakia would
reintroduce bilingual school-leaving certificates already the current school
year.[107] Van der Stoel continued to press for implementation of this promise
in a December visit. In January 1999 the Slovak parliament passed the education act amendment, which made it possible to issue bilingual school report
cards both in the state language and a minority language for the students of
primary and secondary schools. The nationalist opposition unsuccessfully
warned that this would spur irredentism in the south.[108] By the end of January schools once again gave bilingual school reports to some 50,000 pupils
in Slovakia's 350 Hungarian primary and 500 secondary schools.

This school certificate case clearly demonstrates the importance of the
government's disposition and the ability of nationalists to block reform.
Was the new government's decision to reinstate the bilingual reports a
result of international pressure, Hungarian participation in government,
or public demand? Certainly it was not a popular decision. At the time, a
public opinion poll showed that only 36 percent approved of the decision
to reintroduce bilingual school certificates, while 51 percent disapproved.
Of the ethnic Slovak population, only 29 percent approved.[109] Had the
only motivating factor been to please the Hungarian coalition partners, the
coalition partners might have been expected to drag out the issue. Thus,
the international pressure over the last year and a half, and the explicit link
to EU membership, facilitated the solution by providing an easy way for
the new government to signal that it was different from the old government
and that its attention was fully directed toward European integration.

The Role of Leadership: What Can Be Learned from the Case of Slovakia?

Meciar's leadership presents an interesting case for the role leadership.
One reason for Meciar's lack of response to the EU may have been that he

knew that EU membership conflicted with his methods of maintaining personal power, and that in reality it would have been better for Meciar if he had not been subjected to more intense EU criticism than necessary. Thus, his actual attraction and commitment to Western integration was questionable. Even before Slovakia gained independence, Slovak political leaders, and in particular Meciar, exploited nationalist rhetoric as an electoral tactic (Mego 1999). Meciar's governing methods grew increasingly controversial, and at some point he became an outcast for the West (Pridham, 1999). As the EU continued to criticize Slovakia and Meciar, he became the political black sheep among the EU candidate states, which in some ways made it even harder for him to make concessions, even if he wanted to. As one foreign ministry official observed, "Things got worse after the domestic political situation with the kidnapping of the president's son and the failed NATO referendum. . . . [A]fter these events, there was sort of no way back for Meciar. He had crossed a line politically."[110] As a top Slovak policy experts put it, "There was no compatibility between the national government under Meciar and the declared foreign policy goals. Meciar declared the EU as a goal, but for him it was not in practice a priority."[111]

This may have had two causes. First, Meciar was more comfortable with his relations with Russia. He signed a large number of agreements with Russia, trade with Russia was important, and Slovakia depended on Russia for its energy resources. Russia was also a comfortable partner for someone like Meciar who did not speak English, but who did speak Russian. As a journalist and government official put it, "Meciar reached a point where he believed that not being a member of the EU was not the end of the world. In the background he relied on Russia. He believed that if he did not have the EU, then he would have Russia."[112] Secondly, as discussed, Meciar despised the EU's meddling in his governing style and rightly feared that following EU's standards of democracy would undermine his corruption-based clasp on power. Particularly, on his return to power after the 1994 elections, Meciar and his new coalition staged what came to be known as the "night of the long knives." They sacked officials such as the chief prosecutor and the director of Slovak TV, installed their own deputies as head of key parliamentary committees, reassigned the opposition deputies to the least important communities, and canceled host of privatization projects drawn up by the previous government. In short, Meciar and his allies seized the control of almost all areas of political power.[113]

Meciar clearly had good reason to prefer the status quo rather than submission to EU standards of behavior. The government's desire for power took priority when it conflicted with EU demands (Henderson 1999b, 233). The issue of the Slovakian election law, which Meciar fixed along ethnic lines, is a concrete example of how the interests of an authoritarian

leader can conflict with Western democratic standards. Thus, Meciar preferred to not integrate into the EU as long as other countries were also
not being integrated.[114] On the other hand, Meciar did desire the approval
of the West as a statesman and important international actor. If he could
keep his domestic policies out of the EU's agenda, he could use EU membership to bolster his image and subsequently his popularity. That game,
however, did not work for him; as he increasingly realized this, he turned
further from any EU aspirations (Vachudova 1997).

OVERCONFIDENCE, MIXED SIGNALS, AND POOR RESULTS

In addition, the case of Slovakia under Meciar also provides the best example of the hypothesis about a country having "overconfidence" in its admission. One of the reasons for the lack of response to the EU, at least in the
cases of the school certificates and the minority language law, may indeed
very well have been that Meciar believed that the EU would admit Slovakia
without these concessions. He argued publicly that Slovakia was too important for the EU to shun, and he repeatedly reassured the citizenry that
the West "has no other option than to embrace Slovakia."[115] He believed
that Slovakia's geographic location alone was a ticket to the EU. At a rally
in October 1995, Meciar said that there was no need to worry about the
admission of Slovakia to the EU, "because they need us, for we are a country with an exceptionally good geopolitical situation."[116] Also, in the mid-
1990s Meciar relied on Slovakia's economic performance to carry weight
with the EU. Indeed, in 1997 Slovakia's economic performance was on par
with the leading EU candidates. Slovakia's per capita gross domestic product exceeded that of Poland and Estonia, and of all the EU candidates, only
Slovenia and the Czech Republic had a higher purchasing power per head.
Meciar even continued to uphold his public confidence in EU admission
after the release of the EU Agenda 2000 opinion. In August 1998 he asserted in a radio statement that in behind-the-scenes deliberations Slovakia
was still mentioned among those states that would be admitted first to the
EU. He said that Slovakia had already met the criteria for membership and
could not be excluded for geopolitical reasons.[117]

The EU also sent mixed signals to Slovakia, which indeed boosted Meciar's confidence. As chapter 2 argues regarding the credibility of an institution, it is key for institution not to ignore norm violations and, most importantly, not to continue to bestow positive benefits or approval as if
nothing had happened. After the 1994 elections, the EU delivered a diplomatic note voicing concern over the political turmoil in Slovakia.[118] Just one
month later, however, and with no assurances of changes from Slovakia, the
EU granted macrofinancial aid to Slovakia in the form of loan to its balance

of payments. Soon thereafter, the EU concluded the European association agreement with Slovakia. Thus, economic cooperation thrived in the face of grave political concerns, and this probably contributed to Meciar's confidence in EU admission regardless of his behavior.

Although the state of democracy worsened during 1995 in Slovakia, almost a year passed without public EU comments. Then in the fall of 1995 EU criticism became more blunt. First, four EU ambassadors gave an EU demarche to Meciar at a meeting in October 1995, reminding the Slovak authorities of responsibilities Slovakia took upon itself by signing an association agreement with the EU. Also, the EU's parliamentary assembly adopted a nonbinding resolution warning the Slovak government that "if it continues to follow policies which show no respect for democracy, human and minority rights and the rule of law," the EU will have to "reconsider its programme of assistance and cooperation under the Europe Agreement, which might have to be suspended."[119] While the European parliament is weak in policy making on central and eastern European issues in comparison with the council and the commission, the action was nevertheless noted in Europe. A similar warning came a week later at the constituent session of the European parliament and Slovak parliament joint committee in Bratislava.

Again, however, the credibility of the EU's claim that aid and continued cooperation and accession were conditional on political reforms was questionable. Even though Slovakia ignored these warnings and soon thereafter passed a controversial language law, the EU did not withdraw its cooperation and support as it had implied. The following month the EU allocated 200 million ECU in Phare money for 1995–1999 to Slovakia, and 42 million ECU for a 1995 action plan. Support continued in the same way in the spring of 1996. The EU made reproaches; Slovakia took little notice; the EU withheld no benefits.

As the messages from the EU became increasingly critical, however,[120] the EU nevertheless continued to send a mixed message to Meciar. Thus, while van den Broek said that the EU was disappointed with the referendum outcome, he also said that there was no danger of the EU canceling Slovakia's association agreement.[121] Clearly, the "only" leverage being applied now was how the EU would place Slovakia in the accession queue, not whether Slovakia would be in the queue at all. Finally the EU rendered a direct verdict in the Agenda 2000 commission opinion, when Slovakia was the only candidate country deemed as not satisfying the political criteria.[122] Nevertheless, at the Luxembourg Summit the EU decided not to exclude Slovakia from the entry talks as the commission had recommended but merely to relegate it to the second group. Slovakia was clearly experiencing the consequences of the lack of fulfillment of EU requirements. It was credible that the EU would not move Slovakia ahead in the accession process without improvements. Van den Broek's comment that there was "no danger" of canceling the agreement, however, nullified the threat of interrupting the association agreement based on political and human rights concerns, as outlined in clauses in the agreement's preamble.[123] It also seemed clear that Slovakia would be able to keep its foot in the door to the EU, continue a high level of trade, and enjoy financial support regardless of its political behavior. Thus, positive benefits would continue to flow.

Thus, Meciar's overconfidence was to some extent bolstered by the EU's behavior. Between 1994 and 1996 Meciar came to understand that the EU would criticize him but would still continue financial cooperation and trade with Slovakia. When the EU stepped up the criticism in 1997 and 1998, that lesson had perhaps grown too deep to be modified. This explains why Meciar so seemingly carelessly shrugged off EU criticism when it was not convenient for him to pay attention. Thus, although the EU hammered Meciar on the issues of bilingual school certificates and the passage of a minority language law, Meciar either completely ignored these warnings, continued to make empty promises, or even claimed that the laws were already satisfactory.

Naturally, all the blame for why some of the attempts to use conditionality failed in some cases during the Meciar government cannot be placed solely on lack of EU credibility or on Meciar's early overconfidence for admission to the EU. Domestic politics heavily influenced Meciar and often forced his hand—even if he himself may have been willing to compromise with the European institutions. To retain power, he simply sometimes had to put clear priority on domestic authoritarian policies.

CONCLUSION

While Slovakia never had to address issues related to citizenship, as did Latvia and Estonia, issues of language and education were quite contentions. One language issue concerned the use of personal and place names. In this case the CE lost considerable leverage by not having a gradual admission process that allowed the institution to secure some compliance before moving on to full membership. Thus, Meciar happily signed the CE "to do" list upon joining, only for the CE to see the issue shelved completely until there was a change in government and goodwill toward the CE in 1994.

On five separate issues during Meciar's next four years in office the European institutions tried to bring about specific legislative change. Demonstrating that such efforts are less successful with nationalist-leaning leadership, three of these cases—the election law, the school certificate issue, and the minority language law—failed. In these three cases Meciar tried to disconnect his policy from EU membership and portrayed Slovakia's rejection as a product of EU animosity rather than as a result of the government's actual behavior.[124] The benefit he personally derived from the issue politically outweighed any potential personal benefit from the institutions. Thus, in true authoritarian style, he ignored the benefit to the country in favor of personal gain. Underscoring that international efforts are not completely useless with this type of leadership, however, two cases succeeded: the treaty with Hungary, which despite implementation problems was a significant achievement, and the eventual abandonment, after three attempts, of efforts to pass a strict penalty code. On these issues Meciar presumably calculated that his international reputation would be too greatly damaged if he did not cooperate with the EU. These cases also occurred in the mid-1990s—that is, before the EU's publication of the first report on the candidate countries, when Meciar's still believed he had a genuine shot at staying in the first wave of EU candidates. Compared with cases in the Baltic States, where there were also strong domestic opposition, the Slovak cases suggest that narrow extremist opposition, particularly with key leadership riding on its success, is less receptive to external pressure than is broader-based, but less extremist opposition. Taken together, however, the cases suggest that although external engagement is less effective with leaders like Meciar at the helm, it can still work.

Finally, the cases of the language law and the school certificates illustrate how a change of government may facilitate the effectiveness of conditionality, but how it nevertheless may not be sufficient. In both cases the new government was more open to changes to the law, but, particularly in the case of the language law and the struggle surrounding its formulation, it was still evident that passage of the law was not automatically assured just because the government had changed. Some additional impetus from the EU was still necessary.

CHAPTER 7

Romania: The Long Road

THE ETHNIC ISSUE IN ROMANIA centers mostly on the Hungarian population, as it did in Slovakia. In Romania the Hungarians are heavily concentrated in Transylvania.[1] Ethnic Hungarians in Romania comprise about 8 percent of the overall population, and other minorities, mainly Roma, comprise another 5 to 7 percent. Both ethnic Hungarians and ethnic Romanians of Transylvania have been in the minority as well as in the majority, since Transylvania has shifted between Hungarian and Romanian dominance for centuries. After World War I the Romanians took control of Transylvania, but in the compromise dealings with Hitler, Hungary won part of Transylvania back during World War II and lost it again to Romania after the war. Unsurprisingly, perhaps, both peoples, when dominant, have discriminated against the other group.

During Romania's Communist government, Çeausescu conducted a policy of "ethnic homogenisation" (Lovatt 1999), a hate campaign to suspend ethnic differences for the "benefit of international brotherhood." In actuality, however, this campaign was mostly an attempt to deny Hungarians any minority privileges. In 1959 the Hungarian Bolyai University in Cluj was merged with the Romanian Babes University, and by the mid-1980s not a single Hungarian secondary school remained. Bilingual signs all but disappeared, and in 1988 the government ordered Hungarian publications to use Romanian place names only.

POSTCOMMUNIST ROMANIA

On December 22, 1989, Romania's dictator, Nicolai Çeaucescu, and his wife, Elena, fled Communist Party headquarters in Bucharest following a week of popular unrest that had started in Transylvania. Three days later the Çeaucescus were executed following a summary court martial. Romania was the only Eastern European country in which a violent popular uprising overthrew the regime. About one thousand people lost their lives in clashes between the loyalists of the old regime and the National Salvation Front–controlled forces. The National Salvation Front (NSF) had formed under the leadership of Ion Iliescu, a former high-ranking official during the early days of the Çeaucescu regime.

Euphoria initially followed the overthrow of Çeaucescu. The Hungarian minority saw democratization as an opportunity to dramatically improve their situation. Indeed, the new NSF government made promises in January 1990 regarding the use of minority languages in public life and native-language education at all levels. But the tide quickly turned. Many accused the NSF of being the old Communist Party under a new name. The revolutionary move toward democratization fueled—not decreased—ethnic tension. The Hungarians saw themselves as losers in a new Romanian institutional order based on the "unity" of the Romanian people (Verdery 1993, 26; Weiner 1997). Tensions in Transylvania flared and even became deadly in March 1990 in Tirgu Mures, when thousands of demonstrators took to the streets with knives, clubs, and even park benches.[2] One observer noted, "This was the first serious interethnic flare-up in Eastern Europe since the collapse of communism and once again Transylvania seemed to be the paradigm example of an ethnically-based territorial dispute in Eastern Europe" (Gallagher 1997, 29). The remainder of the decade was peaceful however, as ethnic issues remained within the political process.

In 1992 a split of the NSF led to the creation of the Party of Social Democracy in Romania (PDSR). Headed by Iliescu, this party struggled to maintain its hold on government at times, but it generally had a majority until just a few months before the elections in late 1996. From 1992 onward, however, the PDSR had to cooperate extensively with extremist nationalist parties. During this time the opposition formed into the Democratic National Convention (CDR), which initially included the Democratic Union of Hungarians in Romania (HDUR). The HDUR eventually left, however, because even the opposition parties disagreed with what was widely seen as HDUR calls for autonomy. When the PDSR and the nationalists lost power after the 1996 elections, because of a variety of factors and in spite of resistance, the CDR and the HDUR nevertheless joined forces in the first peaceful, democratic change of government. Although nationalist parties had lost both participation in the government and seats in the parliament, however, they remained politically active, vying for a comeback. (See table 7.1.)

Case Studies

In the remainder of this chapter I will discuss several cases of Romanian ethnic politics. The case of the language used in official contacts provides a good illustration of the role of ethnic minorities within the government and of how previous attempts to use normative pressure failed. The prefects issue illustrates of how domestic factors operate in the absence of international involvement.

TABLE 7.1
Romanian governments

Government	Parties*	Seats Parliament	Seats Senate	Total seats (Parliament)	Total seats (Senate)
Petre Roman/Iliescu May 20, 1990–October 1991	NSF	263	92	263/396 (majority)	92/119 (majority)
Theodor Stolojan/Iliescu October 1991–Sept. 1992	Split factions of the NSF	?	?	?/396	?/119
	PNL	29	12		
	Ecological Movement	12	1		
	Others	9	—		
Nicolae Vàcàroiu/Iliescu November 1992–	PSDR	117	49	176/341 (unofficial	74/143
	(PUNR)	30	14	majority)	
	(SLP)	13	5		
	(GRP)	16	6		
January 1995–October 1995	PSDR	117	49	176/341	74/143
	PUNR	30	14	(majority)	
	SLP	13	5		
	GRP	16	6		
October 1995–April 1996	PSDR	117	49	160/341	68/143
	PUNR	30	14		
	SLP	13	5		
March/April 1996–September 1996	PSDR	117	49	147/341	63/143
	PUNR	30	14		
September 1996–November 1996	PSDR	117	49	117/341	49/143
Victor Ciorbea/Emil Constantinescu December 1996–December 1997	CDR	122	53	200/341 (majority)	87/143 (majority)
	SDU	53	23		
	HDUR	25	11		
Victor Ciorbea/Emil Constantinescu December 1997–April 1998	CDR	122	53	147/341	64/143
	NLP		11		
	HDUR	25			
Radu Vasile/Emil Constantinescu April 1998–December 1999	CDR	122	53	200/341 (majority)	87/143 (majority)
	SDU	53	23		
	HDUR	25	11		

Acronyms: NSF: National Salvation Front; GRP: Greater Romania Party; PUNR: Party of Romanian National Unity; SLP: Socialist Party of Labour; PSDR: Democratic National Salvation Front/Party of Social Democracy in Romania; CDR: Political alliances Democratic Convention of Romania; PNL: National Liberal Party; SDU: Social Democratic Union; HDUR: Democratic Union of Hungarians in Romania.

The case of the law on national minorities illustrates how normative pressure proved insufficient, even with many years of concerted efforts. The fact that institutional incentives were never brought to bear on this case makes it a good illustration of the argument that change is not simply a function of duration of institutional involvement but also of the type of institutional involvement. The education law illustrates the strong effect of ethnic minority mobilization and of ethnic minority representation in the government coalition. The case also illustrates that candidacy for EU membership can contribute to anticipatory reforms, even if the EU did not particularly stress the need for those specific reforms. Most importantly, however, the case shows the unique blend of the efforts of the OSCE, the actions of the minorities, and wishes to impress NATO and the EU.

The treaty with Hungary is a case of conditionality overcoming strong domestic opposition, but in this case Romania was much slower to sign the treaty than was Slovakia. Finally, whereas Slovakia and Meciar's case illustrated what may happen when a leader or country is overconfident of admission, the case of Romania illustrates the effect of lack of confidence in admission, when a state's economic or other factors automatically presents it with large obstacles to admission.

A LAW ON MINORITIES

The OSCE and the CE engaged in the issue of a minority law, the CE extracting a promise in connection with admission. The case illustrates how the lack of linkage to tangible consequences, such as EU membership, left both the OSCE and the CE without much ability to influence behavior.

Already in 1991 the ethnic minorities in Romania expressed the need for a national minority law that would in a multitude of ways protect the rights of ethnic groups. Both the HCNM and the CE addressed the issue in 1993. In August 1993, in a speech to the Romanian Council on National Minorities, the HCNM said, "Considering my office of High Commissioner for National Minorities, I was pre-eminently interested in the provisions of the article 6 of the Constitution stipulating the preservation, development, and expression of the identity of persons belonging to the national minorities. . . . I cannot but express hope that, on the basis of this article, further progress will be achieved in the preparation of a law on the national minorities. I understand that both the Council, and its juridical and legislative commission are acting in this direction."[3] In September 1993, in a letter of recommendations, the HCNM wrote, "Even though the Romanian Constitution has a number of Articles laying down principles regarding the position of the minorities, there is obviously a need to elaborate them in greater detail in the form of a law on minorities. I suggest that the Council for Ethnic Minorities gives priority to this question and that the Government will ask the parliament to give priority on its agenda to the draft law. . . . The early adoption of such a law could help considerably in creating an atmosphere of greater confidence among the various minorities."[4]

Friedrich König, a CE parliamentary assembly rapporteur, also supported the OSCE position and told Radio Bucharest after a 1993 visit that Romania needed to pass a law on national minorities.[5] Thus, in connection with inviting Romania to join the CE, in its Opinion 176 the parliamentary assembly wrote, "The Assembly proposes that the Romanian authorities and the Romanian Parliament: 1. adopt and implement as soon as possible, in keeping with the commitments they have made and with Assembly Recommendation 1201, legislation on national minorities and education."[6]

Iliescu, however, was in a precarious position as the economic crisis eroded confidence in the government and increasingly forced Iliescu to rely on the nationalist parties. Thus, despite the promise to the CE, and although the Hungarian minority party, HDUR, had already proposed a draft law in December 1993, very little happened. In March 1994 two CE rapporteurs, Friedrich König and Gunnar Jansson, visited Romania again, and declared that the Romania had only partially fulfilled its obligations to the CE.[7]

Despite rhetoric that the government was working to pass a law, it made no progress.[8] Meanwhile, ethnic tensions continued to simmer. For example, in November 1994, supposedly for an archaeological dig, extremist Cluj mayor Gheorghe Funar tried to remove an important Hungarian statue. Hungarians surrounded the statue; the authorities responded with armed police.[9] The justice minister threatened to outlaw the Hungarian party, and Funar called for authorities to round up any weapons held by the Hungarians.[10] As the Hungarians strove for recognition, they only gave the nationalists more ammunition for their attacks and made the nationalist message of a Hungarian threat seem more credible to ethnic Romanian voters (Weiner 1997, 16). Thus, when the Hungarian party established a national Council for Self-Government with locally elected representatives, Funar even warned of civil war,[11] and soon thereafter he called for an "exchange of citizens," meaning that Hungarians should leave Romania.[12]

The final blow to any hope for a minority law came in January 1995 when the government formalized a tacit agreement that had existed since 1992 with the three more extremist parties. The three nationalist parties tried to make the signing conditional on the outlawing of the HDUR. While the PSDR did not agree, the four-party protocol nevertheless stated that the government would adopt decisions only by consensus and would act "against any chauvinist, racist, anti-Romanian, anti-Semitic, totalitarian, extremist, fascist or Nazi-like manifestations."[13] Thus, during the Iliescu government, the international efforts to persuade the government to pass a law on minorities, although specific and forwarded by both the OSCE and the CE, resulted in no change.

In 1996 Iliescu lost to the centrist Emil Constantinescu, who appealed to the popular desire to join EU and NATO. In parliamentary elections the minority parties performed better than expected, and the extremist Funar and his party lost almost half of its support. The former opposition parties thus formed a government that included the HDUR. In April 1997 Prime Minister Victor Ciorbea met with the HCNM and said that he foresaw the government passing a general minority law. The new government set out a comprehensive reform program with a specific goal to introduce legislation by April 1997 and to achieve results by July 1997, when NATO and EU would make decisions about integration.

Many politicians argued, however, that the CE framework convention was sufficient.[14] Ethnic issues continued to be very controversial, and after a fall that included several problems in Transylvania, the PUNR introduced an anti-Hungarian motion in the parliament calling for a "national program" to prevent the assimilation of the Romanians living in Harghita and Covasna, the two Transylvanian counties with Hungarian majorities. As the government continued to struggle for its survival and eventually fell apart in March 1998, the issue disappeared from the agenda.

Thus, normative pressure was insufficient, even with many years of concerted efforts. Since institutions never brought to bear incentives on this case, it is a good illustration of the argument that change is not simply a function of the duration of institutional involvement but also of the type of institutional involvement.

Prefects

The case of prefects provides a good illustration of how nationalist governments will execute poor policies for the ethnic minorities if either the international institutions are not involved or their admonitions are only mild. It also shows that once a more accommodating government comes into power, ethnic minorities can sometimes push policies through government even without international aid. This case is thus a good illustration of how the domestic factors operate in the absence of international involvement.

In July 1992, months before the general election, controversy evolved over the government's decision to replace ethnic Hungarian prefects with Romanian officials in Covasna and Hargita counties, the two counties where ethnic Hungarians constitute a clear majority.[15] The Covasna County chapter of the HDUR sent a protest to the government regarding the change of the prefect by the government, emphasizing that the Hungarian population accounts for 75 percent of the county's population and declaring the government's act illegal. The Romanian National Unity Party (RNUP) responded, declaring,

> The decision made by Romania's government is absolutely legal; it has this prerogative like any state of law. Prefects are not nominated in accordance with the criterion of communist proportion to which the HDUR was so accustomed. The government of a democratic state is the only one entitled to nominate them in accordance with the country's national interests. Given the fact that the HDUR is not a ruling party, its claims are absurd because they are based on the principles of communist egalitarianism. This ethnic political formation has greatly harmed Romanian democracy and Romania's image in the world and has instigated the population to anti-national and destabilizing actions. From a political and social viewpoint, the HDUR is cultivating ethnic nationalism, chauvinism, territorial isolation and the dogmas of communist democracy. The HDUR ranks among the political formations promoting retrograde and Bolshevik ideas and continues to promote the policy of the narrow-minded and paranoiac proletarian internationalism. We want to advise the HDUR that it assumes full responsibility for the anti-national, ethnic provocations in Covasna and Harghita, which contradict Romania's Constitution and the principles of the state of law.[16]

Prime Minister Theodor Stolojan emphasized that "Romania's government is duty-bound to exercise its authority on each square centimeter on Romanian territory" and that "Prefects are not negotiable."[17] The domestic protests were so fierce, however, that in August 1992 the government compromised and agreed that a Hungarian prefect would be appointed by the government to each of the counties to work jointly with the Romanian prefect.[18] But this solution brought further protest. After elections, when the Vacaroiu government gained power, the issue continued to flare. Despite this, a CE delegation to Romania in mid-March 1993 recommended Romania for admission.

Just weeks after the CE move, the Romanian cabinet discontinued the dual ethnic prefect arrangement and appointed new Romanian prefects in Covasna and Hargihita counties.[19] Tensions mounted. When HDUR senator Gabor Kozsokar sharply criticized the decision before the senate, RNUP senator Valer Suian labeled the HDUR a "political monstrosity, the unique party, of communist inspiration".[20] On April 1 thousands of HDUR supporters held several protests against the appointment of the prefects. The European institutions, however, stayed out of this battle. Indeed, the Romanian government specifically warned the HDUR, which was making accusations likening the situation to ethnic cleansing, not to turn the appointment of the Romanian prefects into an international political affair.[21]

In an example of how the homeland can engage, Hungary now focused international attention on the issue. On April 7 Hungary's foreign affairs committee wrote to the Romanian government, "In our view, this step fails to keep in line with the Romanian statement, repeated several times, that it seeks to guarantee minority rights in the spirit of Council of Europe standards and to smooth relations between peoples living in its territory."[22] Because this had no effect, several Hungarian mayors in Covasna County resigned. When a CE delegation met with President Iliescu in late April 1993, however, Romania still received the green light for admission. Just a few days later, on April 30, 1993, HDUR President Bela Marko brought the HDUR delegation's position to the attention of the CE legal committee. The HDUR president recalled that although the Romanian government had promised to urgently solve the problems of the Hungarian minority, it had taken no concrete steps to this end, and the appointment of Romanian prefects to Hargita and Kovasna counties denied the large majority the right to be represented by a person of its own choice.[23]

Hesitating slightly, the CE deferred the membership decision in May 1993, and two CE rapporteurs called for reform on school language, prefects, and the Hungarian university in Cluj. In response, Romanian spokeswoman Simona Miculescu said,

> We are therefore . . . surprised at the rapporteurs' persistence in bringing up over and over the same matters for which they received comprehensive answers from the Romanian authorities. Moreover, those matters are presented in such a manner that they could be interpreted as a pretext for a delay in receiving Romania in the Council of Europe. We cannot hide our feeling that a different standard is again being applied to Romania, as compared to the other countries in similar situations. After all, the greater part of the problems mentioned by the rapporteurs are common to all the European states in transition.[24]

David Atkinson, chairman of the CE's committee for nonmember European countries, answered the complaint, noting that other former Communist countries had been admitted more rapidly than Romania because, relative to its neighbors, Romania had faced the worst situation and, under Ceausescu, a tougher regime. In meetings with President Iliescu, Atkinson outlines his suggestions for Romania to make before admission.[25]

In early July 1993, however, the political commission of the CE parliamentary assembly recommended Romania for admission.[26] After a September 1993 visit by Catherine Lalumiere, the secretary-general of the CE, the CE admitted Romania with a list of stipulations.

In an attempt to appease the Hungarians, the Romanian government appointed Hungarian vice-prefects. The ethnic Hungarians continued to claim, however, that the prefects were taking abusive measures against the Hungarian minority on issues such bilingual signs and historical sites.[27]

The CE and the OSCE visited but did not move the issue to the top of the agenda. In October 1995, just before the local authority elections and under pressure from Funar's PUNR, the Romanian government appointed a prefect, a member of PUNR, to Tirgu Mures County and dismissed the county's Hungarian sub-prefect. The new prefect was appointed to counterbalance the county seat's Hungarian mayor.[28]

After the nationalist parties lost the 1996 election and Iliescu departed as president, the secretary general of the outgoing PDSR warned the new government that replacing the Romanian prefects would threaten national security.[29] Nevertheless, as a result of their role in the government, the HDUR was given three prefectures, five subprefectures, and six prefecture director generalities. This enabled the HDUR to appoint the prefects of Harghita, Satu Mare, and Salaj counties.

Thus the case of the prefects illustrates the role of the domestic opposition and the bargaining power of ethnic minorities, and underscores how this bargaining may play out in the absence of concerted international attention.

Minority Languages in Official Contacts

The use of minority languages in Romania illustrates a case of how institutions wasted potential leverage and how the absence of persistent institutional involvement resulted in a continuous battle over the outcome. It also shows the role of ethnic minorities within the government. When the issue was finally settled, EU conditionality played some part in the solution, but the compromise mostly resulted from the bargaining power of the ethnic minority party, and the government nearly fell apart over the issue.

Since 1993 the OSCE and the CE had commented on the right of minorities to use their own language in official contacts and urged that the local government law be amended to accommodate this right.[30] Despite these efforts, Meciar's government continually failed to pass legislation that ensured minorities of the right to communication with officials in the minority language. Indeed, in March 1996 Meciar's government had passed a controversial law on public administration, with some details to the contrary.[31]

Because of the bargaining power of the ethnic minority party in the new government, in May 1997 the government approved emergency ordinance number 22, which officially sanctioned the use of Hungarian in local government bodies. The ordinance required local governments in ethnically mixed areas to hire Hungarian-speaking personnel, and ordered government agencies to erect bilingual signs in all towns where the Hungarian population exceeded 20 percent.

The European institutions were only marginally involved with pushing for the decree to become law. But while the EU had not had any input into the decree, with the release of the Agenda 2000 opinion the EU acknowledged the value of the decree, noting, "A new decree entitles members of minorities to deal with the administration and obtain birth, marriage and death certificates in their own language in areas where they account for over 20% of the population. This currently applies to 1624 places in Romania, 1379 of them inhabited by the Hungarian minority."[32]

It was the Hungarian minority party, the HDUR, however, that took the lead in moving from decree to law. Indeed, the HDUR said it would only stay in the government coalition if certain conditions were met. Nevertheless, in March 1998 the senate failed to ratify the decree when certain SDU senators sided with the opposition. The next month the Constitutional Court invalidated the government decree because the government had failed to show that an emergency existed, and held that the issue should be regulated via ordinary legislation. After the Court's decision, the Chamber of Deputies could have recast the ordinance as a law. Indeed, after the March 1998 change of government, the new prime minister, Radu Vasile of the Christian Democrat National Peasant Party (PNTCD), declared that his government would prioritize ordinances on minority language education and local public administration.[33] The chamber, however, left the issue off its agenda.[34]

In the next six months the European institutions did little to help the Hungarian minority party on the matter. In the midst of a conflict in the Balkans, the EU needed Romania's cooperation. Thus, in a May 4, 1999, speech to the Romanian Parliament, British Prime Minister Tony Blair promised Romania that "at the Helsinki European Council in December [1999], Britain will support an invitation to Romania to being negotiations to accede to the European Union."[35] Thus, the government had little reason to fear that failing to address the issue would result in significant EU disapproval.

Indeed, the HDUR itself got results by bargaining within the coalition. In May 1999 the senate adopted a bill stating that minorities would have the right to use their own languages in dealings with local authorities in districts greater than 20 percent minority population.[36] After Hungarian deputies walked out of some sessions in the Chamber of Deputies, the law on the status of the civil service finally passed in June 1999. Thus, the ethnic minorities were to a large extent responsible for moving the legislation forward, while earlier attempts to use normative pressure had failed.

EDUCATION ISSUES

The struggles for the Romanian education law stretched over six years. During Iliescu's reign, until 1996, the case clearly illustrates how a government is likely to renege on promises to an institution after the country is admitted. Thus, the CE found itself frustrated at the Romanian government's failure to fulfill its commitments regarding education for minorities. Indeed, by 1995 the government adopted a strict education law that curtailed some of the constitutional education rights for minorities. Although the HCNM initially said that the law accorded with international standards, he urged caution in its implementation and, a year later, made specific recommendations for changes to the law. Some of the recommendations were accommodated in a temporary decree, mostly because of the mobilization of the Hungarian community. The government, however, did not make the amendments before the 1996 election.

The troubles with minority education in Romania had already begun in 1991 when the minister for education announced that Romanian history and geography would be taught in the Romanian language in national minority schools. In a January 1993 visit, the HCNM discussed minority education, and in May 1993 the CE deferred its decision on Romanian membership because of concerns about several issues, including education. Reacting to a CE report recommending the adoption of an education law, the Romanian government began to discuss a number of draft laws in early June. Teodor Melescanu, the Romanian minister for foreign affairs, wrote a letter to a CE rapporteur in connection with a report on Romania's application for membership, stating that "the parliament is encouraged in its efforts to adopt as soon as possible a draft law on education, which will take care, to a larger degree, of the specific needs of national minorities, in keeping with Recommendation 1201 of the Parliamentary Assembly of the Council of Europe."[37] Weeks later, the political commission of the CE parliamentary assembly decided to recommend Romania for admission.

The intensions of the Romanian government should have been clear to the CE at this pointr. Aside from a proposal adopted by the council on national minorities, absolutely no action followed. Following an August 1993 visit, the HCNM wrote a letter that included specific recommendations related to all levels of education.[38] Nevertheless, the CE admitted Romania in October 1993, stipulating inter alia that Romania reform minority education.[39] By March 1994, however, two CE rapporteurs, Friedrich Koenig and Gunnar Jansson, visited Romania and, after engaging in extensive dialogue, declared that the government had only partially fulfilled the obligations it assumed when admitted.[40] At this time the minister of foreign affairs also replied to the September 1993 letter from the

HCNM. On the education law, he criticized the remarks by the CE rappor-teurs and noted that it was "premature to comment on the draft law of education."[41]

By June 1994 parliament finally began debate on the controversial edu-cation bill, and by the end of June the Chamber of Deputies overwhelm-ingly supported the education draft bill. The draft law required that history, geography, and civics courses be taught in Romanian, even in schools for minorities. In a clear demonstration of the role of domestic ethnic mobili-zation, the HDUR called for civil disobedience to protest the "discrimina-tory" education bill, which in July 1994 led to unrest. Iliescu accused the Hungarians of stirring up ethnic conflict.[42]

In August 1994 the HCNM again visited Romania to discuss the draft law on education and other issues. George Funar, the extremist leader of RNUP, warned that "[van der Stoel] had better stop supporting the ethnic Hungarian claims to all-grade education in their mother tongue that may trigger a major conflict here."[43]

Meanwhile, the Hungarian minority had gathered some 450,000 signa-tures supporting the HDUR's draft of a minority education bill and oppos-ing the current education law. This effort was contested in court. In Febru-ary 1995 the HCNM again held talks with the prime minister. By June, however, the Romanian Parliament endorsed all the outstanding passages of the education bill, including an article specifying that even vocational classes must be taught in Romanian.[44] The law was full of conditions and exceptions, and minority rights were accorded on ill-defined criteria. His-tory and geography had to be taught in Romanian in all schools.[45]

A month later the CE passed a resolution criticizing measures restricting ethnic minorities in the use of their mother tongue.[46] Owing mostly to the intense efforts of the Hungarian minority, however, by August the educa-tion minister signed a decree ruling that in the academic year 1995–96, those completing ethnic minority secondary schools could take entry exams in the minority language.[47] Shortly thereafter, the HCNM visited Bucharest to evaluate the recently adopted law on education. In a follow-up letter from his visit, he noted "the necessity to take into account the specific educational needs of persons belonging to national minorities," and recommended regular reviews of the effects of the implementation of the new law. He also recommended the "addition of socio-economic sub-jects to those which can already be studied in the minority language at public universities," and he argued that, given the interest that ethnic mi-norities had shown in the matter, that the government should also consider "the possibilities for minority language education in vocational schools."[48] Mass protest in the Hungarian communities followed the passage of the law. Several thousand ethnic Hungarians formed a human chain around schools in a town in Transylvania. By October the HDUR submitted proposals for amendment of education law.

December and January brought visits from the CE and the OSCE. The HCNM urged the government to speed up preparations for the implementation of regulations regarding the 1995 law on education. He also recommended that a general revision of the law be undertaken in 1997, after implementation provided some experience. He praised the temporary decree allowing entrance examinations in the mother tongue, urged its extension, and expressed his hope "in the framework of a general revision of the Law in 1997 a return to the old system will be made possible."[49] During Illiescu's government, however, the HCNM's advice fell on deaf ears.

The case of the Romanian education law after the 1996 elections testifies to the effect of minorities' bargaining power in government combined with the government's need to present a good image to the West and intensive OSCE fieldwork. After the 1996 elections, the Hungarian minority were part of a precarious majority government. The new prime minister, Victor Ciorbea, promised changes to the education law. Nevertheless, many members of parliament still preferred to restrict minority rights. The OSCE and the CE continued to be only lightly involved; the HCNM visited in April and May 1997, serving mostly as an intermediary rather than a proponent of specific recommendations. At this stage the international community was not so concerned with securing basic rights as ensuring a resolution of ethnic tension. Thus, most of the movement on the issue came in response to threats by the Hungarian party to leave the coalition.

When the new education law finally passed in June 1999, Bela Marko, chairman of the Hungarian Democratic Union of Romania, gave an interview on Hungarian radio. Although the EU never made any direct linkage to the education issues, he stressed that the major reason the law passed was because of the opposition's need to improve its image in the West. He also said that Romania knew that it was low on the list of candidates for EU entry, and that passage of this law would improve Romania's odds.[50]

Indeed, illustrating the Romanian government's sensitivity to its reputation, the government issued an important decree on July 10, 1997, just before the July 1997 Madrid NATO summit and the release of Agenda 2000. The decree provided for instruction in the mother tongue at all levels of education, and abolished the provision that national minorities must study subjects such as history and geography in Romanian. The decree went into force in September 1997, but, constitutionally, parliament still had to pass the amendments.[51] A week later the EU released the Agenda 2000 report, which stated that it would not include Romania in the first wave of candidates for EU membership. It specifically noted, however, that the new education act should soon replace the 1995 law, which it said had limited the scope of minority education.

Fierce negotiations continued over the new version of the law. After scathing debate, on December 9, 1997, in secret voting, the Romanian Senate rejected a personal appeal by President Emil Constantinescu and voted to ban separate university education in minority languages. It also voted that all history and geography lessons must be taught in Romanian.[52] The Hungarian minority party threatened to quit the ruling coalition but reversed itself after President Constantinescu promised that he would refuse to promulgate a law that infringed the right of minorities to establish independent universities.

In a clear demonstration of how EU admission motivated domestic policy, even when the EU itself was not putting much direct pressure on the government, the president issued a statement asking "the CDR [Romanian Democratic Convention] senators to support, as previously agreed, the amendment of those articles that refer to the ethnic minorities' right to education in their mother tongues." He noted,

> Both strong political alliances and political stability in Romania are essential for the government programme to succeed, in general, and especially today, on the eve of decisions having capital importance for the future European construction. Both at the European and world levels Romanian-Hungarian cooperation is considered a model, which lends Romania an additional chance in view of the decisions that are to be made on 12th and 13th December 1997, during the Luxembourg conference of the heads of EU countries' governments and states.[53]

Three days after the EU summit, where the European Council decided not to open negotiations with Romania, the Romanian senate endorsed, with a 105–19 vote, the draft law for the approval of the emergency ordinance which amended the education law, only to have the decree ruled unconstitutional a few days later, thus leaving the issue unresolved at year's end.

Now having only a minority government,[54] officials met throughout the spring with the HCNM, who made several recommendations.[55] After yet another government reshuffle, the prime minister designate, Radu Vasile, promised to prioritize the education issue, and over the summer the Hungarian Party set clear conditions regarding the education issue for its continued participation in government.[56] Dealing again with this new government, the HCNM visited in August 1998 and again in June 1999, after volatile negotiations and several threats by the Hungarian party to leave the coalition. During his visit, a compromise solution finally passed. History and geography were still to be taught only in Romanian, but Hungarians expressed satisfaction with the compromise, which gave them other rights, particularly education in universities.

What lessons does the Romanian education issue teach? First, it illustrates the strong effect of ethnic minority mobilization and of ethnic minority representation in the government coalition (after 1996). Second, candidacy for EU membership can contribute to anticipatory reforms, even if the EU does not particularly stress the need for those specific reforms. Third, the case illustrate a unique blend of the efforts of the OSCE, of the actions of the minorities, and of wishes to impress NATO and the EU.

A Treaty with Hungary

The treaty with Hungary shows conditionality overcoming strong domestic opposition. When Romania finally signed a treaty with Hungary, it was partly due to European pressure and incentives. The Romanian treaty, however, was much delayed, and like the case of Meciar, Romanian President Iliescu finally responded to EU pressure only to gain popularity as a leader at a time when the domestic popular desire for EU membership was becoming an election issue. In general, Europe had reprimanded Romania less than Slovakia for lack of democratic practices. Thus, President Iliescu did not have the same need as Slovak Prime Minister Meciar to improve his image with the West. Thus, in 1995, with EU membership a fairly distant prospect for Romania because of economic hardship, Romania took its time signing the treaty. When Iliescu finally did sign the treaty, however, he said that the desire to join the EU and NATO "was indeed the most important aspect" driving the cooperation on the treaty.[57]

Negotiations on a treaty with Hungary began in March 1991. In the early 1990s, however, both countries, but Romania especially, were busy with many domestic changes, and neither country exerted great effort to secure a treaty. By 1995, however, the Stability Pact fueled treaty negotiations by making it clear that a bilateral treaty on borders and minority issues was a prerequisite for EU membership. Unfortunately, this coincided with a Romanian government that had just formalized its ties with extreme nationalist parties vocally opposed to the treaty.

The bilateral treaty with Hungary caused tension the entire winter leading up to the March 1995 Stability Pact Conference. As with Slovakia, the pivotal issue was the inclusion of the 1993 CE recommendation 1201. Article 11 of that recommendation pointed to "local or autonomous authorities or a special status" for minorities. Romania feared that such autonomy could lead to unilateral secession, and also refused to include recommendation 1201 because it referred to collective rather than individual rights. This controversy aggravated political tension between Romania's governing PSDR and its extremist allies, who attacked the president and foreign ministry, demanding a national referendum on a treaty with Hungary. Such leaders as Gheorghe Funar, chairman of RNUP, a junior coalition partner in the government, threatened to withdraw RNUP ministers from the government.[58] Opposition to the treaty came not only from extremist parties. All Romanian political parties rejected the Hungarian position on recommendation 1201 and approved their own cabinet's decision to postpone singing the bilateral treaty. The opposition faction, the Democratic Convention of Romania, even issued an official statement of "support for the Romanian government and its prime minister."[59] Thus, Romania and Hungary did not sign any agreement at the Stability Pact Conference, a failure of the EU incentive strategy.

Efforts to produce a treaty continued after the conference, but progress was slow. At the same time the EU was sending Romania ambiguous signals, which decreased the credibility of its demands. Nevertheless, in the fall of 1995 and spring of 1996 the OSCE and the EU continued to stress the importance of the treaty. The HCNM visited Romania and urged officials to sign the treaty. The second EU-Romania joint parliamentary committee called for the treaty's conclusion.[60] In February 1996, on a visit to Romania, European Commissioner Hans van den Broek urged Romania to sign a treaty soon.[61]

The institutions' efforts coincided with propitious domestic developments. In October 1995 Romania's governing PSDR ended its coalition partnership with the nationalist Greater Romania Party, citing a recent spate of verbal attacks by the nationalists against President Iliescu. As elections neared, Iliescu increasingly wanted approval from the West to regain popularity for the elections. Even though EU membership was not imminent, EU approval became desirable. Thus, in March 1996 Hungary and Romania renewed discussions on a treaty in the hope that this would aid the two countries' accession to the EU. Meanwhile, the HCNM practiced shuttle diplomacy between the foreign ministers.

The big breakthrough came in August 1996. Hungarian officials agreed to a clause reaffirming the inviolability of the state borders and annulled the "Budapest Declaration" of July 1996, which had obliged the Hungarian government to protect the rights and interests of all Hungarians residing outside the country. This Budapest Declaration had been a major source of embarrassment for the Hungarian government, who as a result needed to improve its image with the West, contributing to Hungary's willingness to compromise.[62] The Romanians accepted that the CE's recommendation 1201 would become a part of the treaty. Both parties also agreed, however, that the recommendation should not be interpreted to mean either that ethnic minorities have collective rights or that they are entitled to "a special status of ethnically-based territorial autonomy."[63] On September 16, 1996, Romania and Hungary signed the bilateral friendship treaty.[64] The Romanian Senate and the Chamber of Deputies ratified the basic bilateral treaty within a few weeks.

While other factors, for example, various trust-building exercises and the Budapest Declaration, naturally contributed to the signing of the treaty, Hungarian and Romanian officials themselves pointed to the influence of European institutions. After a November 1993 visit to Transylvania, Hungary's foreign minister said that the thaw in relations could be traced back to the requests of the major international institutions. Both parties praised the OSCE's efforts during the negotiating process. At the signing ceremony Romanian Prime Minister Nicolae Vacaroiu emphasized that "the conclusion of the treaty has a special significance for accelerating the process of the joint integration of Romania and Hungary in the European and Euro-Atlantic political, strategic, and economic structures."[65] Most notably, President Iliescu himself said that the desire to join the EU and NATO "was indeed the most important aspect," driving the cooperation on the treaty.[66] Foreign observers confirmed this link between the signing of the treaty and the two countries' desire to integrate. Michael Shafir of Radio Free Europe wrote, "The sudden change can be explained mainly by foreign-policy considerations that have little to do with the long-standing conflict and animosity between Hungary and Romania. The two countries' quest to join NATO and the European Union brought about a compromise on issues that appeared to be insurmountably divisive."[67] Thus, although it took a long time and although it faced many implementation problems, the signing of the Hungarian-Romanian treaty was an important achievement, partly the result of the EU's linkage of the treaty to membership.

ROMANIA'S LONG ROAD TO EU ADMISSION

I argued in chapter 2 that uncertainty about the prospect of membership decreases the chance of successful linkage of membership incentives and behavior. Romania is a good example of how poor economic performance has decreased EU influence in two related ways. First, because Romania was struggling economically throughout the 1990s, Romania increasingly realized that membership in the EU was distant. This gave Romanian politicians less impetus to clear the political hurdles related to ethnic issues. Second, because the EU also realized that Romania's poor economic transition occupied the government's attention, the EU itself initiated fewer demands on Romania regarding ethnic issues. Thus, Romania's poor economic performance decreased both its own confidence in EU membership prospects and the EU's engagement in immediate ethnic issues. The result was twofold: the EU rarely linked membership incentive to behavior on ethnic issues, and when the EU did use incentives the effect was modest.

In the early 1990s the EU used only vague rhetoric regarding Romania's political problems. It seemed that the internal ethnic situation was of little concern to the EU. Soon after Iliescu won the runoff elections for president, Romania and the EU initialed an association agreement providing for closer trade, economic, and political ties. Although the preamble mentioned the protection of minorities, the Europe agreement signed in February 1993 focused on economic reform.[68] Thus, in 1993 the EU did not react to mounting tension and demonstrations over the ethnic issues in Romania. On the contrary, the EU gave Romania generous aid throughout 1993 and 1994. The spring and summer of 1994 brought several legislative changes affecting minorities in Romania, but the EU made no formal comments. Keeping the focus on economics, German Foreign Minister Klaus Kinkel visited Romania and voiced support for its admission to the EU but also warned that Romania had to help itself by making economic reforms.[69] November 1994 brought high profile ethnic tensions in Transylvania when, supposedly for an archaeological dig, extremist mayor Gheorghe Funar tried to remove an important Hungarian statue in Transylvania. The EU again had no official reaction. In January 1995 the Europe agreement entered into force without concern for its political provisions. This sent a message to Romania that the EU was willing to overlook many issues to cooperate economically with Romania.

In the mid-1990s the EU began to criticize Romania, even while continuing economic support and cooperation. The West was sending Romania ambiguous signals, which decreased the credibility of the promise of membership. In March 1995 European Commission President Jacques Santer urged Iliescu to step up Romania's economic and political reforms if he wanted join the EU. On July 18, 1995, after a Paris meeting of the Romanian, German, and French foreign ministers, France and Germany issued a joint statement supporting Romania's drive to join the EU. However, they stressed that it was not possible to set a timetable for Romania's EU membership, adding that intensified economic reform, privatization, and the development of a market economy were key conditions.[70] Thus, in essence the West was saying that Romania would not join the EU in the near future because its economy was too poor.[71] This distant horizon greatly diminished incentive for Romania to act on the EU's concerns.

Although 1997–99 was a period of much closer EU-Romania cooperation, Romania also realized that despite political change, the road to admission was still long. The EU still did not comment much on ethnic issues during this time. Rather, fears that Romania would loose hope made EU officials visit Romania to reconfirm the EU's commitment.[72] Nevertheless, the EU could not deny the economic facts. Thus, although Romania had made several changes since the 1996 elections, the EU commission still gave a rather grave review of Romania in its July 1997 Agenda 2000 opinion. The EU tried to keep Romania's confidence. A year later, however, Gunther Burghardt, head of the European Commission's foreign relations department, said that because economic and other reforms had stalled due to political infighting, corruption, and too much bureaucracy, Romania might be the only country to receive a negative grade in the annual report.[73] Indeed, the first regular report said that Bulgaria and Romania "cannot yet be regarded as market economies." To maintain Romania's confidence the EU issued a presidency declaration in January 1999 reaffirming the EU's "commitment to support Romania in the ongoing difficult transformation process," and stating that the "EU remains fully committed to Romania's accession to the European Union." Again, the declaration especially stressed economic reforms and promised an increase in EU aid.[74]

In summary, although the EU's early treatment of Romania was firm on political reforms, the EU paid little attention to ethnic issues in general as admission criteria. Rather, the EU was preoccupied by Romania's economic ailments. The continued cooperation with Romania on economic issues sent two messages to Romania. First, admission was still a long way off. Second, economic aid and cooperation did not depend on the treatment of ethnic minorities. Thus, the only examples of the EU linking membership to behavior in Romania occurred between 1994 and 1996 on the issue of the treaty with Hungary, and between 1998 and 1999 on the issue of language in official contacts. Iliescu finally responded to EU demands about the treaty with Hungary partly in attempt to capitalize on the issue before national elections. Romania did pass a law allowing the use of minority languages in official contacts, although this was partly due to other factors such as minority representation within government. Thus, in general, while EU membership incentives did work a few times in Romania, the EU did not much use them to influence Romania's ethnic politics. Both Romania and the EU understood that the incentives were not that powerful because of the extant economic hurdles. Thus, the EU only commented on ethnic issues peripherally.

Conclusion

Romania illustrates well what happens when international institutions have only little or weak involvement. Partly because of Romania's poor economic performance and the accompanying long list of necessary reforms, Romania realized that EU admission was distant, at best. Also focused on the long economic "to do" list, the EU largely put questions of ethnic minorities on the back burner, often leaving domestic forces to battle it out.

One of the cases with little to no institutional involvement concerned prefects, the head of local government, which illustrates well how nationalist governments will execute policies that damage ethnic minorities if international institutions are not involved or if their admonitions are only mild. Conversely, once a more accommodating government came into power, ethnic minorities could negotiate policies through government even without international aid. Another issue concerned the passage of a law on national minorities. Here, the CE used the same strategy that it had in Slovakia, and failed in largely the same way. Instead of making admission conditional on passage of the law, as the CE had done in Latvia regarding the citizenship law amendments, the CE invited Romania to join if it would promise to pass a law later. Subsequent efforts to persuade the government to pass the law on minorities, although specific and addressed by both the OSCE and the CE, resulted in no change, and eventually the effort to pass a comprehensive law was completely abandoned.

The separate minority language law provides another good illustration of how the CE largely failed to capitalize on its initial admission leverage and how the absence of persistent institutional involvement resulted in a continuous battle over the outcome. The EU finally did associate the issue with enlargement by including a remark about a related government decree in the 1997 opinion on Romania's application for EU membership. Settling the issue was very much due to the bargaining power of the ethnic minority party in a government, which nearly fell apart over the issue. The treaty with Hungary was one of the few cases in which international institutions actually got their way with the Romanian government. Romania's signing of the treaty with Hungary was clearly the result of European pressure and incentives. The treaty, however, was a long time coming, and, like Meciar, Romanian President Iliescu finally responded to EU pressure only to gain popularity as a leader when the domestic desire for EU membership became an election issue. Thus, Romania paints a good picture of the protracted and often fruitless battles that can occur when the institutions are not using their leverage strategically.

Romania's Hungarian minorities benefited from good organization and electoral support. Many of the results obtained when the ethnic minority parties joined the government after the 1996 elections were partly the result of European institutions and other actors pushing for the inclusion of the minority parties in the government coalition in the first place (Vachudova 2002).

The 1998 elections clearly brought a change of tone toward Brussels, The Hague, and Strasbourg. Although the motives for the policy compromises to accommodate ethnic minorities could be labeled as "shallow"— aiming primarily to satisfy the foreign policy goals of Romania's new government—the change within Romania from the 1980s to the 1990s remains significant, and the initial clashes between Romanians and Hungarians in Transylvania never escalated, as some had feared (Lovatt 1999). European institutions deserve some of the credit for this.

PART III

Evaluation

CHAPTER 8

Alternative Explanations: Russia, Hungary, and Democratic Development

SEVERAL ALTERNATIVE EXPLANATIONS account for the factors that determine a state's choice of ethnic minority policies. As realists argue, the homeland, such as Russia or Hungary, may use economic or military influence to direct policies. As the external actors with the greatest direct stake in the outcome, and as reasonably powerful entities, their efforts plausibly spur the accommodation of ethnic minorities. Regardless of international efforts, policies may simply improve over time as the ethnic problems settle and as democratic institutions consolidate. In this case, causal power could wrongly be attributed to international institutions that simply chose to become involved late in the process, or that were involved for a longer duration. It may also be the case that the type of involvement may not matter so much as the duration of involvement. Thus, if an institution simply persists, it will eventually see the policy outcome it desires, regardless of whether it chooses to use membership incentives. How viable are these alternative explanations?

DEMOCRATIC MATURITY

It might be the case that institutions do not influence policy, but that countries produce better solutions to ethnic issues as they consolidate democracy over time. Finland's and Holland's handling minority issues may illustrate this democratic effect, as these countries resolved tensions between ethnic groups within their borders. The hypothesis makes intuitive sense and appeals if one is willing to overlook such cases as Northern Ireland, where ethnic issues remain contentious. Democratic maturity fails to explain the pattern of outcomes seen in the cases presented in this study. While this theory may predict variation over time, it is poor at predicting variation across issues at one given time. If improvement in policy is the product of the general improvements in democracy in a state, then all issues should become more compatible with international norms over time. This is not the case. Indeed, various governments did not act consistently on the issues at hand. Thus, the same Slovak government that eventually abandoned passage of a penalty code rammed through a controversial election law and other contentious issues. Similarly, while Latvia and Estonia both finally conceded on the issue of allowing stateless children to acquire automatic citizenship, both countries simultaneously made great efforts to pass controversial language legislation. Indeed, this happened toward the end of the decade, when the most democratic experience had accumulated.

Thus, while it may be true that a pattern of improved minority rights reveals itself over time, similar to the stock market's consistent improvement over time, several deviations run counter to such a trend. Another observable implication of the democratic maturity hypothesis would be that Latvia and Estonia, whose politicians had more ambition and desire to act democratically than their Romanian and Slovak counterparts during the early and mid-1990s, should have better records on ethnic minority issues. This, however, is also a vast over-generalization, and such comparison is difficult because of the countries' different democratic histories, their different ethnic issues, and the differences in their ethnic minority-majority demographics.

DURATION VERSUS TYPE OF INVOLVEMENT

What if the duration of involvement by international institutions is decisive rather than the kind of involvement? If issues only improve after sustained institutional involvement, then the method of subdividing issues over time causes a bias in the observation set in favor of incentives, because incentives generally were applied later. For example, if pressure was first consistently used alone and incentives were added only later, it could appear that pressure was never effective alone, while in fact it could be that any kind of involvement simply takes a long time to have an effect.

But this study finds that this explanation is unsatisfactory. The examination of individual legislative cases through process tracing helps distinguish between different temporal phases in the influence process characterized by no intervention, normative pressure only, and normative pressure plus conditionality. If behavioral change occurs only when conditionality comes into play, and if policy actors stress the need to adapt a policy to meet the membership criteria, this strengthens claims that conditionality really was the efficient cause. Indeed, in several instances the institutions used normative pressure alone for an extended period without results, and then achieved their goals when they added incentives. This happened on the citizenship issue in Latvia and Estonia, on the residency issue in Estonia, and in other cases. This supports the hypothesis that incentives are essential, but it does not dismiss the alternative explanation that a good outcome is simply a matter of duration of institutional involvement rather than type.

Thus, it is useful to compare these cases with others in which pressure alone was used for years but incentives were never linked. This happens on the naturalization test issue in both countries, when the OSCE was the primary actor urging simplification of the tests, and on the election law issue in Estonia. The naturalization tests were eventually somewhat improved—the result, some may argue, of financial support (but not conditionality) from such actors as the UNDP—but the election law issue did not meet the OSCE recommendations during the time of this study.[1] When institutions used incentives very early in the process, results followed even though a long period of time had not passed. This happened, for example, with the incentive of CE membership and Latvia's passage of a modified citizenship law. This suggests that in the above cases, in which pressure alone was followed by incentives, it is not just the duration of involvement that caused the outcome but rather the added effect of incentives. Thus, while the alternative explanations that the improvements are a result of general democratic maturity, passage of time in general, or simply the duration of institutional involvement may have some merit, they fail to tell an important part of the story.

HOMELAND EXPLANATIONS

The other category of alternative explanations relates to the homelands, Russia and Hungary. Marshall (1993), Taras (1993), Dawisha and Parrot (1994), and van Houten (1998) articulate arguments about the how powerful external homelands can deter the ruling majorities of other states from hard-line oppression of their minority populations. Brubaker (1995) also argues that minority policies are a product of three factors—the minorities, the majority, and the homeland—that are bound together in a single and highly interdependent relational nexus. The homelands can exert security pressure and make economic threats, and thus create incentives for the states to accommodate the minorities.

Given its power and level of economic interaction with the Baltic States, Russia naturally exerted great influence on Latvia and Estonia. The question, however, is how well this relationship effected the ethnic policy outcomes. Brubaker (1996, 45) writes, "As an unjustly truncated, humiliated Great Power, Russia is a potentially revisionist state. While other successor states, too, are potentially revisionist . . . the presence of nearly 25 million Russians in non-Russian successor states, the enormous military power of Russia, and the uniquely radical decline in status experienced both by new Russian minorities and by key segments of Russian elites in Russia would make a revisionist Russia a potentially much graver threat." He goes on to argue that external incentives—offered, for example, by . . . economically, politically or militarily powerful states—may favor transethnic state- and nation-building strategies, oriented to the citizenry as a whole rather than to one ethnonationally qualified segment of that citizenry. . . . Clearly, the proximity of the (potentially) enormously powerful Russian state, as well as the presence of large Russian minorities in their successor states, other things being equal, would lead prudent successor state elites to avoid alienating their Russian minorities (and provoking the Russian state) by an overzealous program of nationalization. (1996, 47)

Similarly, he notes that "the nationalizing nationalisms of Romania and Slovakia have clashed with the homeland nationalism of Hungary" (1996, 108). With Hungary, however, the security threat was clearly lesser, as Hungary sought NATO admission. Slovakia was also less economically dependent on Hungary, and actually depended more on Russia. Van Houten also argues, "If it is known that the reference state is likely to intervene in the new state if the minority is oppressed, then the ruling majority in the new state has an incentive to protect the minority" (1998, 112). Such theory can help explain variation across both time and issues, since the threats can occur in connection with individual issues and also vary over time.

Both Hungary and Russia played vital roles in ethnic issues in Latvia and Estonia, and Slovakia and Romania, respectively. But they did not primarily present themselves as security threats. Relations with western Europe and the United States made this option highly unattractive for Russia and certainly for Hungary. In the case of Russia, economic pressure may have contributed to a limited number of outcomes. In general, however, the most notable effect of the two homelands was their indirect ability to involve international actors.

Security Threats

Russian officials have stated on several occasions that they would protect Russia's co-nationals in the so-called near abroad (Hill and Jewett 1994; Melwin 1995, 10–22).[2] Thus, the Baltic States have naturally been concerned about reintegration with Russia (Bajarunas et al., 1995; Haab and Viksne 1995; Van Houten 1998). The desire to eliminate this possibility has driven their determination to join the EU and NATO. Their fear is mostly one of economic and political reintegration, however, rather than the fear of a traditional security threat (Hurd 1999, 268–69). If real security threats were the cause of change of policy toward Russians in Latvia and Estonia, then we should expect efforts to push changes to be most effective before Russia withdrew her troops in the fall of 1994; efforts to accommodate ethnic minorities should have declined after that. This does not appear true. Indeed, the United States' and the international community's pressure on Russia to withdraw greatly constrained Russia's ability to leverage change using the security threat. As discussed in the introductions to chapters 4 and 5, about Latvia and Estonia, Russia failed to use its military effectively in the Baltic capitals in the early 1990s, even as these countries called for independence. Russia then agreed to withdraw the one hundred thousand Soviet troops estimated to be in the Baltic States in February 1992. But in October 1992 Russian President Boris Yeltsin suspended troop pullouts because of concerns over the rights of Russian speakers in Latvia and Estonia. In February 1993 the U.S. Congress approved the resolution, which linked the financial aid USD 4000 million to Russia with the withdrawal of troops from the Baltic States. Russia, though, kept trying to get more out of the troop issue from Latvia and Estonia. In April 1993, after a meeting with U.S. President Bill Clinton, Yeltsin said at a press conference, "We will be scheduling the actual withdrawal in line with what [Estonia and Latvia] decide in the human rights field."[3] The United States and other international actors, however, were consistent and uncompromising in their call for withdrawal of Russian troops, and criticized efforts to link it with human rights.[4]

So what did Russia actually get out of the issue of troop withdrawals before Russian troops left in the fall of 1994? Not that much. In both Latvia and Estonia, Russia's main gain was to extract compromises on the issue of residency for retired military personnel. In 1993 Estonia was creating a law on residency that required all ethnic Russians to apply for resident permits. Initially, the law completely excluded retired military personnel from even applying for such permits. The most direct threat from Russia came on June 24, 1993, while this legislation was on the agenda. President Boris Yeltsin declared, "The Estonian government has misjudged Russia's goodwill and, giving way to the pressure of nationalism has 'forgotten' about certain geopolitical and demographic realities," and "the Russian side has means at its disposal to remind Estonia about these [realities]."[5] Just days later Russia and Estonia agreed on terms for the pullout of Russian troops from Estonia by the end of August 1994, overcoming a crisis that had poisoned bilateral relations. In negotiations with the OSCE, and most likely as a result of a trade-off on the issue of the withdrawal of Russian troops that fall, Estonia later agreed to allow for individual applications by military personnel.

In July 1994, however, defying pressure from the West and reneging on a commitment made earlier, Yeltsin told G-7 leaders gathered in Italy that Russia would not withdraw the last of its military forces from Estonia by the August 31 deadline. Yeltsin attributed the decision to what he purported were very crude violations of human rights in Estonia and to that nation's unwillingness to grant citizenship to and to provide housing for Russian military retirees still living in Estonia. Apparently at the request of Washington, Yeltsin did agree to meet with Estonian President Lennart Meri in the hope of resolving the issue. The *New York Times* suggested that Yeltsin's hard line on the withdrawal represented a negotiating tactic; it was also undoubtedly aimed at Russians domestic political arena, where aggressive assertions of Russia's national interests had increasingly become the rule.[6] Three days later the U.S. Senate approved an amendment to a foreign aid bill that linked USD $839 million aid to Russia and the CIS with the withdrawals of Russia troops from the Baltic States by August 31, 1994. West German Chancellor Helmuth Kohl added his support for withdrawals.

A few weeks later, after last minute talks on troop withdrawal in Moscow between Yeltsin and Meri, Russia agreed to withdraw the remaining two thousand troops by the deadline. In exchange, Estonia signed an agreement on "Matters Related to Social Guarantees for Military Pensioners of the Russian Federation on the Territory of the Republic of Estonia," agreeing to allow all military retirees to apply for residency in Estonia on the condition that a special Estonian commission review each individual application. The commission would include a representative from the OSCE, and Estonia would reserve the right to reject any applicant considered a threat to Estonian security. Russia would pay a pension to the military retirees, regardless of citizenship, offering some social guarantees to the retirees. This was the only case in Estonia in which Russia was able to exert some compromise due to the military presence. Russia tried to extract some leverage from an on-going border dispute with Estonia, but this was also largely unsuccessful and met with EU criticism.[7] EU officials noted that the absence of a border treaty with Russia should not effect Estonia's chances of becoming a full EU member. Thus, even Van Houten (1998, 136), who makes the argument that Russia as a reference state helped prevent ethnic conflict in Estonia by giving Estonia incentives "not to treat the Russians too poorly" is able to give few concrete examples of how Estonia toned down ethnic politics in direct response to Russian pressure.

In Latvia, Russia got similarly little out of any efforts to link the troop withdrawals to improvements in legislation for ethnic Russians. In March 1994 Latvia and Russia signed four basic agreements, stating that Russia would completely remove its troops by the same August 31, 1994 deadline. The agreements also included social protection for the withdrawing troops and social guarantees for Russian military pensioners who had retired before January 28, 1992, when Russia officially transferred the former Soviet army to its jurisdiction. Latvia would grant the pensioners the status of permanent residents, and they could be naturalized as Latvian citizens under Latvian law. The U.S. secretary of state, Warren Christopher, confirmed in a letter the United States' "active engagement on behalf of the withdrawal of Russian forces from Latvia."[8] The EU added its approval.[9]

In July 1994, however, Yeltsin linked troop withdrawals to the citizenship legislation. According to a statement released by the Russian president's office, Yeltsin said that if the Baltic States cancelled discriminatory legislation, Russia would be prepared to sign a schedule for withdrawing its troops.[10] U.S. President Clinton tried to mediate Yeltsin's attitude with a speech in Riga, urging tolerance on both sides and disconnecting the citizenship and withdrawal issue. Hinting that Latvia would not suffer Russian occupation again, President Clinton told a cheering crowd, "The chain that binds our nations is unbreakable. We will be partners so your nations will be forever free."[11]

Thus, while Yeltsin's renewed reluctance came amidst Latvia's passage of a citizenship law, Russia had little real leverage in the case: the compromises in the citizenship law were largely driven by the international institutions (see chapter 4). Yeltsin, kept in check by widespread international disapproval, was dissatisfied with the outcome negotiated by the institutions. He issued a statement denouncing the Latvian citizenship law, and although Russian troops were still present in Latvia, he extracted no further concessions. Indeed, because of immense international pressure, Russia abided by the August 31 troop withdrawal deadline, even before Latvia and Russia had ratified the March 1994 agreements.[12] Thus, the early security threat from Russia's remaining troops yielded few results for Russia.

Likewise, Hungary might have used military pressure with Slovakia and Romania to push those countries on minority rights. In fact, military cooperation was good between these countries, and no military threat occurred. On the contrary, because of the aspirations of Hungary, Slovakia, and Romania to join NATO, the countries were eager to display their ability to cooperate militarily. In 1992 a reporter commented to Hungary's defense minister, Lajos Fuer, "It was surprising for many that out of the neighbors, Hungary concluded the first military co-operation agreement with Romania, whereas our inter-governmental relations and other links are burdened with a lot of political problems." Fuer replied, "The military relations were not burdened by these and are still not burdened today."[13] In 1995 the Hungarian ambassador to the United States told the *Washington Times* that Hungary's conflict with Romania "is not a thing of crisis. . . . We have signed a political declaration. The relationship is moving. There is excellent cooperation between the two militaries of the two countries."[14] Hungarian and Romanian defense ministers described Hungarian-Romanian military cooperation as exemplary.[15] Thus, security threats do not explain the outcomes satisfactorily. Indeed, such international organizations as the OSCE and the CE as well as individual countries, including the United States, were alert and able to flag any security threats, and effectively removed military options from the table.

ECONOMIC THREATS

Economic threats from Hungary were not an issue since Hungary, Slovakia, and Romania all wanted to enter trade relations under EU terms. Russia, however, certainly tried to use economic threats in several instances, although again, this was perhaps as much a show for domestic politics as a real effort at influencing Latvia and Estonia. In June 1996 the Russian State Duma adopted a resolution to impose restrictions on trade-economic relations to protest Latvian efforts to pass an education law, which the Duma characterized as the beginning of a program to forcefully integrate the Russians in Latvia. The education law was already mostly dead by then, because it was stuck in parliament with hundreds of proposals for amendments.[16] A few months later the Duma approved an appeal to the government and president to impose economic sanctions against Latvia to protest the Latvian parliament's declaration on occupation, which the Duma called anti-Russian. This declaration stood, however, and Russian sanction threats faded.

One case in which Russian sanction threats may have actually contributed to the resolution of an ethnic issue in Latvia took place in the spring and summer of 1998. In Riga in March 1998 many older Russian residents protested the pension policy, and the police had responded with some physical crowd control methods. After this, Moscow's mayor accused the Latvian authorities of "pursuing a consistent policy of genocide" against the Russian-speaking population. He compared Riga's policies to events in Cambodia during Pol Pot's rule.[17] He expressed concern about the treatment of Russian-speakers in Latvia during meetings with acting Russian Prime Minister Sergei Kirienko and UN Secretary-General Kofi Annan on March 25 and 29, respectively.[18] A week later, President Yeltsin announced practical economic measures to pressure Latvia on its treatment of the Russian-speaking minority.[19] Russian pressure and threats of sanction continued in April and May 1998.[20] As in the case of military threats, however, the international community widely condemned Russia's approach. EU Commissioner for Foreign Relations van den Broek urged Russia to stop applying economic pressure on Latvia over the issue. "We've made it clear to Russia that we do not accept their attempts to mix political and economic issues. . . . We resist unjustified pressure on an EU candidate," he commented.[21] Thus, while the process tracing of the case reveals a very deep concern in Latvia with the European institutions' actions, the threat of

Russian sanctions both contributed to internal political crisis in Latvia and increased the European institutions' focus on the issue. As discussed, Latvia amended the citizenship law after intense pressure from the EU and other international actors.

In July and November 1999 Russia again threatened Latvia with sanctions, when Latvia was debating a new language law.[22] The European institutions had already been extensively involved, however, long before the Russian threats. The outcome, which included concessions specific to EU concerns, was, as discussed and as also demonstrated by the timing (right before the EU summit), driven by the united European pressure, linked to the admission to the EU.

In Estonia, Russia also threatened economic and even political sanctions at times. The ultra-nationalist Vladimir Zhirinovsky's Liberal Democratic Party often initiated the threats.[23] In a case not included in this study because it concerns an individual, rather than general policy, the Duma passed the resolution on sanctions against Estonia on March 24, 1995, to protest Tallinn's decision to deport Russian nationalist Petr Rozhok. Yeltsin ignored the Duma's recommendation, but Russia remained very involved with the case. A year and a half later, a court ruled in Rozhok's favor.[24] This is the only case in which sanctions were linked to the outcome. Van Houten (1998, 139) argues that Russia's halt of natural gas supplies to Estonia at the end of June 1993 to protest the law on aliens was somewhat successful because it achieved some concession in the law. These concessions were moderate, however, and the linkage to the actions by the international community explain these modifications just as well—if not better.

Thus, economic threats, mostly in the case of Russia, did at times catch the attention of the Latvian and Estonian governments. But a direct effect is rarely visible, and in many cases Russia made no targeted effort. Consider also that Latvian and Estonian trade shifted significantly toward the West, the Russian threats were ambiguous, and the Baltic governments knew that the threats were often mostly domestic Russian electioneering.[25]

CONCLUSION

Alternative explanations for these four states' ethnic policies may center on the argument that policies naturally improve over time, perhaps because democracy within the state is improving in general, leading to policy improvements. A time factor could also represent the argument that it is not the type of institutional involvement that matters but simply the duration. Thus, as institutions naturally tend to use normative pressure as a first resort and then add incentives later, the analysis could be picking up the effect of the incentives in error when the real cause is just the persistence of involvement. This explanation is not satisfying because several cases contradict such a time pattern.

I also largely dismiss the effect of homeland explanations as direct explanatory factors for changes in ethnic policy. While Russian relations with the Baltic States was complex and while Russia remained a key geopolitical actor, in reality, Russia was able to solicit very few concession on ethnic minority policy. Russian security threats achieved few concessions, and its economic threats were often seen as a Russian domestic political propaganda. As Latvian Prime Minster Gunters Krasts himself said, the EU provided a greater incentive than did Russia provide pressure: "There was no other way to get a positive progress report from the EU. We were forced to go ahead—well, forced wouldn't be the right word. It was reasonable from our side to go ahead with changes. . . . Not to get a positive report *would be more negative than current instability or current pressure from Russia.* In that case, we would be out of the game entirely" (emphasis added).[26]

Nevertheless, another effect occurred: Russia indirectly influenced the ethnic issue in Latvia and Estonia, just as Hungary did in Slovakia and Romania. Russia and Hungary helped place the ethnic issues on the agenda of the European institutions and at times motivated the institutions to take action. Thus, for example, Russia frequently handed the CE memorandums about the violations of the rights of Russians in the Baltic States. Russian members of the CE parliamentary assembly also initiated some resolutions, which primarily the Russian parliamentarians themselves would sign.[27] Also, in all the countries the minorities themselves joined the homelands in using the international institutions as a forum for their grievances. Thus, the Hungarian minority, for example, always met with representatives visiting the countries, and at times sent letters of complaints to the institutions.[28] In connection with Slovakia and Romania's admission to the CE, Hungary, as a CE member, was able to make a lot of noise. Hungary's threat to veto Slovakia's and Romania's admissions ensured that ethnic minority concerns were part of the commitments the countries had to make to the CE when joining. Russia, however, was not a CE member at the time of Latvia and Estonia's admission. As an OSCE member, however, Russia was able to discuss issues frequently with the HCNM, who made several trips to Moscow. Indeed, Latvians and Estonians sometimes criticized HCNM van der Stoel for siding with the Russians.[29] Further, as discussed, in the spring of 1998, the tensions between Russia and Latvia helped propel European institutional involvement.[30] Thus, for example, in April 1998 Italian Foreign Minister Lamberto Dini said at a joint press conference with Russian Foreign Minister Yevgenii Primakov in Moscow, that "events like those of recent days distance Latvia further from the process of preliminary membership."[31]

In sum, Russia and Hungary both used international institutions to turn the spotlight on ethnic minority problems. In these cases, however, the homelands did not pose security threats and rarely used real economic leverage. Rather, the advocacy of Hungary and Russia helps explain why and how the institutions were involved in some issues. This is consistent with theory proposed by both Brubaker (1995) and van Houten (1998). Thus, the role of the homeland is not an alternative explanatory factor but in some cases an antecedent explanatory factor for the involvement of the institutions. This finding is also consistent with a study on the role of neighboring states on citizenship policy in the newly independent states of Ukraine, Lithuania, Latvia, and Estonia. This study concludes that neighboring states did not have a large significant effect, but rather that they were only effective when working through international organizations (Barrington 1995).

CHAPTER 9

Conclusion

ALTHOUGH SEVERAL INTERNATIONAL ORGANIZATIONS participated actively in eastern Europe's ethnic politics over the last decade, research on their role has focused on a single institution and the particular strategy it applied. The OSCE has been praised for easing ethnic tensions, but studies have not focused on its concrete policy effects or they have ignored the role of the EU (Michalchuk 1999; Kemp 2001; Ratner 2000). Studies of EU conditionality similarly have disregarded the vast diplomatic efforts of the CE and the OSCE or they have focused on broad democratic trends rather than particular policies (Grabbe 2001; Fierke and Wiener 1999; Grabbe and Hughes 1998, 41 ff; Amato and Batt 1998; De Witte 2000). This book has sorted out the institutional effects for the first time by using extensive new data to compare how the OSCE, the CE, and the EU influenced the governments of Latvia, Estonia, Slovakia, and Romania to pass certain ethnic minority legislation during the 1990s.

The flurry of European institutions' activities motivated the analytical division of external engagements into the use of normative pressure and the use of incentives. Drawing on theory from both rationalist and constructivist approaches, I developed hypotheses about the mechanisms and conditions of institutional influence. In the context of the recent histories and the domestic political battles within each government, I tracked all the legislation and events related to ethnic minorities from 1990 to 1999, performed quantitative analysis, and examined the relationships between variables through case studies. Finally, I also explored alternative hypotheses about the role of time, timing, and homelands.

I found that—despite prevalent pessimism about the ability of international actors to mitigate ethnic issues—international institutions can influence policy in states with sizable ethnic minority groups. Contrary to the ambiguity about the effects of aid conditionality and sanctions, membership conditionality has been a surprisingly effective way for international institution to shape minority-related policy, even in the face of considerable domestic opposition. Indeed, to change policy in most instances the institutions must link membership with the country's behavior. Despite the widespread use of purely diplomatic approaches relying on persuasion and social influence, such efforts alone rarely change policies. Further, the domestic context plays a large role not only directly but also indirectly by influencing the usefulness of international efforts. Domestic opposition, however, debilitates normative pressure more than it debilitates conditionality. Specifically, authoritarian leadership or strong nationalist opposition in parliament decreases and sometimes even blocks institutional success. Similarly, having ethnic minorities in government improves success. Indeed, these domestic factors are key in explaining ethnic policy. But neither of these factors predicts the outcomes well: international institutional efforts still matter. Finally—and importantly for the policy implications of the study—not only does the chosen mechanism determine the efficiency of international efforts, but the international institutions' credibility and the nature of their admission process does so as well.

Three key tasks remain. First, to discuss the findings in greater depth and try to disentangle the effects of normative pressure and conditionality. Second, to extend the analysis to relevant theory. Third, to draw some policy lessons and to discuss several questions raised by the findings, for example, durability, applicability, and implementation. I conclude by suggesting further research.

Explaining the Influence of European Institutions on Ethnic Politics

The Role of International Institutions

International institutions were active and effective participants in the domestic policy process. In numerous cases institutions influenced domestic governments to bring about the institutions' desired policy outcomes. Further, governments tried to or actually did tighten laws when institutions were not involved. This happened even in the late 1990s, when these countries were considered more democratic and tolerant. All four countries passed various types of legislation that were unfavorable to ethnic minorities. Thus, the Latvian election laws used language requirements to bar many people from running for office in both national and local elections. At times local representation was completely lost because the vast majority of the population in certain areas failed to meet citizenship or residency requirement that would have allowed them to vote. Another example were efforts in Latvia and Estonia to pass stricter language laws—efforts that really took hold between 1997 and 1999. The quantitative data also confirmed that positive changes to policy occurred more often with institutional involvement than without, and this finding maintained a high statistical significance even when controlling for the influence of domestic opposition. Indeed, without external intervention governments only rarely resolved an issue favorably for minorities, and when they did, there were

TABLE 9.1
Predicted probabilities for a compatible outcome

	Institutions not involved (percent)	Normative pressure only (percent)	Conditionality and normative pressure (percent)
Strong domestic opposition	0	3	57
Moderate domestic opposition	3	23	93*
Weak domestic opposition	24	74*	99

For calculations, see table 3.7.

* These calculations are based on fewer than five observations and should be interpreted with extra caution.

other apparent explanations. Thus, the evidence confirmed that institutional engagement was effective.

The Type of the Institutional Involvement

Clear differences marked the effectiveness of the two institutional strategies. The combination of incentives and normative pressure was much more effective than the use of normative pressure alone, even though several of the conditions that scholars hypothesize as favorable for the effectiveness of such softer socialization efforts were present.[1] Ordered logit analysis did identify normative pressure as a significant explanatory variable. Further investigation, however, suggested that normative pressure alone was decreasingly effective as the domestic and institutional policy preferences diverged. Table 9.1 suggests that when institutions relied solely on normative pressure and when domestic opposition to the institutional policy preferences was strong, the improvement in the probability of a compatible outcome was minimal. Membership conditionality on the other hand had a consistently large effect above both the absence of involvement and the use of normative pressure alone.

The qualitative case studies provide several examples of normative pressure's failure to improve policy. On a general note, in the case studies policy makers clearly did not take advice seriously or were not concerned with displeasing the institutions that offered the advice.[2] Some of the reply letters that the HCNM received from states reflect this view. For example, once after the HCNM had admonished Slovakia about a draft election law, Slovakia's foreign minister replied, "I have the honour to inform you that this draft law has already been adopted in the National Council of the Slovak Republic. It can also be said that through this law the Slovak Republic safeguards the right of 'the national minorities to govern the affairs they are concerned with.' "[3]

Normative pressure alone also suffered from implementation flaws, such as poor timing and lack of coordination among institutions. Even when institutions executed normative pressure well, however, it often went unheeded. Thus, the OSCE did not persuade the Estonian president to veto the introduction of language requirements for local and national candidates. Similarly, pressure from the HCNM, which included detailed recommendations and extensive meetings, also failed in the end to shape the education law in Latvia, where the point of contention was the language of instruction. Although many of his recommendations made it into intermediary drafts, illustrating that they were given some consideration, the final draft omitted most of the recommendations despite the detailed efforts. Similarly, in 1994 the OSCE and the EU called in vain for Estonia to issue permanent residency permits immediately to those who were residents before July 1990 and to pass legally binding provisions to ensure the rights of temporary residents. Most notably, both Latvia and Estonia for many years ignored continuous pressure by the OSCE to allow stateless children to acquire citizenship, although it was a point of criticism raised from the early 1990s . Thus, in these cases, diplomatic pressure alone produced no results. The general pattern was that normative pressure had little to no effect on policies, or that the opportunity to use such pressure was wasted because it was not executed well.

Nevertheless, in a few cases, normative pressure did seem to have some effect. While the data in table 9.1 is only descriptive because it is based on an additive logit model, the figures suggest that an interactive effect may exist: normative pressure alone appears increasingly effective the weaker the nationalist influence. Indeed, successful use of normative pressure alone tended to occur in the context of moderate or weak domestic opposition, such as the passage of the laws on names and places passed by the interim Moravcik government in 1994 in Slovakia. This government was eager to please the West and relied indirectly on the support of ethnic minorities. On the other hand, some of the cases in which normative pressure alone failed also suggest other obstacles apart from the fact that no incentives were used: institutions often did not support one another, they became involved in cases at late stages of policy formation, and they were sometimes perceived as biased, as in the Baltic States, where the opposition in particular tended to portray the HCNM as pro-Russian.

Importantly, however, although institutions rarely changed policy with normative pressure, they often had other related goals at which they were indeed quite successful. Such additional goals have included calming of ethnic tensions, monitoring of the implementation of the naturalization process, and facilitating language learning and communication.

Membership Incentives

Institutions increased their influence significantly if they linked membership incentives to policy behavior. First, the ordered logit analysis showed that the combined use of membership incentives and normative pressure was an extremely significant explanatory factor. Indeed, compared to the cases in which institutions were not involved at all, the predicted score of a compatible outcome rose between 57 to 90 percent across the different levels of domestic opposition when institutions used membership incentives (see table 9.1). While these figures should be interpreted with care, they do strongly suggest that the use of incentives is a vast improvement over the use of normative pressure alone.

The qualitative analysis raised confidence in the quantitative results by providing sound illustrations of how the added effect of the membership incentives produced more favorable outcomes. Thus, for example, in 1994 in Latvia during the Birkavs government, the OSCE and CE experts were able to push through the changes in the citizenship law only because this behavior had been tied to admission to the CE. Prime Minister Birkavs perhaps most pointedly stated that the cause of the revision of the law was European pressure and membership in European institutions. When Latvian President Ulmanis returned the law to parliament, Birkavs said, "We shall not allow the Latvian people to perish because of the citizenship law. We shall not allow this law to bar our way to Europe, the only place where Latvia can survive."[4] Likewise, the OSCE and the CE had little success in improving the citizenship laws in Latvia and Estonia in 1995, 1996, and 1997, when they could not equate compliance with specific payoffs. Not until the EU threw its weight behind their various recommendations did change occur.

Similarly, the ambitions to join the EU drove both Slovakia and Romania to sign treaties with Hungary despite strong domestic opposition. Romanian President Iliescu underscored that the desire to join the EU and NATO "was indeed the most important aspect, motivating the cooperation on the treaty."[5] Likewise, Slovakian Prime Minister Meciar said, "We are aware, as one of the [EU] associated countries, that the Stability Pact, through its course and actual results, will speed up our bona-fide participation in the European Union."[6] Although the implementation of the agreements was problematic, the conclusion of the agreements was nevertheless an important achievement for the European institutions. Also, membership incentives shaped policy in both Slovakia and Romania after the changes of governments there in the late 1990s. Although Slovakia's government actually included ethnic minority representation, the opposition to the minority language law was still formidable, and institutional conditionality played a key role in facilitating a compromise. The EU membership incentive not only propelled the non-Hungarian coalition partners to pass the law,[7] but also softened the ethnic Hungarian position. Lajos Meszaros, spokesman for the Hungarian Coalition Party, said frankly, "[W]e are prepared for a compromise because the law is one of the basic conditions for Slovakia beginning talks on the admission to the European Union."[8] Summing up the logic of policy makers facing pressure from admission requirements, Toomas Ilves, Estonian foreign minister commented, "In dealing with laws that are the norm of the organization you want to join, your choice is to abide by them or decide not to join. If you don't want to join, fine, do it your way. But you can't say, 'We'll take the EU subsidies, but we won't meet them on standards.' "[9]

Sorting Out the Effects of Socialization and Conditionality

The key remaining challenge is to sort out the relative impact of normative pressure vis-à-vis conditionality when these efforts are used simultaneously. Naturally, conditionality alone is not sufficient, given that even some cases of conditionality failed—particularly during Meciar's Slovakia, such as Meciar's refusal to allow issue bilingual language certificates, his insistence on changing the election laws, and his failure to pass a minority language law. But in the cases in which the institutions were effective, would they have failed if socialization-based efforts had been absent? That is, is normative pressure necessary when the institutions use membership conditionality? This is a complex question, since institutions never applied conditionality without also relying on softer efforts.

First, variation in the level of normative pressure may make it possible to say whether socialization-based efforts condition the effect of membership conditionality. However, in all but one of the nineteen conditionality cases, the OSCE and the CE were active participants and comparing their levels of engagement is difficult. This brings up another important point, which is that the relationship between the OSCE, the CE, and the EU often became intertwined because the EU relied on the OSCE and the EU for evaluation and information. Thus the very *character* of the normative pressure changed once behavior was linked to admission in an organization: even the normative actors indirectly gained instrumental leverage through their relationship with the admitting organization.

Counterfactual analysis is a more effective way to assess how pivotal normative pressure was. Does systematic examination of each case suggest that the socialization efforts created links in the process of change that would not otherwise have been made? This does not seem to be the case. Although the normative pressure framed the problems, facilitated dialogue, and helped formulate solutions, the conditionality appeared to be such a strong motivating factor that it is plausible that the results would have come about eventually even if these supportive actions had been absent. Three examples follow.

Would the case of stateless children in Estonia have turned out differently without OSCE involvement? Probably yes. Would the EU have been able to change the policy without the OSCE? Probably yes. The OSCE clearly was highly active, yet the legislative movement toward a compromise occurred in a pattern consistent with the EU actions regarding membership: before EU meetings, drafting of EU reports, and interaction with EU officials. It is quite possible that the EU would not have framed the issues the way it did without the OSCE involvement, or—more generally— that the softer actors influenced the content of norms that the more instrumental actors apply. Given the strong EU membership ambitions and the open EU support for the OSCE, however, the high level of OSCE involvement itself does not necessarily mean that the OSCE efforts were necessary. They were no doubt helpful. For example, as the Estonia citizenship issue was drawing to a close in 1998, OSCE staff visited Talinn urging specific swing policymakers to change their position. The reasoning of the OSCE staff may have been instrumental rather than moral, or more likely with the swing voters: a mixture.[10] Their efforts, regardless, helped build the necessary coalition to pass the amendments. Thus, that one-on-one engagement was beneficial in this case both in framing the issues and in building coalitions. Judging from the timing of events, however, the EU conditionality, not the OSCE efforts, was the motivating factor.

In the case of Slovakia's rejection of the penal code, the OSCE was again highly active and may indeed have flagged the attention of the EU on the matter. While the OSCE and EU were mutually supportive, the fact that the rejection happened as the EU was preparing the Agenda 2000 report and after the EU officially linked the law to admission suggests that the relative causal impact of conditionality was larger than that of normative pressure. Indeed, parliament rejected the law because a few members of the governing coalition finally defected from the party line on the third attempt to pass the law. Several factors make it unlikely, however, that these politicians had changed their beliefs drastically since the two earlier votes: only a few months had passed since those votes and there were little to no socialization efforts during that time. Further, the law had been slightly softened since the two previous attempts; this should have made the law more acceptable to any swing voters, not less. Thus, it makes most sense to interpret the rejection of the law as a response to the EU pressure in the light of the upcoming evaluation for admission.

Counterfactual analysis is more challenging in Latvia's 1994 change to the citizenship law, because the membership incentive came from the CE, which is also a heavily norm-based institution. Thus, one cannot simply separate the actors and ask if the CE would have succeeded without the

OSCE. Both the CE and the OSCE clearly helped define a solution to the problem of naturalization at the time. The question, however, is whether the *willingness* to compromise resulted solely from the CE's conditionality or whether it indeed depended also on the CE norm-based efforts. Understanding this requires a more in-depth examination of the CE efforts themselves. While the CE had made seven visits between 1991 and 1993, it made only two in 1994 before the passage of the citizenship law, first in January, but then not again until August 1994, just a few days before approval of the final draft. The CE did not issue formal documents on Latvia during the spring of 1994. The absence of visits in the spring of 1994 suggests that the main activity of the CE was not intensive persuasion efforts. Recall, too, that the Latvian Parliament actually passed an unsatisfactory version of the law in June 1994 and then reversed itself only two months later. During these two months, however, the relationship with the CE seemed very much to be one of negotiation, not about what was "right" but about what was sufficient to gain CE approval. As the opinion on membership stated later, adoption of the law had been a "major pre-condition for accession."[11] Thus counterfactual analysis suggests that while normative pressure by the CE and the OSCE were integral to the outcomes in many ways, conditionality was the motivating factor. The leverage this conditionality provided did not depend on the concurrent efforts to shape the solutions.

The last way to get at the question of the relative causal power of membership conditionality vis-à-vis normative pressure is to examine what rhetoric accompanied the policy changes. If the normative pressure was important, one might expect some rhetoric about the moral imperative of the changes rather than just comments linking the changes to EU membership. Indeed, politicians may prefer to present the policy positions as their own to avoid being seen as puppets. Of course, this effect could be distorted by the fact that policy makers might prefer to blame the international institutions for unpopular moves, even if they actually agreed with them. Given these contradictory expectations, it might be fair to predict a mix of public rhetoric on the causes for the changes. The comments by policy makers, however, rarely ever reflected any moral support for the policies at all. Indeed, when Slovak Prime Minister Mikulas Dzurinda drew fire for making concessions to Hungarians on a minority language law, he almost excused himself from his action: "I am not responsible for the fact that someone has suggested that the law on the usage of ethnic minority languages in public administration be drafted. I repeat, it was not me who made sure this law was embodied in the constitution and it was not me who concluded the basic treaty with Hungary in France."[12] This was hardly a ringing endorsement. In contrast, returning from a working meeting in Brussels, EU chief negotiator Jan Figel said that if Slovakia did not adopt a law on ethnic languages a "big question mark" would hover over EU membership negoti-ations. The conditionality, not the norms, was in the forefront here. This book has provided numerous similar examples where policy makers frankly explain their actions as moves to gain EU or CE admission.

While these inquiries do not prove that conditionality would have worked in isolation, they do suggest that conditionality did most of the heavy lifting. Nevertheless, it may be that the efforts to persuade, while rarely effective alone, help explain why political conditionality appears to be more effective than economic conditionality, which often fails to both engage the actors and provide what the scholars term "ownership" of the reforms (Killick 1996). The case studies illustrate how the international institutions cooperated. For example, the EU relied heavily on the HCNM to explain key concepts, soften the attitudes of key policy makers, and sug-gest solutions. Indeed, the EU very much wanted the HCNM to play this role, especially since EU member states, wary of implications for them-selves, preferred not suggest too detailed a solution. The EU also relied on CE and OSCE standards and recommendations as benchmarks for per-formance and as reference points for the validity of EU entry requirements. Different institutional representatives met or invoked one another's stan-dards or rewards several times. Thus, the case studies show a dense cooper-ation that suggests normative pressure played an integral part, even when conditionality fueled the policy engine.

How Domestic Factors Matter

Domestic opposition was consistently a statistically significant factor in explaining policy outcomes. The case of prefects in Slovakia is a good illus-tration of how domestic factors operate in the absence of international involvement. In this case, a nationalist government removed ethnic Hun-garian political authorities in areas with extremely high Hungarian popula-tions. After a more accommodating government came into power, however, Hungarians managed to regain these seats of authority even without direct international help.

But the study suggests some interesting subtleties about the interaction between domestic opposition and institutional involvement. The basic in-teractive hypothesis was supported in that institutional involvement in gen-eral did decrease in effectiveness with an increase in nationalist influence. The effect of domestic opposition, however, may not be the same for the two institutional strategies. Thus, domestic opposition seemed to have a greater debilitating effect on the use of normative pressure than on the use of incentives. Most noticeable, incentives seemed able to affect policy *de-spite the degree* of nationalism. Table 9.1 showed that even when the domes-tic opposition was strong, the probability that membership conditionality was likely to be associated with a compatible outcome was 57 percent. Even when applying a good deal of caution to the statistical findings, this is remarkably high, considering that the institutions had no threat of force at their disposal. It is even more noteworthy when compared with the 3 percent probability of a compatible outcome in cases in which institutions used normative pressure alone. Thus, while domestic opposition clearly did decrease the effectiveness of institutional involvement as hypothesized, the international institutions could to a surprisingly great extent use membership incentives to override strong domestic constraints.

The qualitative analysis supported the statistical analysis on domestic opposition. When the institutions did not get involved, nationalist politicians and parties could easily be traced as active factors in exacerbating the outcomes. When the institutions were involved, however, the case studies illustrated how institutional efforts sometimes spurred solutions despite strong domestic opposition. The most startling examples were when, in several instances, a parliament actually went so far as to pass legislation contrary to the institutions' recommendations only to have the president veto it, after which the parliament followed the institutions' recommendations in a final revision. This happened, for example, when the president vetoed a harsh law on the citizenship in Latvia in 1994, and also when the Estonian parliament eventually revised a harsh law on residency in 1993 after a presidential veto. Similarly, in 1996 in Slovakia the president repeatedly blocked a harsh penalty law, and in 1999 the Latvian president returned a strict language law. Finally, the opposition to Latvia's 1998 citizenship law amendments was so strong that the nationalists called a referendum and ran a strongly negative campaign that just barely failed in undoing the accomplishments of the parliament.[13] Yet in all these cases of strong domestic opposition, the institutions linked membership to behavior and eventually managed to bring about their desired outcomes.

The interactive effect of domestic opposition and institutional involvement was particularly well illustrated by the quasi-experimental designs provided by the changes of governments. Thus, in several cases international institutions were clearly unsuccessful at getting governments to change their policies until a change of government. This was the case, for example, after the elections in Slovakia and Romania, with governments more eager to comply with European institutional norms. Before these changes, Slovakia's and Romania's governments mostly shrugged at institutional pressure on several issues. Pressure on Romania to pass a law on minorities and to allow the use of bilingual road signs was largely ineffective. And Slovak Prime Minister Meciar's government proceeded with local administrative reform and passed a strict language law despite institutional pressure. After the elections, however, ethnic minorities in these countries gained the protective legislation they had been coveting on language and other issues.

Authoritarian Leaders and Minority Parties in Government

While it is a key explanatory factor, the influence of domestic opposition alone does not fully explain the failure and success pattern of the incentives. One factor that can add more understanding is the presence or absence of a strong authoritarian leader. The study found that 71 percent of cases with authoritarian leadership had incompatible outcomes, compared to only 53 percent of cases with no authoritarian leadership. Case studies further illustrated how authoritarian leaders blocked the effect of institutions. Thus, for example, Slovak President Meciar resisted institutional efforts to reinstall bilingual school certificates, pass a law on minority languages, and amend the election law. He was clearly guided by the political benefit he achieved from the issue outweighing any potential personal benefit from the institutions. In true authoritarian style, he was not concerned with the benefit to the country; his desire for power took priority when this conflicted with EU demands (Henderson 1999b, 233). As the EU continued to criticize Slovakia and Meciar, he became the political black sheep among the EU candidate states, making it even harder for him to make concessions, even if he wanted to. As one foreign ministry official observed, "Things got worse after the domestic political situation with the kidnapping of the president's son and the failed NATO referendum. . . . [A]fter these events, there was sort of no way back for Meciar. He had crossed a line politically."[14]

There are also cases, however, in which incentives worked, even with leaders such as Meciar. In the case of Slovakia's treaty with Hungary, for example, a barrage of international actors urged the singing of the treaty via letters, personal contacts, and so on. Although Meciar was generally prone to shrug off international critics, the social influence and incentives worked in this case because at this stage he still saw it in his own personal interest to improve his image with the West and his legitimacy as a statesman. This is why the role of authoritarian leadership is not clear cut. The key to getting political conditionality to work in the presence of strong authoritarian leadership is to aim the rewards at the interests of this leadership.

Similarly, the presence or absence of minority representation in the government coalition is naturally an important factor. Thus, although the number of actual cases is quite small in this study, 75 percent of cases with minorities in government had compatible outcomes contrary to only 21 percent of cases with no minority representation. The case studies showed how it was frequently possible to attribute a good outcome to the bargaining power of minorities in a coalition government. For example, when the education law in Romania eventually passed in a version that satisfied the minorities in 1999, this was primarily because of the bargaining power of the minorities within the government. The situation was similar when

Romania finally passed a law on the status of the civil service in 1999, allowing Hungarians to communicate with officials in Hungarian. In 1998 ethnic Hungarians in the Slovak government also helped push for the reinstatement of bilingual school certificates and the passage of a minority language law.

On the surface, an explanation relying on the presence of minorities in government downplays the role of international institutions. First, note, however, that minorities were rarely part of the government coalition, and were never part of the government in Estonia or Latvia. Thus, this factor cannot explain the general pattern of outcomes. Second, that the reason the Slovak and Romanian governments included minorities in the first place was partly because of expectations and earlier influence on the opposition parties.[15] Thus, the international community had an indirect effect even in these cases. Finally, as discussed in the cases and under alternative explanations, domestic ethnic groups (as well as their homelands) also influenced the outcomes by using international institutions as forums for articulating their grievances and demanding greater respect for their rights.

Finally, the case studies show that the ethnic minority representation in government is no guarantee for such policies. In Slovakia and Romania, the minorities did not get what they wanted on language and education issues, and they themselves stressed that the influence of the international community was key to the cooperation achieved.

In summary, it would be an omission to discount either the ability of authoritarian leaders to block a positive response to institutional membership incentives or the bargaining power of minorities in government. Minorities only participated in governments in eight of sixty-four cases in this study. Likewise, an authoritarian leader was present in only seventeen. Thus, naturally, the explanatory power of these variables is limited. Indeed, perhaps due to the smaller size of the data set, regression analysis finds that the factors are not statistically significant. Noticeably, however, even when controlling for authoritarian leaders or ethnic minorities in government, the size and significance of the other explanatory variables—normative pressure only, incentives and pressure, and domestic opposition—remain consistent. This suggests that the findings about these variables are robust.

Confidence in Admission

The case studies suggest that other factors influence the effectiveness of conditionality. The ideal circumstance for the use of conditionality is when countries believe they have a fair chance of admission but cannot take it for granted. Both overconfidence and too great pessimism about admission prospects decrease the effectiveness of membership incentives. Thus, for example, when states consider themselves geopolitically significant or if institutions or individual member states frequently support their admission for other reasons, issue linkage is less effective. Subsequently, outcomes are less favorable for minorities. Similarly, when states struggle economically and institutions or member states rarely support their admission or specifically express concerns about their admission for other reasons, issue linkage is less effective. Slovakia and Romania best displayed these tendencies.

In the case of Slovakia, the government often took CE and EU admission for granted. Meciar believed that the EU would admit Slovakia without these concessions. He argued publicly that Slovakia was too important for the EU to shun, and he repeatedly reassured the citizenry that the West "has no other option than to embrace Slovakia."[16] He believed that Slovakia's geographic location alone was a ticket to the EU. At a rally in October 1995, Meciar said that there was no need to worry about the admission of Slovakia to the EU "because they need us, for we are a country with an exceptionally good geopolitical situation" (Wlachovsky 1997, 46). As a result, Slovakia questioned some of the EU "threats" of withholding admission. While the high degree of domestic opposition naturally was a key source of some of the conditionality failures in Slovakia, this overconfidence further decreased the effectiveness of the membership conditionality.

In Romania, on the other hand, the economic situation dimmed hopes of admission. On July 18, 1995, after a Paris meeting of the Romanian, German, and French foreign ministers, France and Germany issued a joint statement supporting Romania's drive to join the EU. They stressed, however, that it was not possible to set a timetable for Romania's EU membership, adding that intensified economic reform, privatization, and the development of a market economy were key conditions.[17] Thus, in essence the West was saying that Romania would not join the EU in the near future because its economy was too poor.[18] This greatly diminished the power of the incentive for Romania. Indeed, this resulted in a sort of preemptive blow to the use of membership incentives as a tool because it made the EU more hesitant to even use conditionality in Romania.

In Latvia and Estonia, however, politicians believed in their EU admission prospects but also understood that they were competing with other candidates and could not take admission for granted. Thus, the EU membership conditionality was credible and effective, and indeed never failed to produce at least some improvement.

Structuring Incentives

The case studies made it particularly clear that issue linkage is more effective when institutions use a gradual admission process. Thus, the greater the use of a series of steps in the admission process and the greater the use of pronouncements, declarations, demarches, and other communication clearly linking action and admission progress, the easier it was for institutions to encourage reform. If an institution relied extensively on reports, meetings, and other tools to evaluate a state's status in the admission process, this increased the ability of the institution to reward or punish, and thus to encourage reform. Efforts to meet the institutional requirements increased as such events neared. Frequently, a parliament would schedule important decisions just before key institutional events. The case of stateless children in Estonia is a particularly good illustration of the usefulness of the EU's gradual accession process. The issue received a marked increase in attention after the EU entered the debate and connected the issue to membership and linked the timing of policy changes to EU summits and upcoming important decisions. Indeed, the government's decision to discuss the amendments came just a few days before the EU summit that would decide which countries would be invited to open negotiations with the EU. This type of dynamic was also evident in the case of the language law in Latvia. The Latvian parliament finally approved an amended version of the controversial language law on December 9, 1999, just as the EU was meeting in Helsinki to decide candidates' status on the admission process.

Thus, several cases demonstrated the effect of the EU gradual admission process while other cases displayed the inverse effect: how the CE lost leverage because it lacked such gradual steps. For example, although Friedrich König, a CE parliamentary assembly rapporteur, had told Radio Bucharest after a 1993 visit that Romania needed to pass a law on national minorities, the CE invited Romania to join based on the government's promise to pass such a law later. Subsequently, the law never passed. Similarly, in Slovakia, the Meciar government completely reneged on commitments to pass legislation on the use of ethnic personal and place names, and indeed withdrew legislation on the table after Slovakia joined the CE. The changes did finally pass, but only because of a change in government. Illustrating that this was not just an institutional difference between the EU and the CE, the CE did effectively use more preadmission monitoring in Latvia, which introduced a series of meetings and stages of approval necessary before admission. The modification of the citizenship law was directly linked to the CE's aggressive involvement via extensive monitoring and negotiations before admission.

Extending the Analysis: Theory, Policy Lessons,
   and Remaining Questions

This study has addressed the debate about when and why states comply with international laws and norms as well as the more recent debate about the domestic effect of international institutions. Evaluating the findings on both persuasion and conditionality, it has contributed to the more general debate between the rational choice and constructivist approaches to international institutions and has advanced it beyond "either/or" by actually including both approaches and submitting them to unified testing. As such, this study has been unique in its treatment of actors as both norm-guided and cost-benefit-calculating individuals. By including both approaches in a common framework, the study has been able to give a more complete account of the relevant events and relationships.

As argued in chapter 1, the use of normative pressure in the form of persuasion or social influence is a subcase of socialization. Thus, by examining several specific instances of international institutions' effort to use normative pressure to change state behavior, the study provided new empirical data about socialization. While the study did not address the traditional debate about whether socialization efforts work via a constructivist or rationalist mechanism, the case studies provided evidence of the behavioral effects (or lack thereof), and cast new light on the conditions for when socialization efforts can change policy. Specifically, the study probed whether socialization efforts can work in the absence of further incentives and, if so, what domestic political conditions makes this possible. The study found that in most cases socialization efforts by themselves only worked when the domestic opposition was weak and the beliefs and calculations of the key actors did not require major adjustment. For cases of stronger domestic opposition, however, the findings suggested that the addition of incentives was necessary. This finding aligns with the work of some scholars who have suggested that socialization primarily works only in tandem with material incentives (Ikenberry and Kupchan 1990; Sikkink 1993; Klotz 1996).[19] Thus, the study deepens our understanding of conditions for when socialization can change behavior.

The study also contributes to the body of research on positive incentives and specifically on political conditionality (Davis 2000; Bernauer 1999, 157). While research has often focused on negative incentives such as trade sanctions, deterrence, military intervention, and so on, the relatively high success rate for membership conditionality outlined here suggests that positive incentives promote policy change by facilitating constructive dialogue, greater interaction, and greater understanding (Cortright 1997, 11; Long 1996). Case studies reveal how states communicate extensively with international institutions about domestic legislation. Besides engaging in extensive meetings and correspondence, legislatures at times even send drafts for comments to the international institutions or directly solicit their input by inviting them to participate in the formulation of policy. This was the case, for example, with the participation in 1990 of the CE in the formulation of the Romanian Constitution and also with Latvia's implementation policy on the language law.[20] Thus, contrary to the more skeptical research on economic conditionality by the World Bank and the IMF (Killick 1996; Gilbert, Hopkins, Powell, and Roy 1997, 509n; Nelson 1996; Collier 1997; Killick with Ramani and Marr 1998), this study argues that the use of political conditionality by European institutions has been quite successful—even though the requirements intruded into the core socio-political attributes of these states. Most importantly, while domestic opposition does impede the effect of positive incentives, when membership conditionality is very attractive—as in the European case—politicians are willing to compromise on even quite controversial issues. This suggests that institutions can apply conditionality to require "peace reforms" that will decrease conflict (Boyce and Pastor 1998; Reinicke 1996; World Bank 1997, 5, 19; Boyce 1996).

Further, the study has some particularly interesting implications about the benefit of an incremental membership admission process. The findings suggest that a series of gradual admission steps provides opportunities to build trust and confidence, and ultimately increase the effectiveness of the conditionality.

Finally, the study contributes to the study of ethnic minority politics, both by expanding the empirical case studies but more importantly by integrating the often-neglected factor of the international community to the study of domestic ethnic minority policies (Brubaker 1995). The study also has added to more general international relations research by examining in detail how and when institutions have been able to influence the domestic politics of candidate states and new member states.

Policy Lessons

John Harsanyi, recipient of the 1994 Nobel Prize in Economics, noted in 1962 that "one of the main purposes for which social scientists use the concept of A's power over B is for the description of the policy possibilities open to A" (Harsanyi 1962). The primary policy implication of this study comes from the evidence that links institutional membership incentives to behavior as an effective tool for intervention in domestic political situations. Also, not only is membership conditionality effective in the case of ethnic politics, but it can be employed preemptively (Hurlburt 1997, 226). Thus, the study is an argument for the international community to consider more carefully how it can use the incentive of membership in international institutions to achieve its goals. Indeed, institutions may also be able to retain leverage after admission if institutions can create additional credible incentives for member states.

Notably, even though many domestic situations appear difficult and it may be tempting to ignore them, the appeal of membership can overcome even quite strong domestic opposition. Conversely, to minimize their failure to influence domestic policy, institutions should limit the use of normative pressure alone to "easier cases"—that is, where the policy gap is small, where nationalists have only a weak influence, or where ethnic minorities already are part of a government coalition.

To maximize their influence, member states and international institutions should keep several things in mind. First, directly linking policy and incentives is important, but this does not mean that normative pressure can be abandoned. Indeed, in this study the European institutions always used conditionality in addition to normative pressure not as a substitute for it. Thus, institutions continued efforts to persuade even after they linked membership to policy change, and the case studies suggest a dynamic relationship between these two approaches. While membership conditionality drives policy changes, normative efforts often guide them. Thus, combining the two methods seems not only effective, but also wise.

Second, the message must be clear and preferably formal. The institutions cannot expect states to produce favorable policy outcomes just because they are candidates for membership in international institutions. Institutions need to specifically formulate requirements. An institution's silence often results in poor outcomes, even if membership is being discussed at the same time. Tacit assumptions and ambiguity beget evasion rather than results.

Third, coordination and cooperation between institutions is crucial, and their messages must align. If one institution declares a policy satisfactory, a country can use this as a shield against the criticism of other institutions. This happened in some cases in which the OSCE and the Council of Europe sent contradictory signals.

Fourth, the more the merrier: as many institutions as possible should criticize worrisome policies. If one institution, the OSCE, for example, is alone in its criticism, the silence of the others diminishes the authority of the recommendation. This happened in several cases in which, for example, the EU did not participate in criticism. States can easily interpret the lack of full institutional involvement, while it may have other causes, as a tacit lack of agreement with the proffered recommendations.

Fifth, timing matters. Forwarding advice early in the policy process is best. In the early 1990s for example, owing to the timing of the establishment of his office, the HCNM sometimes criticized policies quite late in the process. This was seldom effective. Nevertheless, institutions should not give up just because a law has already been passed. The case studies showed several instances of a president returned a law to parliament for successful revision.

Sixth, institutions should be consistent. If an institution forwards a criticism, the failure to follow-up decreases the credibility of the institutions. To its detriment, the CE often raised concerns in the early 1990s only to abandon the issues later. This not only decreases the effectiveness of the specific recommendation, but also of future ones.

Seventh, and related to the above, membership conditionality works best when the recipient must make the changes before membership. When institutions use a post-admission strategy, states often fail to keep their promises. This happened repeatedly in connection with commitments states made when joining the CE. Thus, institutions should consider carefully what they are actually achieving by admitting states based purely on promises of changed behavior.

Eighth, if institutions have monitoring privileges in a candidate state or even in a member state, as do the CE and the OSCE, criticism should be transparent, formal, and preferably connected to some consequence. Indeed, it may be ideal for institutions if they can actually suspend membership or the admission process or otherwise withdraw membership or association benefits. This point was apparent in the EU's use of annual reports, which always received great attention from candidate countries eager for favorable assessment. Since implementation tends to lag behind policy, institutions should continue to monitor and take appropriate measures if the implementation is not consistent with the adopted policy. Thus, for example, it took several steps of revisions of the citizenship legislation in the Baltic States before the international institutions were satisfied with both the policy and the implementation. Indeed, challenges remain.

Ninth, institutions should pay attention to the structure of their admission process. An extended process with multiple concrete steps maximizes the opportunities for influence because it builds confidence while retaining future incentives. Thus, the EU's extended process provides many more opportunities for influence than does either the CE's process or the OSCE's easy process. While the size of their carrots differed, even the Council of Europe showed variation in its ability to influence policy depending on how it approached the admission process.

Remaining Questions: Durability, Sui Generis,
  Paper Compliance, and Future Research

Since this study concludes that membership conditionality is a highly effective strategy, the question of the durability of the policy changes naturally emerges. The conformance may just disappear with the incentive. Particularly in the case of membership incentives, should we not expect to see changes reversed after admission? In connection with EU conditionality, that may be a particular concern, as the entry requirements related to ethnic minorities were never generalized and are not components of the EU body of law.

Actually, both constructivists and rationalists have to answer the question of durability. Rationalists can ask constructivists whether the policy changes will not just disappear if the persons whose belief change drove the policy fall out of power.[21] Thus, the question about durability is general (Fearon and Wendt, 2002).

The answer depends on factors driving the initial change in behavior. If changes in belief drove the policies, the durability should be ensured if the socialized actors stay in power, or if the actors replacing the socialized actors have similar normative beliefs (Vachudova, 2001; Pridham 1999, 1236–38). If payoffs calculations drove behavior change, then the durability of the behavior should be assured if an incentive structure stays in place. This may happen even after admission if membership benefits or membership itself may be suspended or sanctioned, and if the country has a high reliance on those benefits with few or no alternative providers of this benefit. In either case, however, the policy changes may endure even if these conditions are not met. This may be the case if the behavior has become routinized in the country (Feason and Wendt 2002, 62) or if the policy is logistically difficult to reverse because, for example, it may take larger majorities to reverse a policy than it did to adopt it. Such "status quo bias" is particularly prevalent in systems with multiple veto points (Tsebelis 1995). There may also be audience costs of reversing policies for politicians who have publicly committed to the policy (Fearon 1994).

Testing the durability of the policy changes and the factors that influence it would be a good topic for further research. Indeed, some research suggests that the current members of the EU continue to respond to various "adaptational pressures" from the Union (Cowles, Caporaso, and Risse 2001). The Copenhagen Criteria on the "respect for minorities," however, is not part of the *aquis communitaire*, and thus the truth shall not be fully known, of course, until some years after these countries join the EU in May 2004.

Sui Generis

While history may repeat itself, this seldom means that we can expect much actual resemblance over time. Thus, asking how well these findings transfer to other institutions, non-European regions, and other uses of conditionality is entirely appropriate. First, the EU is clearly unique. But there have been similar uses of conditionality in NATO and in WTO entrance negotiations. The Organization of American States and Mersocur (Southern Common Market) have also had human–rights related requirements. The Organization of Economic Cooperation and Development (OECD), which has used political criteria in its development assistance committee, is also debating more overt membership criteria for the swelling applicant pool. Thus, "clubs" will continue to play a large part in global cooperation. Lessons about inclusion and exclusion may apply to them. As the United States promotes a free trade area in the Middle East and in general, and as free trade areas arise in other regions, the natural impulse will be for inclusion. This study implies that the point of leverage is greatest before entry. Thus, while the creation of other attractive organizations depends on the inclusion of key states, their establishment may also build potential for promoters of political liberalization to use a more gradual admission to encourage democratic reforms. Thus, a careful balance exists between inclusion to build an organization, and exclusion to exert leverage. In sum, the lessons of normative pressure and membership conditionality promise to have increasing relevance as nations reshape global cooperation.

Second is the question of whether these findings are limited to the European arena. Even if this is the case, this would not make the study meaningless because Europe continues have great implications for the rest of the world. Also, the insights apply to broader European regions as such candidates as Turkey and the Balkan States queue for membership. To date, however, the use of political conditionality in other regions is scant. Like the IMF and World Bank "good governance" requirements, which in some cases includes respect for human rights and political freedoms, most uses of political conditionality in other regions are related to economic assistance, as for example the human rights clauses in the EU aid program. This complicates parallels to political conditionality in connection with organizational membership. Regional organizations are changing rapidly, however, and comparative work on their design and efficacy is emerging.[22] Further, while current regional comparisons are weak, the findings may extend to other geographical regions in the future.

Finally, the theoretical implications about membership conditionality may extend to other incentive use. The model of in-depth engagement and clear conditionality may align well with evaluations of aid conditionality, that suggest an increased need for "ownership," which, though different from normative pressure, is not unrelated in that it points to the need for engagement and dialogue.

Paper Compliance

All studies of compliance have to confront potential discrepancy between policy and implementation. Indeed, this study did consider implementation in several cases. Thus, cases such as Baltic citizenship policy as well as the treaties with Hungary specifically discuss implementation failures. Not all ethnic minority problems are results of implementation failures per se vis-à-vis the European institutions. In some cases they were simply casualties of institutions selective engagement. The most obvious example here is the treatment of the Roma, which at least until recently, was low or even ignored on the institutional agenda (Vermeersch 2002). Generally, however, implementation of the policies on ethnic minorities is lagging, which can be either good or bad for ethnic minorities, depending on the character of the legislation. In an education policy in which the parliament may vote to enforce the state language as the only language of instruction, slow implementation benefits minorities. Likewise, in a language policy in which the state language may be required to hold certain positions, it benefits the ethnic minority if the state does not have the capacity to enforce that policy. On the other hand, lagging implementation on the right to travel documents will harm minorities who depend on such documentation. Thus, the implementation lag goes both ways and does not bias the analysis systematically. Even if one takes the study at face value, for policy impact only, such changes are still significant steps in the right direction. The future of the countries within the EU makes adherence to these policies more likely.

Future Research

Future research should first focus on disentangling the effects of normative pressure and conditionality further. This may occur in two ways. First, future scholars can try to isolate the causal *pathways* of constructivist and rationalist change, as indeed several scholars are trying to do. Second, from a policy perspective it would be useful to isolate the *effects* of conditionality and softer diplomatic tools. This study has only done so only partly, as discussed, because whereas normative pressure sometimes occurred alone, conditionality always occurred together with normative pressure. The case studies addressed this weakness to some extent by teasing out the chain of events and permitting for counterfactual analysis. Ironically, case study may be the only available method to isolate effects. That is, finding a topic in which the data would allow for statistical isolation of the conditionality effect from the effect of normative pressure is unlikely. It would be useful, however, if future research could find cases of conditionality applied in the absence of more persuasive efforts. One potential comparison of the two levels of engagement would be of specific human rights clauses that various national or institutional donors attach to aid. Such data exist in the framework of "good governance" studies, but a specific examination of stated policy goals and careful process tracing, as in the case of this study, would be needed. If there are cases in which donor engagement is not very extensive, then such cases may provide evidence of the independent effect of conditionality. Indeed, governments on the receiving end of aid with human rights clauses have repeatedly criticized donor of interference in sovereignty and paternalism, suggesting that there is perhaps more "ordering" than "communicating." A study of political conditionality in Zambia specifically stresses the need for more human rights education and training—apparently a criticism of too-blunt conditionality lacking engagement.[23]

The other viable strand of future research is to study the interactive effects between domestic factors and international engagement. Here, research may benefit from extension to other issues such as the death penalty, for example, or even to economic or environmental areas,[24] where the domestic factors would tend to vary greatly from those in this study. Such studies may cast further light on the relative importance of broad domestic opposition versus narrow extremist opposition, and on the role of authoritarian leadership and organized domestic interests.

A FINAL WORD

The process of admitting new states to international organizations presents a unique opportunity: in an environment in which international actors often find it difficult to implement global policy priorities on the domestic policy level, linking membership to behavior is a powerful tool. While domestic opposition to institutional goals naturally hampers their influence, international institutions can nevertheless be extremely effective—even when the domestic opposition is strong or the prevailing leadership is uncooperative. Thus, as regional institutions outside Europe may imitate elements of the EU in the future (Keohane 2002), they may take membership requirements seriously and incorporate gradual levers into the admission process. Importantly, however, norm-based efforts always accompanied membership conditionality, often guiding the substance of the requirements. Thus, while international institutions wishing to duplicate the European model should not rely solely on persuasion, social influence, and other forms of normative pressure, they risk weakening their impact if they neglect these approaches.

Methods

Table I.a
Type of involvement by domestic opposition

	Weak	Weak to Moderate	Moderate	Moderate to Strong	Strong	Total
No involvement	4	2	8	5	1	20
Normative pressure only	0	1	9	1	14	25
Membership conditionality	1	4	2	4	8	19
Total involvement	1	5	11	5	22	44
Total	5	7	19	10	23	64

Table I.b
Determinants of involvement (regression I) and determinants of using membership incentives (regression II)

Independent variable	Regression 1	Regression 2
Constant	-1.681891	-1.271023
Nationalism	0.7219523**	0.1120849
n	64	64
log likelihood	-34.53426	-38.789465
Pseudo R^2	0.1312	0.0035
Model	logit	logit

Table I.c
Involvement by country

	Estonia	Latvia	Romania	Slovakia	Total
No involvement	7 (39%)	9 (43%)	4 (36%)	0 (0%)	20 (31%)
Normative pressure only	6 (33%)	7 (33%)	5 (45%)	7 (50%)	25 (39%)
Membership conditionality	5 (28%)	5 (24%)	2 (18%)	7 (50%)	19 (30%)
Total	18	21	11	14	64

Outcome Classification Scheme

TABLE II

	Not compatible	Partly compatible	Compatible
Institutional involvement	The legislature worsened the policy or left a poor policy at the status quo ignoring recommendations	The legislature made moderate improvement in accord with some recommendations (enticement) or partly modified some negative changes (restraint)	The legislature followed the institutions' recommendations by either making a recommended improvement (enticement) or (in a few instances) by not passing a criticized proposal (restraint)
No institutional involvement	The legislature worsened the policy or left a poor policy at the status quo	The legislature made some moderate improvement to the status quo or partly modified some negative changes	The legislature made some significant improvement or dropped a plan to pass a worse law

For a discussion of enticement versus restraint, see chapter 2.

Predicted Probabilities

Table III
Predicted probabilities for a compatible outcome: expanded

	Not compatible (probability)	Partly compatible (probability)	Compatible (probability)
Strong domestic opposition			
Institutions not involved	.99	.01	.00
Normative pressure only	.90	.07	.03
Membership conditionality	.18	.25	.57
Moderate domestic opposition			
Institutions not involved	.90	.07	.03
Normative pressure only	.49	.28	.23
Membership conditionality	.02*	.05*	.93*
Weak domestic opposition			
Institutions not involved	.47	.29	.24
Normative pressure only	.09*	.17*	.74*
Membership conditionality	.00	.01	.99

*These calculations are based on fewer than five observations and should be interpreted with extra caution.

Interviews

Aija Priedite, Director, Latvian National Language Training Programme
Martins Mits, Assistant Director, Latvian Institute on Human Rights
Dr. Ineta Ziemele, Director, Latvian Institute on Human Rights
Heidi Bottolfs, Member, OSCE Mission to Latvia
Zeneta Ozolina, Assistant to Geoffrey Barrett
Geoffrey Barrett, First Councilor, Delegation of the European Commission to
    Latvia
Inga Reine, Lawyer, National Human Rights Office
Juris Cibuïs, Deputy Head, Department of Foreign Relations and Press,
    Naturalisation Board
Inese Birzniece, MP, Latvia's Way
Boris Tsilevich, MP, For Human Rights in United Latvia
Aleksandrs Kirsteins, MP, People's Party (previously a member of LNNK)
Dr. Andrejs Pozarnovs, MP, TB/ LNNK, faction leader
Andrejs Pantelejevs, MP, Latvian Way
Janis Jurkans, MP, For Human Rights in United Latvia, faction leader and party
    founder
Pauls Raudseps, Managing Editor, *Diena* (Latvia's main newspaper)
Anna Stroja, Journalist covering ethnic Russian issues, *Diena*
Nils Muiznieks, Director, Latvian Center for Human Rights and Ethnic Studies,
    Program Director, Human Rights and Tolerance Program, Soros Foundation
Baiba Laizane, Advisor to the Prime Minister
Kristine Kruma, Head of the Unit of International Organisations and Human
    Rights Policy, Latvian Foreign Ministry
Mark Dayton, Advisor to the Foreign Minister
Eriks Leitis, Director, NGO Centre
Ilmars Mezs, Head of the Office, IOM International Organisation for Migration
    in Latvia
Leonid Raihman, Cochairman, Latvian Human Rights Committee

Falk Lange, Advisor to the HCNM
Craig Oliphant, Advisor to the HCNM
Gajus Scheltema, Personal Assistant to the HCNM

John Packer, Personal Assistant to the HCNM
Zdenka Machnyikova, Deputy Legal Advisor to the HCNM
Larissa Gabriel, Foundation on Ethnic Relations

IN BRUSSELS, OCTOBER 1998 (EU)

Katarina Areskoug, Latvian Desk Officer in the European Commission, DG1A
  (Directorate General for External Relations)
Ana Blanca Gallo Alvarez, Estonia Desk Officer, European Commission, DG1A
Michael Rupp, European Commission, DG1A
Georg Ziegler, European Commission, DG1A
Gianluca Brunetti, Administrator, Committee on Foreign Affairs, European
  Parliament
Rosa Maria Guida, European Commission, DG1A
Franz Cermak, Political Counsellor in Charge of Coordination of Political
  Relations—Central Europe
Catherine Magnant, European Commission, DG1A, the Czech Republic
Mr. Josep Lloveras, Team Leader, Slovak Republic, European Commission, DG1A
John Penny, Human Rights and Democratization, European Commission, DG1A
Axel Walldén, Desk officer, Balkan countries, European Commission, DG1A
Jean Trestour, Desk officer, Poland, Baltic States, European Commission, DG1A
Graham Avery, Commission official, held various key positions during the 1990s
  enlargement
Michael Leigh, Chief Negotiator with the Czech Republic
Fraser Cameron, Political Adviser, European Commission, DG1A.
Helen Cambell, European Commission, Member of Cabinet of Commissioner
  Hans van den Broek
Adam Isaacs, Documentation Task Force on Enlargement, European Parliament
Soveiga Silkalna, First Secretary, Mission of the Republic of Latvia to the European
  Union
Peter Javorcik, First Secretary, Mission of the Slovak Republic to the EU

IN BRUSSELS, JUNE 1999 (EU)

Katarina Areskoug, Enlargement Process, Pre-accession Strategy and Europe
  Agreements, European Commission, DG1A
Ricardo Pascal Bremon, Deputy Head of Unit, Enlargement porces, Pre-accession
  strategy and Europe Agreements, European Commission, DG1A
Drs. Ion Jinga, Minister-Counsellor, Deputy Head of Mission, Mission of Romania
  to the European Union
Hans Christian Stausbøll, Administrator, Desk Officer, Romania, European Com-
  mission, DG1A
Dr. Angel Vinas, Director, Multilateral Relations, European Commission, DG1A

Anne Härmaste, Second Secretary, Press and Information, Mission of Estonia to the European Union

Allan Rosas, Principal Legal Advisor, European Commission, Legal Service

Miroslav Adamis, First Secretary, Mission of the Slovak Republic to the European Union

Bettian Dosier, Desk Officer, Latvia, European Commission, DG1A

Ana Blanca Gallo Alvarez, Estonia Desk Officer, European Commission, DG1A

Gerd Tebbe*, "Planning & Analysis" Unit Directorate-General "External Relations: Europe & the new independent States, common foreign & security policy & external missions," European Commission

Marc Jorna*, Assistant to the Director-General of the Accession Negotiations Task Force, European Commission

Leon Brittan*, Vice-President of the European Commission

ESTONIA

Vello Pettai, Lecturer at Tartu University, Department of Political Science

Katrin Savomägi, Head of the Foreign Relations and European Integration Department, Estonia Citizenship and Migration Board

Klara Hallik, Former Minister of Ethnic Affairs, Former Deputy of the Supreme Soviet, Professor, Talinu Pedagogical University

Andra Veidemann, Chairman, Balance Non-Governmental Organization

Kai Willadsen, Advisor, EU Phare Programme, European Union, Delegation of the European Commission in Estonia

Tanel Mätlik, Counsellor to the Minister of Ethnic Affairs

Dr. Aleksandr Dusman, Director, Ida-Virumaa Integration Center

Aleksei Semjonov, Director, Legal Information Centre for Human Rights

Neil Brennan, First Secretary, OSCE Mission to Estonia

Sulev Valdmaa, Head of the Centre, Jaan Tönissoni Instituut

Henrik Hololei, Head of the European Integration Office, Ministry of the Interior

Kristina Mauer, Programme Officer, United Nations Development Programme

Eino Tamm, Former Member of Paliament 1993–1999

Liia Hanni, Member of Parliament since 1990

Mart Nutt, Member of Parliament since 1992

Marten Kokk, Director of the Bureau of Human Rights in Estonian Ministry of Foreign Affairs

* These were small group meetings with question and answer opportunities

Notes

1. Not until May 2002, outside the timeframe of this study, did Latvia finally abolish the language proficiency requirements for elections (Saeima [Latvian Parliament], bills 1258 and 1259).

2. Chapter 4 discusses these cases in greater depth.

3. International legal documents provide no authoritative definition of what constitutes a minority. In this study I treat as minorities Hungarians in Romania and Slovakia, as well as Russians and Russian speakers in Latvia and Estonia. Although the EU was formerly known as the European Community, I refer to it as the EU in all instances. Similarly, I refer to the OSCE at all times, although the OSCE was formerly the Conference on Security and Cooperation in Europe before 1995.

4. One notable exception is the work of Checkel 2000a and 2001. Efforts to systematically study the impact of OSCE missions and the HCNM are also under way.

5. In the case of the EU, for example, aid and association status are also part of the path to membership and may be used strategically in the conditionality framework.

6. Article 93 of the Versailles Treaty and Articles 39, 40, and 46 of the Treaty of Neuilly specifically addressed the issue for Poland, Greece, and Yugoslavia. Diplomatic recognition of Czechoslovakia was contingent on acceptance of terms regarding ethnic minorities. The minorities treaties subjected all successor states to international scrutiny of their treatment of ethnic minorities (Raitz von Frentz 1999).

7. See, for example, Brubaker 1989.

8. For example, Michalchuk's thesis (1999) compares four countries and focuses specifically on minority rights but examines only the work of the OSCE and does not frame questions in the light of the literature of international institutions or of international influences on domestic politics. The same is true for Kemp 1999.

9. For a review of this literature see Horowitz 1985 and Brown 1997c.

10. "Bulgarian PM Admits Long, Hard Way Ahead to EU," *Reuters Wire Service*, April 14, 2000.

11. See Johnston 2001 for a good overview of socialization theories. See also Cortell and Davis 1996 (452–553) for a review of socialization theory. Scholars from multiple schools of thought have focused on such international norms and rules in the last decades. See for example Axelrod 1986; Nadelman 1990; Goertz and Diehl 1992; Finnemore 1993; Goldstein and Keohane 1993; Sikkink 1993b; Klotz 1966; Cortell and Davis 1996; Legro 1997; and Ikenberry and Kupchan 1990.

12. For a good discussion about the common ground of constructivist and rationalist methods and explanations, see Fearon and Wendt 2002.

13. Jacek Kucharczyk, a Polish political scientist, notes that popular support for joining the EU has dropped and that "the EU displays a kind of take-it-or-leave-it attitude. It gives the impression that enlargement is just a technical process. I like the idea of an enlarged political Europe: I would say that the candidate countries should be involved more closely as partners in the construction of a new Europe." John Lloyd, "A new wall for Europeans to climb over," *Financial Times*, January 11, 2000.

14. Recently, for example, Thomas Bernauer and Dieter Ruloff (1999) edited a volume on the politics of positive incentives in arms control. While this volume has made a significant contribution to the research on the use of positive incentives, it focuses on how states can use positive incentives to pay others to collaborate internationally and thus does not discuss how incentives can influence domestic politics as such.

15. Cartwright (1959, 33–34, n. 32) argues that such impressions profoundly influence the outcome of external influence attempts–.

16. "Austrian Parliament head wants European committee to watch government," *Agence France Presse*, March 15, 2000; "World News—Europe: Austria looks for end to political isolation in EU," *Financial Times*, April 13, 2000.

17. The primary documents are the Convention for the Protection of Human Rights and Fundamental Freedoms (1950, CE), the European Social Charter (1961, CE), the International Covenant on Civil and Political Rights regarding persons belonging to ethnic linguistic or religious minorities (1966, UN), the Universal Declaration of Human Rights (1948, UN), Recommendation 1201 (1993, CE), the European Charter on the Protection of Minority Languages (1992, CE), the Framework Convention for the Protection of National Minorities (1994, CE), the Copenhagen Document (OSCE, 1990), the Hague recommendations regarding the Education Rights of National Minorities (OSCE, 1996), and the OSCE recommendations regarding the linguistic rights of minorities (OSCE, 1998).

18. The percentage of ethnic Latvians and Estonians peaked in the post-Holocaust years. In the 1930s the relative share of each population had been about 10 percent lower.

19. Welsh 1993 discusses domestic politics and ethnic issues.

20. Latvia and Estonia "circumvented" the 1961 Convention on the Reduction of Statelessness because they asserted their status as continuous states (Gelazis 2000).

21. Determining the causes for this variance is outside the scope of this chapter, but one could argue that it was a product of demographic differences and perhaps differences in the personalities of political leadership.

22. FF and LNIM merged in 1997 to become FF/LNIM, often referred to as TB/LNNK, the Latvian acronym.

23. In 1994, 46 percent of ethnic Latvians thought either definitely or possibly that conflicts between Latvians and Russians living in Latvia were a threat to peace

and security. This changed to 42 percent in 1995 but rose again to 45 percent in 1997. In Estonia the comparable percentages were 69, 50, and 57, respectively. When asked whether hard-line nationalist politicians were a threat to peace and security in Latvia, 45 percent of ethnic Latvians in 1995 thought definitely or possibly; by 1997 this had risen to 48 percent. In Estonia the comparable percentages were 35 and 40, respectively, displaying a rise in both countries. Ethnic Russians showed even greater concern in both countries (Rose et al. 1994a; Rose et al. 1994b; Rose et al. 1995; Rose et al. 1997).

24. The circumstances of this incident are still debated, and there is no agreement on the exact numbers of wounded or dead, estimates of the death toll ranging from four to twelve ("Power of the pulpit: Politics: Laszlo Tokes used his role as a minister to speak against the corrupt Romanian regime, now he speaks on behalf of Romania's fledgling democracy," *Los Angeles Times*, March 26, 1990.

25. Peter Gross and Vladimor Tismaneanu write, "In September 1997, the Greater Romanian Party, the Socialist Labor Party, and representatives of the Party of Romanian National Unity—all nationalistic, xenophobic, and outspokenly anti-liberal parties—announced they would form a coalition to 'put a stop to the crisis situation and anarchy' in the country" (1997, 30).

26. Author's interview, Gregorij Meseznikov, President of the Slovak Institute for Public Affairs, Bratislava, February 8, 2000.

27. Author's interview, Juraj Hrabko, General Director, Section on Human Rights and Minorities, Slovak Government, Bratislava, February 10, 2000.

28. Author's interview, members of the Slovak Foreign Policy Association, Bratislava, February 8, 2000.

29. All but Romania, who was already a member, joined the OSCE when they became independent, without any substantive conditions attached.

30. For more information, see Helsinki Document 1992, chapter III, paragraphs 12–16.

31. See the Helsinki Decisions of July 1992. The HCNM's role is to identify—and seek early resolution of—ethnic tensions that might endanger peace, stability, or friendly relations between the participating states of the OSCE. His mandate describes him as "an instrument of conflict prevention at the earliest possible stage." Operating independently of all parties involved, the HCNM is empowered to conduct on-site missions and to engage in preventive diplomacy at the earliest stages of tension.

32. Council of Europe opinion no. 183 (1995) and opinion no. 170 (1993).

33. Article 11, the most debated of the articles in the recommendation, states, "In the regions where they are a majority, the persons belonging to a national minority shall have the right to have at their disposal appropriate local or autonomous authorities or to have a special status, matching this specific historical and territorial situation and in accordance with the domestic legislation of the State." There have been controversies over the interpretation of this article, which most states emphasize neither suggests territorial autonomy nor grants collective rights to minorities. For extensive discussion on this issue, see *Report on the Protection of the Rights of Minorities*, Rapporteur: Mr. Bindig, June 5, 1996, Doc. 7572, including its appendixes.

34. *Report on the Protection of the Rights of Minorities*, Rapporteur: Mr. Bindig, June 5, 1996, Doc. 7572.

35. Full text of the treaty exists on the Internet at http://www.coe.fr/eng/legaltxt/148e.htm.

36. Only after six years did the charter fulfill the conditions of five ratifications before it finally entered into force on March 1, 1998.

37. For a list of signatories, see http://www.coe.fr/tablconv/148t.htm.

38. Full text of the treaty exists on the internet at http://conventions.coe.int/treaty/EN/cadreprincipal.htm.

39. Articles 24 and 26, *Framework Convention for the Protection of National Minorities*.

40. To date, Estonia, Slovakia, and Romania have provided such a report, but Latvia has not. See http://www.humanrights.coe.int/minorities/Eng/FrameworkConvention/StateReports/Toc.htm.

41. Initially, in the Treaty on European Union, member states undertook to uphold the principles of democracy and respect for human rights. Before 1990, however, there was no specific mention of minority rights. Indeed, some member states specifically emphasized the unity of the state rather than special minority arrangements (Estonaez 1995, supra note 1, 133–). France, for example, formulated a reservation to Article 27 of the International Covenant on Civil and Political Rights regarding persons belonging to ethnic, linguistic, or religious minorities (*Human Rights: Status of International Instruments* [1987]: 35). Greece ratified the covenant only in 1997.

42. European Council in Copenhagen, June 21–22, 1993, Conclusions of the Presidency, SN 180/93, p. 13.

43. Author's interview, Allan Rosas, Principal Legal Advisor to the European Commission, Brussels, June 1999.

44. *Conclusions of the European Council*, PE 167.145, paragraph 25.

45. This started with the 1997 Agenda 2000 and continued with the accession partnerships and commission reports released every fall.

46. The 1998 Eurobarometer survey of policymakers in ten EU candidate countries found that 80 percent had a positive view and 3 percent had a negative view of the EU, a considerably more positive perspective than found among the general populations of the candidate countries, of which 50 percent had a positive view, 29 percent a neutral view, and 6 percent a negative view (*Central and Eastern Eurobarometer*, no. 8, March 1998, European Commission). This view is also evident in politicians' rhetoric and in the programs of all the parties.

47. " 'Good Shepherd' gathers E. European states to the gold: As Council of Europe Secretary General, Catherine Lalumiere works to bring former East Bloc members into her organization to help them smooth their transition to democracy," *Los Angeles Times*, March 19, 1991.

48. "Council of Europe leader pledges support to Latvia," *Baltic News Service*, January 10, 1995.

49. "Council of Europe Secretary-General in talks on council membership, minorities," *BBC Summary of World Broadcasts*, September 3, 1993.

50. "The Slovak Republic: Meciar on IMF 'compromise,' Slovakia's admission to Council of Europe," *BBC Summary of World Broadcasts*, June 22, 1993.

51. "Latvia to join Council of Europe in early 1995," *Euro-East*, November 15, 1994.

52. *Activities of the Council of Europe*, 1990 Report, Strasbourg: Council of Europe Press, 1991, 6; Manas 1996, 106–11.

53. "Slovakia asks for Italy's support in European integration," *CTK National News Wire*, October 19, 1993.

54. For quotations from CE officials stressing the importance of their place in the candidate queue, see Schimmelfennig 2000a, 130.

55. The note of caution, of course, is that each observation is not wholly independent. Nevertheless, the outcomes on most issues can be observed separately and I find that they are often not correlated. If an issue was already solved, or if it was not yet part of the political discourse and agenda in a certain government period, then I do not treat that instance as an observation.

CHAPTER 2
THEORETICAL FRAMEWORK

1. While this distinction may be debatable on the level of individuals, this is less true on an aggregate or government level, where individual policy makers cannot automatically translate their individual beliefs into aggregate behavioral change.

2. Various incentives such as side payments, material goods, and compensation payments have long been used in international affairs. Only recently, however, has there been empirical analysis of the effectiveness of incentives in fields such as international development, international trade, environmental policy, and arms control (Oye 1992; Keohane and Levy 1996; Bernauer and Ruloff 1999).

3. This definition is consistent with Bernauer 1999.

4. For an excellent discussion of different international relations theories on rationality and constructivism, see *International Organization* 52(4) (1998), and in particular, Ruggie 1998, Kahler 1998, and Finnemore and Sikkink 1998.

5. See Johnston 2001 for an example of a classification of the use of material incentives as a type of socialization. See Cortell and Davis 1996, 452–553, for a review of socialization theory. See also Alderson 2001.

6. Full version of European Union démarche towards Slovakia, *BBC Summary of World Broadcasts*, November 30, 1994.

7. See also Kenneth Waltz (1979, n. 63), who has suggested that socialization occurs via praise and ridicule or via censure.

8. While some may argue that international norms and institutional preferences are not always consistent, I nevertheless find them to be quite consistent. What sometimes proves inconsistent is the demand the institutions make on candidate states and the behavior of some of the member states.

9. Walter Schwimmer, CE Secretary General, "Building fortress Europe." Speech delivered at the Forum, Kennedy School of Government, Harvard University, April 13, 2000.

10. For an extensive discussion of this dichotomy and the literature, see Checkel 1997.

11. It should be noted that institutions that exert normative pressure and rely mostly on low-key methods do not have as their single or even foremost goal to change policy. While such change is certainly part of the agenda, the institutions also have other goals that they indeed may meet whether or not the institutions contribute to actual policy changes. Thus, to conclude that normative pressure alone does not produce policy change is not equivalent to deeming it useless.

12. See Checkel 2001 and Johnston 2002 for a discussion of the factors that influence the effectiveness of persuasion and social influence efforts.

13. Checkel 2001b has recently begun to develop scope conditions and hypotheses about when constructivist socialization may work.

14. This definition is consistent with Bernauer 1999.

15. Institutions typically do not use incentives without also trying to use their diplomatic capital to persuade and cajole. Thus, this study contains no cases of conditionality use without the accompanying efforts to persuade or use social pressure.

16. See the discussion in the introduction.

17. Classic works on rational choice include Arrow 1951, Schelling 1978, and Axelrod 1986.

18. As opposed to Ikenberry and Kupchan's 1990 article about socialization, in which they study the ability of "external inducements" to eventually alter norms.

19. Bargaining theory begins to explain how incentives operate at the structural level of international exchange when one state wants political concessions for economic benefits (Wagner 1988).

20. Tony Killick argues,
"Conditionality frequently fails because it is not accompanied by an adequate incentive structure. In the face of often substantially differing donor-recipient goals and sometimes large recipient participation constraints, the BWIs do not have enough assistance to offer, nor sufficiently large or dependable catalytic effects, to offer sufficient incentives to governments asked to execute measures of whose desirability they are not convinced. Still less do the BWIs offer a credible system of sanctions against delinquency, compounding the ever-present danger of moral hazard" (1996, abstract). See also Collier et al. 1997, and Leandro, Schafer, and Frontini 1999.

21. "Bank aid strategy flawed says departing chief economist," *Financial Times*, November 29, 1999; "The bumpy ride of Joe Stiglitz," *Economist*, December 18, 1999.

22. "Development Finance: Old Battle; New Strategy," *Economist*, January 8, 2000; "Koehler's Quest," *Economist*, July 29, 2000; "Bash the IMF for the Right Reasons," *International Herald Tribune*, March 11–12, 2000.

23. See, for example, the contributions in Brown 1997c.

24. Checkel also explores other reasons why economic conditionality has failed to produce compliance.

25. Martin and Sikkink (1993) point out that in U.S. efforts to improve human rights in Guatemala, congressional limitations on President Carter's power to compromise made the threats against Guatemala ineffective.

26. Thus, in a May 4, 1999 speech to the Romanian parliament, British Prime Minister Tony Blair promised Romania that "at the Helsinki European Council in

December [1999], Britain will support an invitation to Romania to begin negotiations to accede to the European Union" (transcript obtained from the Romanian mission to the EU in Brussels).

27. One could replace the assumption of risk neutrality with one of risk aversion on the grounds that the state may be cautious given the high stakes. This could affect the state's decision in different ways, depending on the relationship between the cost of compliance and the benefit of admission. For simplicity, this model stays with the assumption of risk neutrality, since this illustrates the practical insights sufficiently.

28. Schimmelfennig (2001) suggests that an institution may put itself in a position of admitting a state it does not want to admit because the institution is caught in it's own rhetoric—a rhetorical trap, so to speak.

29. Schelling's concepts of intersecting and continuous negotiations are also relevant to how European institutions have dealt with postcommunist states. Intersecting negotiations can be defined as an actor negotiating with several parties simultaneously and thus claiming that his actions are constrained because they have implications for the other negotiations. Similarly, whereas intersecting negotiations refer to multiple cases with multiple parties at a single time, continuous negotiations refer to multiple negotiations with one party over time. In continuous negotiations, the party can claim his actions are constrained because they have implications for later negotiations.

30. For a similar focus on elites in socialization studies see Ikenberry and Kupchan 1990.

31. For a review of this literature, see Horowitz 1985, Brown 1997c.

32. For reference, this study relies on Rogers Brubaker's (1995 and 1996) definition of a nationalizing state. Nationalist politicians are those who take just such a view of the state and who see the repression of other ethnic minorities as a necessary ingredient for success. Even in states in which strong nationalists groups do not operate in racist or xenophobic ways, parties do exist that have patriotic goals and resist efforts to accommodate ethnic minorities. For a review of different theoretical concepts of nationalism, see Özkirimli 2000; Kellas 1998; Mego 1999, 20 ff.

33. For a discussion of research, see Evans 1993, 412–414.

Chapter 3
Quantifying and Exploring the Data

1. I do not use lagged variables because the institutions directed their efforts specifically at the current governments, and the governments did consider their efforts and respond. Requiring the change to occur in the same period of observation actually presents a more stringent test for the effectiveness of the tools. If engagement by external actors occurs in period t, but not in t - 1 or t + 1, and a change occurred in period t, this would suggest that the external action was effective. If there was no change in period t, but a lagged change in period t + 1, however, then the applied method would conclude that the efforts of period t were not effective, and that change occurred in the absence of such action in period t + 1; thus,

it was completely uncorrelated. If socialization occurred in t - 1, conditionality was added in t, and a change was observed in t, however, then this change could wrongly be attributed to conditionality when it was really a lagged effect of socialization-based efforts. In several cases, however, actors used socialization-based efforts for multiple consecutive periods without changes in behavior until conditionality is added. If socialization-based efforts were effective, change should also be observed in these cases. Similarly, in several cases conditionality was never applied, or institutions were never involved at all. Further, the issues and involvement was followed over time for all issues, allowing for inferences about lagged effects if they seemed apparent in the case studies.

2. See chapter 1, n. 18.

3. Ibid.

4. For an overview of how the views of the general population of Latvia, Estonia, Slovakia, and Romania vary across issues, see Abele 1996.

5. In the data I actually use a five-level variable to get more exact variation, but for presentation in tables, I collapse these into three basic levels.

6. For a list of interviews, see appendix IIIb.

7. The quantitative analysis in the paper yields almost the same results for probit as for logit regressions.

8. Indeed, if we take only these 45 variables and do not control for domestic opposition, the variable pressure is insignificant.

9. A few calculations are based on fewer than five observations, as noted below table 11.

CHAPTER 4
LATVIA: OVERCOMING OPPOSITION

1. For a good discussion of the Soviet period, see Nørgaard 1995.

2. For more information, see Dreifelds 1996, 147–149.

3. Ibid. 157.

4. Ibid. 162.

5. "Crowds attack Estonian, Latvian Parliaments," *United Press International*, May 15, 1990.

6. "Chronology of developments in the Baltic Republics," *Associated Press*, January 22, 1991.

7. On the legal context of the statelessness created by Latvia and Estonia's independence, see Gelazis 2000.

8. For more on strict ethnic policy, see Nørgaard 1995, 101.

9. Even when the Siegerists did well in elections, they were excluded from coalition building, as were, for that matter, the ethnic Russian parties.

10. Law "City Dome, District Council and Rural District Council Election Law," Act 13 of 1994, January 13.

11. Ibid, article 9.

12. Ibid, article 17.

13. In 1996 the parliament twice rejected amendments to grant voting rights to noncitizens in local elections.

14. "Parliament adopts election law in second reading," *BBC Summary of World Broadcasts*, March 30, 1995.

15. Law on National Elections, 1995, article 11, paragraph 5.

16. Saeima (Latvian Parliament) bills 1258 and 1259.

17. "Law change clears path to NATO." *Baltic Times*, May 16, 2002.

18. For example, the case is completely omitted from Kemp's supposedly comprehensive treatment of the high commissioners activities in Latvia. (2001)

19. "The Republic of Latvia Education Law," Act 174 of 1991, June 19.

20. Article 5, paragraph 1 of the education law stated that "the rights to acquire an education in the state language is guaranteed," but with regards to other languages, the law stated, "The state makes every effort to guarantee this right."

21. Article 5, paragraph 4 of the education law, Riga, June 19, 1991.

22. Article 5, paragraph 2 of the education law, Riga, June 19, 1991.

23. In essence the amendments constituted a new language law, because it declared that the new text entirely replaced the old law.

24. Article 11, paragraph 2. Law "On Amendments and Additions to the Language Law of the Latvian Soviet Socialist Republic," Act 136 of 1992, March 31.

25. Law, "Amendments to the Republic of Latvia Education Law," Act 211 of 1995, August 10.

26. Legislators had submitted 709 amendments to the education, science ,and culture committee after the law passed in the first reading. "Latvia parliament speaker calls for new education law, *Baltic News Service*, June 28, 1996.

27. The party formed as a merger of the Freedom and Fatherland party and the Latvian National Independence Movement in June 1997 to become LNNK/TB.

28. The General Programmme of the Latvian Conservative Union, "Tezemei un Brivibai"/ LNNK, 1997.

29. The last government had already passed the law in the first reading.

30. "Latvian parliament passes official language law in first reading," *Baltic News Service*, June 5, 1997; Draft Law on the State Language, adopted in the second reading by the Sixth Saeima, April 29, 1998,.

31. Written comments from the HCNM dated September 7, 1998.

32. Letter from the HCNM to Mr. Dzintars Abikis, September 23, 1998.

33. Article 9 of the education law, Act 217 of 1998, October 29.

34. Education law, Act 217 of 1998, October 29.

35. Author's interview, Aija Priedite, Director, Latvian National Language Training Programme, March 5, 1999.

36. Text of a report by the Latvian newspaper *Diena* on its web site, http://www.diena.lv/,April 9, 2003.

37. "New party in Latvia," *RFE Newsline*, June 23, 1997.

38. The meeting was held on October 21, 1997. "Latvia panel to send language draft law to European institutions," *Baltic News Service*, October 22, 1997.

39. Draft Law on the State Language, adopted in the second reading by the Sixth Saeima, April 29, 1998, unofficial translation.

40. Letter to Guntis Ulmanis, President of Latvia, from van der Stoel, November 10, 1997; Statement by the HCNM, April 17, 1998; CE, "Report prepared by team of experts visiting Latvia on March 24–25,1998 on the Draft law on the State

Language and the proposed amendments to the Labour Code," Strasbourg, March 30, 1998; CE, Honouring of obligations and commitments by Latvia, Doc. 8426, May 24, 1999, "Information report Committee on the Honouring of Obligations and Commitments by Member States of the Council of Europe (Monitoring Committee)," Co-rapporteurs: Mr. Terry Davis, United Kingdom, and Mr. Gunnar Jansson, Finland; "CE slams Latvia over citizenship, death penalty," *RFE Newsline*, May 19, 1998; Addendum I to the "Progress Report of the Bureau of the Assembly Conclusions of the fact-finding visit to Riga," April 29–May 1 1998) by Mr. Terry Davis, United Kingdom, Socialist Group, and Mr. Gunnar Jansson, Finland, Liberal, Democratic and Reformers' Group, rapporteurs of the Committee on the Honouring of Obligations and Commitments by Member States Doc. 8136 Addendum I June 9, 1998; "Latvia-OSCE clash over language rights, *Agence France Presse*, August 26, 1998; Letter from HCNM, September 7, 1998, Addendum.

41. UK Presidency of the European Union, Statement on Latvia, Permanent Council, May 28, 1998, PC.DEL/222/98.

42. "Latvian committee rejects proposals for language law," *Baltic News Service*, June 10, 1998

43. "Since the controversy at the heart of the citizenship law was that all applicants for naturalization should speak the language well to prove their loyalty, the language law provided a way to compensate for the 'leniency' of the citizenship law on the language issue. Thus, the State Language Law should also regulate the use of Latvian in the private sector," Saeima Culture, education and science commission chair, Dzintars Abikis (TP), told journalists after meeting with van der Stoel. He said that his committee would not give in to European experts on the draft state language law. Abikis noted that it was not possible to apply in Latvia all European norms concerning language legislation because Latvians have become a minority in many places in their country. "Parliamentary panel not to give in to European experts on language issue," *Baltic News Service*, August 25, 1998.

44. Letter from HCNM van der Stoel to Mr. Dzintars Abikis, September 23, 1998.

45. Though not word for word, about half of van der Stoel's recommendations were clear in the draft. Draft for the third reading, Law on the State Language, Submitted by the Committee of Education, Culture and Science, October 8, 1998. Author's interview, Heidi Bottolfs, Member of the OSCE Mission to Latvia, March 15, 1999.

46. "Latvia hears reassurances at joint parliamentary meeting," *Europe Information Service, Euro-East*, February 23, 1999

47. Article 6, Law on the State Language, adopted in the second reading, March 18, 1999. Due to Saeima procedures, the new parliament had to once again pass the law in the second reading.

48. Letter to Foreign Minister Valdis Birkavs from HCNM van der Stoel, March 22, 1999; letter to Latvian Minister of Foreign Affairs Valdis Birkavs, April 13, 1999. "Latvian social democrat leader, OSCE Commissioner discuss Latvia's human rights obligations," *Baltic News Service*, January 12, 1999; "Stoel supports Latvian efforts to strengthen position of Latvian language," *Baltic News Service*, January 13, 1999; "Stoel urges Latvia to point attention to definitions in language law," *Baltic News Service*, May 25, 1999.

49. Honouring of obligations and commitments by Latvia, Doc. 8426, May 24, 1999 Information report Committee on the Honouring of Obligations and Commitments by Member States of the Council of Europe (Monitoring Committee) Co–rapporteurs: Mr. Terry Davis, United Kingdom, and Mr. Gunnar Jansson, Finland; "CE Parliamentary Assembly: Latvia as not achieved substantial progress in eliminating drawbacks," Latvian National News Agency *LETA*, June 25, 1999.

50. "Latvia hears reassurances at joint parliamentary meeting," *Europe Information Service, Euro–East*, February 23, 1999. There were also some meetings with EU Foreign Affairs Commissioner Hans van den Broek, the President of the EU Commission Jacques Santer and the Latvian Prime Minister in Brussels. "Latvian Premier discusses EU enlargement and language law with EU officials," *BBC Monitoring Former Soviet Union—Political*, April 23, 1999.

51. "Latvian Premier discusses EU enlargement and language law with EU officials," *BBC Monitoring Former Soviet Union—Political*, April 23, 1999.

52. Danish Foreign Minister Niels Helveg Petersen visited Latvia and urged politicians not to let the issue become an obstacle to an invitation to talks on admission to the EU. "Kristopans, Danish foreign minister urge caution on language law," *BBC Summary of World Broadcasts*, July 0, 1999. Several foreign politicians participating in the World Economic Forum in Salzburg warned Latvian Prime Minister Vilis Kristopans that the state language law could prevent Latvia from getting an invitation to the EU membership talks at the end of the year. Kristopans said that each foreign official in Salzburg began conversation with the state language law, even the European Commission Agriculture Commissioner Franz Fischler. "It is everywhere like this. And now, too, during the meeting with Austrian Chancellor Mr. Klima the first question will be—what will you have there with the language law," the premier said. "Latvia gets next warnings about state language law," *Baltic News Service*, July 2, 1999.

53. "Latvian Prime Minister warns of link between language law and EU," *Baltic News Service*, July 3, 1999.

54. "Foreign commissioners concerned over Latvian language law development," *Baltic News Service*, June 29, 1999.

55. In the midst of all this tension surrounding the language law, the FF/LNNK, a member of the governing coalition, signed a cooperation agreement with the opposition People's Party. The contract listed seven steps of economic reform needed to overcome what it described as the "financial and economic crisis" gripping the country, worsened by "the prime minister's inability to provide leadership for the country's long term interests." Two days later, Prime Minister Kristopans resigned, and the scramble to form a new government began. "Kristopans quits, political spectrum in flux," *Baltic Times*, July 8–14, 1999.

56. "Coalition parties vow to promote language despite criticism of law," *BBC Summary of World Broadcasts*, July 19, 1999.

57. First, the EU country ambassadors resident in Latvia met with Saeima deputies to talk over compliance of the State Language Law with international norms and to recommend postponing adoption of the law until this fall. "Latvian government tumbles under the weight of Russian crisis," *Agence France Presse*, July 5, 1999. Second, EU Commissioner van den Broek sent a letter to the Saeima suggesting

that the adoption of the state language law be postponed. He said that the EU still was concerned that the law was poorly formulated, and that it was are likely to damage implementation of the rights and freedoms that the European Agreement provides for, e.g. the business activities of enterprises in EU member states. "Saeima receives van den Broek's letter on state language law," *LETA*, July 5, 1999. Third, the Wall Street Journal quoted European Commission press secretary in Brussels Niko Wegter, who said: "We are very critical of the drafted [language] law. We are planning to discuss the issue with Riga [today]. It is an essential issue and I hope Latvia will treat it as such." "WSJ: Western observers concerned about Latvia," *Baltic News Service*, July 6, 1999. Finally, Guenther Weiss, the head of the delegation of the European Commission in Riga, said that Latvia should not emulate Estonia on the language policy and urged revision and postponement. "Latvia warned not emulate Estonia on language," *ITAR/TASS News Agency*, July 7, 1999.

58. That the law was passed in the strict version could have several explanations. First, nationalist-leaning politicians wanted to pass a strict language law in compensation for the liberal citizenship law. Second, the law became intertwined with the formation of the new coalition. Voting yes on the law became a pre-requisite for coalition participation. The first official negotiations on forming a new government were launched by the FF/LNNK, the People's Party, the Latvian Social Democratic Party, and the New Party. The day before the final reading of the language law, three Saeima factions—the People's Party, FF/LNNK, and the Latvian Social Democratic Party, together representing 55 deputies—signed a joint protocol on the adoption of the state language law. Meanwhile the New Party's faction proposed postponing review of the state language bill. The faction's deputy chair Ingrida Udre protested attempts to link the language law with the formation of the new government. She said that TB/LNNK representatives had said that if the New Party joined the agreement on the language bill, it would be asked to join the ruling coalition; otherwise "the doors will be shut." Udre protested that the "The language law cannot be tampered with in setting up the new government." "Three parties sign agreement on adoption of state language law; new party urges bill be postponed," *LETA*, July 7, 1999. While the New Party thus moved out of the coalition formation, Latvia's Way party, eager to participate in the government, also agreed to vote for adoption of the State Language Law in its third reading, and to take no counteraction that could hinder promulgation of the law. " 'Latvia's Way' supports new government's program in principle, will vote for state language law," *LETA*, July 7, 1999. However, Latvia's Way was open to voting for some amendments to the law that would lessen the international criticism.

59. Van der Stoel also asked her by telephone to review the law carefully. "Van der Stoel expresses concern to Vike-Rfeiberga on implementation of language law," *LETA*, July 13, 1999. Van der Stoel's personal advisor John Packer met with the President to discuss the details of the law. "Advisor to Van der Stoel substantiates commissioner's object to language law." *LETA*, July 13, 1999.

60. "In its present shape this law is not in line with Latvia's international commitments, particularly the European Convention of Human Rights, which recognizes the freedom of expression and association and the right to privacy," Tarschys said in a press statement. The secretary general added that the CE had been actively

engaged in promoting the Latvian language and the integration of the non-Latvian population. It has also provided its expert advice during the drafting of the language law. "The Saeima should get another chance to look into this matter," "Tarschys said. Council of Europe voices concern over language law," *BBC Summary of World Broadcasts*, July 13, 1999.

61. "Language law may create problems for EU membership—EC official," *BBC Summary of World Broadcasts*, July 13, 1999; "EU ambassador meets Latvian President over language law," *Baltic News Service*, July 13, 1999.

62. "Halonen advises Latvia against strict language law," *Deutsche Presse-Agentur*, July 14, 1999.

63. "If we took the road to Europe, we should prove our ability to harmonize our laws with European norms," she said in a special broadcast of TV news, explaining her decision. "There is no sense in donning clothes with drawbacks in the belief that they will be patched later. It is better to mend holes right away or to sew something new, and then appear before the public," she added. "Latvian president turns language bill back to parliament," *ITAR/TASS*, July 14, 1999; "Vike-Rfeiberga objects to seven points in language law, says decision was 'difficult'," *LETA*, July 14, 1999. She reiterated the concern for the EU decision soon thereafter. "President Vike-Freiberga addresses first session of new government," *BBC Summary of World Broadcasts*, July 23, 1999.

64. Press Release, HCNM, July 15, 1999; "International organizations appreciate Vike-Rfeiberga's decision on language law," *LETA*, July 15, 1999; "Blair welcomes Vike-Rfeiberga's decision on language law," *LETA*, July 23, 1999; "U.S. State Department welcomes return of language law to Saeima," *LETA*, July 16, 1999.

65. "Latvia's chances to be invited to EU talks good—Finnish ambassador," *Baltic News Service*, August 13, 1999; "Latvia has realistic chance to join EU talks: ambassador," *Baltic News Service*, July 24, 1999

66. The head of the People's Party parliamentary faction, Gundars Berzins, said that the parliament should adopt an amended law in November because "it is important [for Latvia] to demonstrate an ability to act." Fatherland and Freedom and Latvia's Way, on the other hand, wanted to see consideration of any new amendments delayed until early next year. *RFE/RL Newsline*, August 19, 1999.

67. "EC delegation to Latvia head emphasizes role of language law," *Baltic News Service*, October 14, 1999; "Foreign Minister Berzins discusses language law with British minister," *BBC Summary of World Broadcasts*, November 17, 1999.

68. "OSCE experts support efforts to strengthen Latvian language," *Baltic News Service*, November 15, 1999.

69. "Latvia's FF/LNNK calls on People's Party to implement agreement on national issues cooperation," *Baltic News Service*, November 27, 1999; "Latvia's People's Party says not to yield to coalition partners concerning language law," *Baltic News Service*, November 27, 1999; "Latvia's FF/LNNK dissatisfied with implementation of agreement with People's Party," *Baltic News Service*, November 27, 1999.

70. *RFE/RL Newsline*, August 30, 1999.

71. Comment by the parliament's Education, Research and Culture Committee head Dzintars Abikis. "Latvian parliament panel head not sure about language law adoption." *Baltic News Service*, December 1, 1999.

72. The bill split the ruling coalition, forcing the government to rely on a moderate opposition party to muster a slim majority of 52 in the 100-member chamber. "Latvians adopts controversial language law, anger Russian minority," *Agence France Presse*, December 9, 1999. EU enlargement commissioner Verheugen noted "with satisfaction that Latvia has thus followed recommendations made by the Commission" in its progress report worked towards compliance of the text with international standards. The HCNM said that the law was "essentially in conformity" with Latvia's international obligations. "EU Commissioner approves of language law adopted in Latvia," *Baltic News Service*, December 9, 1999; "OSCE Commissioner finds language law compatible with Latvia's obligations," *Baltic News Service*, December 9, 1999.

73. Resolution on the Organization of the Working Group for the Working Out the New Working of the Republic of Latvia Constitution and Citizenship Conception Projects of the Republic of Latvia., Act 116 of 1990, July 31, 1990.

74. Resolution on the Renewal of the Republic of Latvia Citizens Rights and Fundamental Principles of Naturalization. Act 308 of 1991, October 15, 1991.

75. Article 3.5 (8).

76. Resolution on the Republic of Latvia Draft Law On Citizenship, Act 328 of 1991, November 12, 1991.

77. See Paragraph 4 of opinion no. 183 (1995) on the application by Latvia for membership to the CE. Also, Doc. 7169, Report on the application by Latvia for membership of the Council of Europe, October 6, 1994.

78. "Council of Europe Assembly to probe human rights in Baltics," Associated Press, September 21, 1991.

79. Dzintra Bungs, Lalumiere in Latvia, *RFE/RL* February 19, 1992.

80. Author's interview, Boris Tselevich, March 19, 1999.

81. Saulius Girnius, "Council of Europe delegation in Latvia," RFE September 16, 1993.

82. After attending the September CE parliamentary Assembly meeting in Strasbourg, Latvian delegation head, Aleksandrs Kirstein, said that Latvia's entry into the CE in 1993 was excluded because the council was concerned about the Russian reaction to Latvia's laws on citizenship, aliens and labor and so on. "Saeima's failure to vote on noncitizens' status may hamper entry to Council of Europe," *BBC Summary of World Broadcasts*, October 24, 1994.

83. "CSCE's Max van der Stoel on visit to discuss citizenship law," *BBC Summary of World Broadcasts*, September 24, 1993.

84. Latvian Radio, Riga, in Latvian 1800 GMT 27 Sep 93, "Latvian National Independence Movement on citizenship issue," *BBC Summary of World Broadcasts*, September 29, 1993.

85. "Latvian Chronology," *Monthly Survey of Baltic and Post-Soviet Policies*, October 1994.

86. Letter to Georgs Andrejevs, Minister of Foreign Affairs of the Republic of Latvia, December 10, 1993. CSCE Communication no. 8/94.

87. The Council of Europe made these comments on the draft of the citizenship law, which passed in the first reading on November 25, 1993. Council of Europe, Strasbourg, 24 January 1994, Comments on the Draft Citizenship Law of the Republic of Latvia.

88. Latvian nationalists were victorious, although twelve other parties also won seats. The major winners were the LNIM with 22 of the 60 seats in the Riga council, the Saimnieks entrepreneurs with 11, and For Fatherland and Freedom with 6. The ruling coalition, Latvia's Way and Farmers' Union, won only 2 and 3 seats, respectively.

89. On June 9, 1994.

90. Dzintra Bungs, "Latvian draft citizenship law not endorsed by CE representatives," *RFE/RL*, June 15, 1994. This was also confirmed in March 1999 Author's interviews with members of the delegation.

91. "EU and CSCE express reservations on citizenship bill before amendments," *BBC Summary of World Broadcasts*, June 23, 1994.

92. "Britain asks Latvia to review restrictions in citizenship law," *ITAR/TASS*, June 23, 1994.

93. "Latvia votes in tough citizenship law," *United Press International*, June 21, 1994, Tuesday, BC cycle.

94. Presidency communiqué on behalf of the European Union on the draft Latvian citizenship law, European Union, DN: PESC/94/58, June 21, 1994.

95. "The European Council expects Russia, in conformity with earlier commitments, to complete its troop withdrawals from Latvia and Estonia by 31 August 1994. The European Council attaches importance to the efforts made by the Baltic States to develop legal and regulatory frameworks which conform to inter alia the recommendations of the CSCE High Commissioner and of the CE. It notes with concern the adoption by the Latvian Parliament of a citizenship law incompatible with these recommendations and hopes that the draft law will be reconsidered." European Council at Corfu, June 24–26, 1994, Presidency Conclusions, European Union, European Union, DN: DOC/94/1, Date: June 25, 1994.

96. "Government asks president not to approve law on citizenship," *BBC Summary of World Broadcasts*, June 24, 1994.

97. "President returns citizenship bill to Saeima for reconsideration," *BBC Summary of World Broadcasts*, June 30, 1994.

98. According to author's interviews with Lativan politicians, on July 11, 1994, the Farmers Union faction left the governing coalition because of disagreements with Latvian Way (LW) over agrarian issues. LW continued as a minority government. Two days later, the LW faction approved amendments to the citizenship law replacing the quotas with a system of categories for naturalization giving priority to those born in Latvia and to younger people. Meanwhile Prime Minister Valdis Birkavs announced that his cabinet was resigning, but that LW would be willing to form a new government.

99. Law on Citizenship, Act 144 of 1994, July 22, 1994.

100. Only persons with a special "grade I invalid status'" were exempted from the language test.

101. Article 12, part I, paragraph 7.

102. "The Union considers this law to be a good basis for progress in the integration of ethnic minorities and the development of inter-community relations in Latvia. The Union welcomes that the law takes account of the recommendations of the CSCE and the Council of Europe and of appeals from the Union." Presidency

statement on behalf of the European Union on Baltic-Russian relations, European Union, DN: PESC/94/75, July 28, 1994.

103. Doc. 7193, Opinion on the application by Latvia for membership of the Council of Europe, 8 November 1994.

104. "Working group formed to submit amendments to citizenship bill," *BBC Summary of World Broadcasts*, June 30, 1994.

105. Author's interviews, members of parliament, March 1999.

106. Author's interview, Aleksandrs Kirsteins, MP for the Latvian National Independence Movement and then presently with the People's Party, March 19, 1999.

107. Author's interview, Inise Birzniece, MP from Latvia's Way, March 14, 1999.

108. Patrick Lannin, "Latvia set to swing right in weekend elections," *Reuter European Business Report*, September 26, 1995, Tuesday, BC cycle. See also, the pre-election program of the TB.

109. "Parliament factions sign agreement on forming government," *BBC Summary of World Broadcasts*, December 22, 1995.

110. HCNM, letter to Mr. V. Birkavs, Minister for Foreign Affairs of the Republic of Latvia, 14 March 1996, Reference : No 516/96/L.

111. Ibid.

112. In September 1996 the head of the Naturalization Board, Eizenia Aldermane, meet with president Ulmanis to explain that about 550,000 permanent residents could apply for membership, and that out of those who could, under 2 percent had done so. She said that for example, in 1996, only 450 out of 33,000 eligible people had applied. Aldermane noted that the Naturalization Board had proposed several amendments to the citizenship law, but the parliamentary committees never reacted.

113. Andres Kahar, "Ulmanis puts citizenship on front burner," *Baltic Times*, April 10, 1997; "Citizenship pole-arity," *Baltic Times*, March 6, 1997.

114. Latvian Radio, Riga, in Latvian 1300 GMT 23 Aug 97, Latvian Radio, Riga, in Latvian 1300 GMT 23 Aug 97; "Latvian organizations protest at Soviet links of army officers," *BBC Summary of World Broadcasts*, August 26, 1997

115. Krast' interview, the newspaper *Diena* on August 5, 1997. Cited in Nils Muiznieks, "A Gap in the Government Declaration, *Diena*, 12 August, 1997.

116. The first time was in October 1997, and the second was in February 1998. Latvian Radio, Riga, in Latvian 0900 GMT 16 Oct. 97; "Parliament rejects amendments to citizenship law," *BBC Summary of World Broadcasts*, October 17, 1997; "Latvian lawmakers reject amendment to citizenship law," RFE *Newsline* February 13, 1998.

117. Author's interview, Mr. Geoffrey Barrett, First Councilor, Delegation of the European Commission to Latvia, March 16, 1999.

118. The amendments also proposed abandoning the practice of granting citizenship for special service of benefit to Latvia. Latvian Radio, Riga, in Latvian 1600 GMT 9 Mar 98, "Major nationalist group proposes tightening of naturalization rules," *BBC Summary of World Broadcasts*, March 11, 1998

119. For a detailed discussion of the events of March, 1998, see *East European Constitutional Review* (Spring 1998): 15–17.

120. "Eric Jansson, Guntars Krasts and the silent treatment," *Baltic Times*, April 23, 1998: 5.

121. "TB/LNNK almost stalls citizenship amendments," *Baltic Times*, May 21, 1998.

122. UK Presidency of the European Union, Statement on Latvia, Permanent Council, 28 May, 1998, PC.DEL/222/98.

123. Deputies from Latvia's Way and the Saimnieks were joined by scattered MPs from the Christian Democrats, the Farmers' Union, the National Reform and Green Parties, the People's Harmony Party, and some independents in support of the proposal. FF/LNNK led the charge against the amendments that also included independent deputies and members of the For Latvia faction. One MP abstained, and 15 did not vote. The chief opponent of the amendments, Prime Minister Guntars Krasts (TB/LNNK), left in the morning for the United States and was not present. Steven C. Johnson, "Parliament closes in on citizenship amendments," *Baltic Times*, June 11, 1998

124. Declaration by the Presidency on behalf of the European Union on Latvia, European Union, DN: PESC/98/55, June 11,1998.

125. Law "Amendments to the citizenship Law," Act 135 of 1998, June 22, 1998. Parents had to apply on behalf of their child before the child turned 15. Also, applicants over age 65 were finally exempted from the language exam, albeit only from the written part.

126. Memo from the European Union Delegation of the European Commission in Latvia, Press and Information Unit, regarding "Commissioner Hans van den Broek's visit to Latvia July 20," July 23, 1998. Also, in a public speech entitled: "The enlargement of the European Union and Latvia" at the Riga Stock Exchange, van den Broek gave strong words of support for the integration of Latvia's noncitizens. He said, "We believe that the amendments to the Citizenship Law adopted by the Parliament on 22 June are crucial." "Second Draft: The EU Enlargement Process and Latvia, Version: July 19, 1998 23:50."

127. Outside the timeframe of this study, both Estonia and Latvia eventually amended their election laws in 2001 and 2002, respectively. Again, this occurred through a citizen's appeal to the European Court of Human Rights and through external pressure—this time from NATO. "Law change clears path to NATO," *Baltic Times*, May 16, 2002.

CHAPTER 5
ESTONIA: RELUCTANT COOPERATION

1. In the 1934 census, Estonians formed 88.2 percent of the population, Russians 8.2 percent; Germans 1.5 percent, and Swedes 0.7 percent. See http://www.ciesin.ee/ESTCG/POPULATION/

2. See, for example, http://www.europeanforum.net/cup/estonia/

3. See "Russians in the Baltics, a 1991 survey," VCIOM, Studies in Public Policy number 287, University of Strathclyde, Glasgow: 1997; Richard Rose et al., "Nationalities in the Baltics, a survey study," Studies in Public Policy number 222, University of Strathclyde, Glasgow: 1994; Richard Rose et al., "Conflict or Com-

promise in the Baltic States? What do peoples there think?" Studies in Public Policy number 231, University of Strathclyde, Glasgow: 1994; Richard Rose et al., "New Baltics Barometer II: A Survey Study," Studies in Public Policy number 251, University of Strathclyde, Glasgow: 1995; Richard Rose et al., "New Baltics Barometer III: A Survey Study, Studies in Public Policy," number 284, University of Strathclyde, Glasgow: 1997.

4. At that time the OSCE was still the CSCE.

5. The Coalition Government's Program of the Coalition Party and the Rural Union (KMÜ) and the Estonian Centre Party, Web edition: http://www.vm.ee/eng/estoday/1995/9504vsgov.html

6. Under the existing 1993 municipal elections law, aliens legally residing in Estonia had to register themselves one month before the elections to participate. As a positive move, the new bill aimed to eliminate this requirement. Also, to correct for the Estonian bureaucratic processing problems, the changes would mean that the filing of a petition for Estonian citizenship would be regarded as equal to a valid residence permit allowing the person to vote.

7. "Estonian cabinet discusses municipal elections bill," *Baltic News Service*, January 30, 1996.

8. "Estonian parliament amends local elections law, eases language requirements," *Baltic News Service*, May 16, 1996.

9. Ibid.

10. Author's interview, Mart Nutt, Member of Parliament since 1992, and author of legislation on citizenship and residency, September 22, 1999.

11. "French President backs EU membership for Estonia," *Baltic News Service*, April 4, 1996.

12. "Netherlands' Prime Minister says Estonia's EU membership due after the year 2000," *Baltic News Service*, March 26, 1996.

13. This was initiated in the language law, not the election laws. Apparently, although HCNM van der Stoel visited Tallinn at the time, he did not formally comment on the law. Nevertheless, the president vetoed it, only to have the parliament reapprove it without alteration. President Meri subsequently submitted the language law matter to the constitutional review chamber. Finally, in February 1998, the State Court pronounced the amendments in conflict with the constitution. The court ruled that language requirements for new deputies must be included in the electoral law, not in the language law.

14. Draft on amendments and changes to the laws on parliamentary elections, local elections and language. second reading, November 24, 1998.

15. "Estonia amends laws imposing language requirement on MPs and local councillors," *BBC Monitoring Former Soviet Union—Political*, December 15, 1998.

16. "Van Der Stoel: Non-Estonian-speakers must have right to run for election," *Baltic News Service*, January 8, 1999.

17. Author's interview, Neil Brennan, First Secretary, OSCE Mission to Estonia, September 21, 1999.

18. Author's interview, Liia Hanni, Member of Parliament since 1990, September 21, 1999.

19. "Prime Minister: OSCE mission to leave Estonia soon." *Baltic News Service*, November 30, 2001.

20. The new amendments said, "For meeting the requirements of workplace environment and consumer protection and in the interests of environment, health and safety, the employees of firms, non-profit organizations and foundations as well as entrepreneurs being natural persons, shall by offering goods or services and by forwarding information use the Estonian language for the fulfillment of work tasks at the level required." Amendment Act of the Language Act and State Fee Act, approved February 9, 1999.

21. Author's interview, Marten Kokk, September 23, 1999.

22. Author's interview, Liia Hanni, Member of parliament since 1990, September 21, 1999.

23. Author's interview, Henrik Hololei, Head of the European Integration Office, September 20, 1999.

24. Regular Report from the Commission on Progress towards Accession—Estonia, October 13, 1999, 1.3 General Evaluation.

25. "Premier Laar defends amendments to language law," *BBC Summary of World Broadcasts*, October 19, 1999.

26. "PM says Estonia a middler among first-tier EU hopefuls," *Baltic News Service*, October 20, 1999.

27. *RFE/RL Newsline*, October 21, 1999.

28. Finnish President Martti Ahtisaari, speaking in Tallinn on Novmeber 5 at the conference, "Estonia and the EU," *RFE/RL Newsline*, November 8, 1999.

29. "Premier Laar defends amendments to language law," *BBC Summary of World Broadcasts*, October 19, 1999.

30. "Foreign minister says language law must be relaxed to join EU," *BBC Summary of World Broadcasts*, February 3, 2000.

31. Third meeting of the Association Council between the European Union and Estonia, RAPID, February 23, 2000.

32. "Estonia asks for EU experts' opinion on language law," *Baltic News Service*, February 15, 2000.

33. "European Commission's estimate of Estonian language law positive-official," *Baltic News Service*, March 27, 2000.

34. "Estonian language law adjusted to European norms," Interfax Russian News, May 16, 2000.

35. "German chancellor highlights need to change language law," *BBC Summary of World Broadcasts*, June 8, 2000.

36. "Estonia improves reputation in EU's eyes—FM," *Baltic News Service*, June 8, 2000.

37. The law still requires knowledge of Estonian for those working in those parts of the public and service sectors deemed vital, such as emergency services. But no language knowledge requirement will apply to private sector jobs, such as at shops and stores.

38. Enlargement Commissioner Guenter Verheugen praised the passage of amendments to the Estonian language law on June 14, saying the language law is

now in total compliance with all OSCE and EU norms. *RFE/RL Newsline*, June 15, 2000. In a statement welcoming the adoption of amendments to the Estonian language law, HCNM van der Stoel immediately issued a statement saying, "Analysis of the amended text of the Law on Language leads me to the conclusion that the text of the law is largely in conformity with Estonia's international obligations and commitments. I trust that the Cabinet of Ministers will follow the letter and spirit of the amended law in elaborating implementing regulations, as foreseen in certain provisions of the law, and in supervising public administration of the law." Also the European Union's Enlargement Commissioner Guenter Verheugen welcomed the amendments and affirmed that the Estonian language law amendments fully met the standards set by the EU and the OSCE. "Van der Stoel hails changes in Estonian language law," *Baltic News Service*, June 15, 2000.

39. Author's interview, Vello Pettai, September 24, 1999.

40. Not until February 1993 did the parliament pass a law on the language requirements. The law stated rather broadly that applicants should have a listening comprehension of general information, and should be able to hold a conversation and read and write some everyday language texts. The government was then to establish an examination procedure. There were some exemptions for those educated in Estonian language schools, and the possibility existed that the government could establish a simplified language examination procedure for those born before January 1, 1930 and for some disabled persons. Law on Estonian Language Requirements for Applicants for Citizenship, February 10, 1993.

41. "Human rights situation; CSCE commissioner calls for citizenship issue to be solved in Latvia and Estonia," *BBC Summary of World Broadcasts*, Part 1. The USSR; 2. Eastern Europe; SU/1597/A2; January 27, 1993.

42. The other requirements were that certain precautions should be taken in the implementation of the Law on Estonian Language Requirements for Applicants for Citizenship, that those who had failed to meet the language or residency requirements should not be precluded from applying again, that it should be made explicit that the requirement that applicants have a steady legal income to qualify for citizenship will not apply to unemployed people.

43. Author's interview, Mart Nutt, Member of Parliament since 1992, and author of legislation on citizenship and residency, September 22, 1999.

44. "Opinion on the application of Estonia for membership of the Council of Europe," Doc. 6824, 5 May 1993, Rapporteur: Mr. Bindig.

45. According to an expert: "The new law on citizenship made a number of changes to the naturalization process which generally made it more difficult for persons to become citizens" (Visek1997, 337). First, the law increased the residency requirement from two years or permanent residence to five years with a permanent residence permit. This would apply, however, only to those who had settled in Estonia after July 1, 1990. Also, the new law retained the requirement of the knowledge of the Estonian language and included in the law some specifications of the test. The law narrowed the waiver provisions for the language test and eliminated the waiver eligibility for stateless persons with ten years of residency (see article 8(2)). The new waiver provision applied only to hearing or visually disabled applicants, and the exemption from the writing requirement only applied to those

born before 1930. In an entirely new provision, the law set out an additional requirement for the knowledge of the country's constitution and citizenship law. Applicants also had to take a loyalty oath and have a permanent lawful income sufficient to support the applicants and his dependents. Of utmost relevance to those
who had entered Estonia as part of the Soviet armed forces, the law stated clearly
that citizenship could not be granted to person who had acted against the State of
Estonian and its security, or been employed by the intelligence or security service
of a foreign state, or served in a career position in the armed forces of a foreign
state.1995 Law on Citizenship, article 21(2). The only exception is persons who
have been married for five years (and nor divorced from) to a person who is an
Estonian citizen by birth.

46. Author's interview, Mart Nutt, Member of Parliament since 1992, and author of legislation on citizenship and residency, September 22, 1999.

47. "Estonian MP finds Stoel's proposal potentially dangerous," *Baltic News Service*, April 9, 1997.

48. Ibid.

49. "Danish foreign minister pleased with moves on ethnic minorities," *BBC
Summary of World Broadcasts*, October 27, 1997; "EU holds first joint parliamentary
committee meeting with Estonia," *Europe Information Service, Euro-East*, November
27, 1997.

50. Author's interview, Andra Veidemann, Member of government 1992–1999,
Minister of European Affairs 1996–1997, Minister of Ethnic Affairs 1997–1999,
September 23, 1999.

51. Author's interview, Aleksei Semjonov, Director, Legal Information Centre
for Human Rights, September 21, 1999.

52. "Estonian PM and OSCE representative discuss language law," Agence
France Presse, November 24, 1997.

53. On December 4, 1997, the European Parliament adopted a resolution essentially supporting the conclusions of Agenda 2000. In its resolution on the communication from the commission for Agenda 2000, 1997—for a stronger and wider
Union' (A4-0368/97), the parliament called for accession negotiations to be started
with all applicants, while raising specific concerns. On Estonia, the parliament
stated "that efforts have to be sustained fully to implement the acquis, to improve
the quality of public administration and to further extend citizenship to members
of minority groups."

54. The EU Presidency declaration said,
The European Union welcomes the Estonian Government's decision of 9 December to lay before Parliament an amendment to the law on citizenship to the effect
that Estonian citizenship will be granted on request to children born to stateless
parents in Estonia. The decision is a constructive step towards the integration of
Estonia's non-citizens in the spirit of the UN Convention on the Rights of the
Child and an important confidence-building measure. The European Union supports and appreciates the Estonian Government's decision.

Declaration by the Presidency on behalf of the European Union on the draft law
concerning stateless children in Estonia, December 15, 1997.

55. "Proposal to ease citizenship rules to meet heavy resistance in parliament,"
Baltic News Service, December 12, 1997.

56. Briefing No. 8, Estonia and the Enlargement of the European Union, Luxembourg, 8 October, 1998. PE 67.409/rev.1 Or.EN.

57. Author's interview, Marten Kokk, Former head of the MFA Human Rights Department, September 23, 1999.

58. Author's interview, HCNM staff, November, 1998.

59. Declaration by the Presidency on behalf of the European Union on Estonia, September 12 1998.

60. Author's interview, Kristina Mauer, UNDP in Estonia, September 20, 1999.

61. Author's interview, Mart Nutt, Member of Parliament since 1992, and author of legislation on citizenship and residency, September 22, 1999.

62. Author's interview, Liia Hanni, Member of parliament sinc1990, September 21, 1999.

63. "Estonian Chronology," *Monthly Survey of Baltic and Post-Soviet Politics*, July, 1993.

64. "The Russian President's Statement on Estonian 'Ethnic Cleansing' and 'Apartheid,' " *ITAR-TASS News Agency*, June 25, 1993, as translated in the *BBC Survey of World Broadcasts*, SU/1726, June 28, 1993, A2/1.

65. "Estonian Chronology," *Monthly Survey of Baltic and Post-Soviet Politics*, July, 1993.

66. July 6, 1993, "Opinion on the law of Aliens in Estonia." The opinion is a confidential document, but some information can be deduced from: Information report on honoring of commitments entered into by new member states(1) : ESTONIA–Addendum IV to the Progress Report of the Bureau of the Assembly and the Standing Committee, Doc. 7080 Addendum IV, 31 May 1994

67. *Estonian Review*, July 5–11, 1993

68. On August 24, 1993, the government approved regulations for issuing and extending living and work permits for resident aliens. On August 19 the government adopted the resolution on alien passport as a basis for the government's plans to issue passports residential permits to aliens. The guidelines simplified the procedure for obtaining passports or resident permits for aliens living permanently in Estonia. Resident aliens had until July 12, 1994, to apply for a resident permits. The old Soviet passports would become invalid on July 12, 1995. On September 21 the government adopted two decrees complementing the law on aliens establishing the procedures for issuing and renewing aliens' residence and work permits, and establishing some of the procedures for aliens' passports, respectively.

69. "Citizenship law amended, but with little significant change," *Agence France Presse*, July 8, 1993.

70. Author's interview, Klara Hallik, Minister of Ethnic Affairs, 1992, September 23, 1999.

71. *RFE/RL Newsline*, July 14, 1993.

72. Author's interview, Mart Nutt, Member of Parliament since 1992, and author of legislation on citizenship and residency, September 22, 1999.

73. Law on Amendments to the Republic of Estonia Supreme Council Resolution "On the application of the Law on Citizenship." February 18, 1993.

74. Their registration cards were green as opposed to the blue ones given to citizens.

CHAPTER 6
SLOVAKIA: THE MECIAR HURDLE AND BEYOND

1. For example, in accordance with the urban integration policy, houses could only be built in so-called "central settlements" and not in smaller villages. This resulted in school mergers and closure of schools in the countryside, which had benefited minorities. Thus, the number of students in schools with Hungarian language teaching almost halved between 1970 and 1989.

2. The Czechoslovak Federal assembly passed a law terminating the federation on November 25, 1992.

3. For a map showing the territorial distribution of the Hungarian population in Slovakia, see the results of the 1991 census at http://www.geowiss.uni-hamburg.de/home/mandzak/hung.gif.

4. For a good overview of Slovak politics, see Pridham 1999; Bútora et al. 1997, 1998, and 1999; Meseznikov, Ivantysyn, and Nicholson 1999.

5. "Premier confirms Slovak counterpart proposed population exchange." *BBC Summary of World Broadcasts*. September 8, 1997. EE/D3018/C.

6. Indeed, by March 2003 Slovaks still regarded Meciar as the second most trustworthy politician in the country. "Slovak opposition party head increases poll lead as trustworthy politician." *BBC Monitoring Europe—Political*, March 19, 2003.

7. "Slovakia to meet Council of Europe's demands," *The Independent*, May 13, 1993; "Slovakia accepts European Council's recommendations—minister," *CTK National News Wire*, May 27, 1993; "The diplomatic maneuvering of a new state Slovakia has its sights set on joining the EC," *Irish Times*, June 8, 1993.

8. Parliamentary Assembly of the Council of Europe, Report on the application by the Slovak Republic for membership of the Council of Europe, Rapporteur: Mrs. Halonen, Doc. 6864, 11 June, 1993, paragraph 37.

9. The CE issued opinion no. 175 (1993) on the application by the Slovak Republic for membership of the Council of Europe. Among other concerns, the opinion noted that

[The assembly] takes note of the Slovak authorities' commitment to adopt a legislation granting to every person belonging to a minority the right to use his/her surname and first names in his/her mother tongue and, in the regions in which substantial numbers of a national minority are settled, the right for the persons belonging to this minority to display in their language local names, signs, inscriptions and other similar information, in accordance with the principles contained in Recommendation 1201 (1993).

Opinion No. 175 (1993) on the application by the Slovak Republic for membership of the Council of Europe, paragraph 9. See also Council of Europe, Committee of Ministers, Resolution (93) 33, Invitation to Slovakia to become a member of the Council of Europe, Adopted by the Committee of Ministers on 30 June 1993.

10. The law enabled a person born on the territory of the Slovak Republic to register several names and surnames, including foreign language names. Names and surnames could be used in their foreign language forms in accordance with the rules of Slovak spelling and without transcription into Slovak. Women were allowed to omit the Slavic ending "-ova" from their surnames. In official contacts, a Slovak citizen would be able to use one surname only. If there were several names

in the register, it would be the name listed first. Seventy-seven of 105 deputies present voted in favor of the amendment. "Deputies pass law on names, meeting condition of Council of Europe membership," *BBC Summary of World Broadcasts*, July 12, 1993; "Chairman of ethnic Hungarian Coexistence movement praises law on names," *BBC Summary of World Broadcasts*, July 12, 1993.

11. "Premier to ask president to send back law on names," *BBC Summary of World Broadcasts*, July 15, 1993.

12. Law on the Names and Surnames No. 300/1993 Coll., adopted September 24, 1993.

13. "Name law not to be discussed again-Parliamentary leadership," *CTK National News Wire*, September 28, 1993.

14. "European Council to sent [*sic*] mission in Slovakia," *CTK National News Wire*, November 12, 1993.

15. "Austria to propose further CE observation of Slovakia," *CTK National News Wire*, November 26, 1993.

16. "President signs law on names," *BBC Summary of World Broadcasts*, December 9, 1993.

17. "The Slovak Republic; Minister not considering bilingual place names," *BBC Summary of World Broadcasts*, June 3, 1993.

18. "Premier Vladimir Meciar on the controversy over road signs," *BBC Summary of World Broadcasts*, August 16, 1993.

19. Letter from the HCNM to Minister for Foreign Affairs Jozef Moravcik, The Hague, 8 November 1993, Reference: No 1320/93/L

20. "Government approves bill on bilingual Slovak-Hungarian signs," *BBC Summary of World Broadcasts*, May 12, 1994.

21. Author's interview, Bela Bugar, chief of the Hungarian Party Coalition and longtime deputy, February 7, 2000. Such a view was confirmed in an author's interview, foreign policy experts at the Slovak Foreign Policy Association, February 8, 2000.

22. The pact's purpose was "to resolve the problem of minorities and to strengthen the inviolability of frontiers. . . to promote good neighborly relations. . . to facilitate rapprochement between those States and the Union and their cooperation with it by helping them to fulfill the condition listed by the European Council in Copenhagen." European Commission, *The European Councils: Conclusions of the Presidency 1992–1994*, Luxembourg: Commission of the European Communities, 1995, 117.

23. "Hungary likely to sign treaties with Slovakia, Romania: Holbrooke," *Agence France Presse*, February 24, 1995.

24. Article 11 of the CE Recommendation 1201 says, "In the regions where they are in a majority the persons belonging to a national minority shall have the right to have at their disposal appropriate local or autonomous authorities or to have a special status, matching the specific historical and territorial situation and in accordance with the domestic legislation of the state." Recommendation 1201 (1993) 1 on an additional protocol on the rights of national minorities to the European Convention on Human Rights.

25. "Talks on Slovak Hungarian treaty blocked," *CTK National News Wire*, March 5, 1995.

26. "Hungarian spokesman on Slovak Hungarian Bratislava talks," *CTK National News Wire*, March 6, 1995.

27. "Prime Minister Horn's reply to European leaders," *MTI Econews*, March 10, 1995.

28. "Two open questions hamper signing of Slovak Hungarian treaty," *CTK National News Wire*, March 10, 1995.

29. " Hungary to sign basic treaties only if minority rights guaranteed," *BBC Summary of World Broadcasts*, March 10, 1995.

30. "Meciar, Horn to discuss bilateral treaty," *Deutsche Presse-Agentur*, March 15, 1995.

31. "Six open questions between Slovakia and Hungary-foreign minister," *CTK National News Wire*, March 15, 1995.

32. "Is Hungarian Slovak treaty ticket to NATO and EU," *CTK National News Wire*, March 17, 1995.

33. "Hungarian Romanian talks fail Slovak radio," *CTK National News Wire*, March 16, 1995.

34. The agreement included Recommendation 1201, with an addendum clarifying that the recommendation applied to individual, not collective, rights.

35. "Premier Meciar speaks at the Stability Pact conference in Paris," *BBC Summary of World Broadcasts*, March 21, 1995.

36. "Is Hungarian Slovak treaty ticket to NATO and EU?" *CTK National News Wire*, March 17, 1995.

37. "Treaty costs Meciar some friends," *Prague Post*, March 29, 1995.

38. Balogh, 1995, 839; Chmel 1996; Dunay 1995a, 26–7; Póti and Dunay 1995, 442. Cited in Williams 2000. See also Fisher.

39. "Meciar speaks on his first 100 days," *CTK National News Wire*, March 29, 1995.

40. "Foreign affairs; Interview, premier on political benefit of treaty with Hungary," *BBC Summary of World Broadcasts*, March 25, 1995.

41. "Slovak National Party leader 'dreads' treaty with Hungary," *BBC Summary of World Broadcasts*, March 22, 1995; "Ethnic Hungarians on the brink of high treason—Slota," *CTK National News Wire*, April 27, 1995.

42. In June 1995 the HCNM visited Slovakia and stressed that the ratification of the Slovak-Hungarian basic treaty would help solve ethnic minority issues. The fall 1995 EU-Slovak joint parliamentary committee meeting discussed the ratification of the Treaty, as did van der Stoel in a January 1996 visit.

43. For a full text of the treaty and the Slovak addendum, see Ministry of Foreign Affairs of the Slovak Republic, Treaty on Good Neighborliness and Friendly Cooperation between the Slovak Republic and the Republic of Hungary (and the Statement by the Government of the Slovak Republic on the Treaty with the Republic with Hungary) and the situation of the Hungarian Minority in the Slovak Republic (a Comparison with the International Documents), June 1995.

44. A Slovak political analyst wrote, "The SNS is a "single-issue" party having the Hungarian minority in Slovakia as its main theme. . . . The SNS argued that the Slovak Republic, a young state, was confronted with the threat of a united opposition, the leaders of the Hungarian minority and the numerous foreign ene-

mies. . . . Following this line of argument were also statements of party leaders that opposition parties were preparing 'political disturbances' (March 1995) or a 'palace coup' (July 1995), the proposal to forbid the Slovak branch of the Open Society Fund, and the suggesting of beginning the criminal prosecution of leader of the Hungarian parties for treason." *Global Report* 1995–1996, 22.

45. "Ethnic Hungarians on the brink of high treason—Slota," *CTK National News Wire*, April 27, 1995.

46. Letter from HCNM van der Stoel to Slovak Minister for Foreign Affairs Schenk, February 26, 1996.

47. "EU still dissatisfied with state of human rights in Slovakia," *CTK National News Wire*, February 27, 1996.

48. The government proposed that deputies' speeches in the debate be limited to ten minutes each. The Opposition Christian Democratic Movement (KDH) leader. Jan Carnogursky, spoke against passing a law drawn up by "a thrice-punished cop," for which Slota described him as "human ruin." Harsh words dominated the debate, although Bartolomej Kunc (SNS) called on deputies to be nonconfrontational, defending the amendment on the grounds of "the mission of the state as the supreme organisor of a free and democratic society." Peter Weiss, leader of the opposition Democratic Left Party (SDL), which is the successor to the Communist Party, also described the law as a "conscious return" to former habits, allowing for expedient interpretations and suppression of rights and freedoms. The SDL believed the amendment negates any good gained by ratifying the basic bilateral treaty with Hungary and puts Slovakia into a difficult position regarding eventual membership in the EU. The amendment has been seen as one of the conditions set by the SNS in exchange for support of the Slovak-Hungarian bilateral treaty, another point on the agenda of the current parliament. The treaty was to settle differences in relations between Slovakia and Hungary, and was considered vital for both countries' EU-membership bids. Weiss said the amendment was not for the "protection" of the republic, but rather "a whip to use on people who have different viewpoints." But he said the opposition would not be intimidated, and that the SDL would support handing the amendment to the Constitutional Court for consideration. KDH Deputy Ivan Simko also described the amendment as "criminal" and compared it to a law drawn up in 1948, shortly after Communists seized power in Czechoslovakia. Simko's party colleague Frantisek Miklosko said that the ideology of the "patriots" had been drafted by former StB (communist secret police) agents. He warned that the next stage would be the removal of political opponents and their imprisonment. Hungarian Christian Democratic Movement (MKDH) leader Bela Bugar said the amendment was intended to "muzzle" anyone with different opinions, while Jan Langos, leader of the nonparliamentary Democratic Party (DS), said the government was behaving like a foreign occupier. "Parliament approves 'protection of republic' amendment," *CTK National News Wire*, March 26, 1996.

49. Law on the protection of the republic, Article 92 b sub 1.

50. "Slovaks protest as their freedoms are whittled away fear freedoms are under threat; New anti-subversion law confirms fears of drift towards totalitarianism, writes Adrian Bridge," *The Independent* (London), April 1, 1996.

51. Declaration by the Presidency on behalf of the European Union on Slovakia, April 3, 1996. See http://ue.eu.int/pesc/article.asp?lang=en&id=19606253.

52. "President does not sign law on 'the protection of the republic,' " *CTK National News Wire*, April 9, 1996.

53. "EU/Slovakia: Joint Parliament Committee hears strong words from Van den Broek," *Europe Information Service, Euro-East*, June 18, 1996

54. "Slovakia's political image different than the economic one—EU," *CTK National News Wire*, July 1, 1996

55. "National party session; Party criticizes Hungary, wants new debate on Penal Code," *BBC Summary of World Broadcasts*, July 22, 1996.

56. National party session; Party criticizes Hungary, wants new debate on Penal Code, *BBC Summary of World Broadcasts*, July 22, 1996.

57. Letter from HCNM van der Stoel to Slovak Minister for Foreign Affairs Schenk, August 13, 1996.

58. "Slovak parliament passes protection of republic amendment," *CTK National News Wire*, December 17, 1996.

59. Referring to Article 87 of the constitution, Kovac claimed that parliament had not fulfilled its duty of discussing the law once it was returned by the president in April. Consequently, parliament could not discuss a further amendment before having discussed the previous version of the law.

60. "EU warns Slovakia on minority rights," *Limited Reuters World Service*, February 14, 1997.

61. Author's interview, Bela Bugar, February 7, 2000. Author's interview, Grigorij Meseznikov, President for the Institute for Public Affairs, February 9, 2000.

62. Author's interview, Peter Hunzik, Founder of the Hungarian Civil Liberal Party, February 9, 2000.

63. Author's interview, Frantisek Sebej, Chairman of the Committee for European Integration, February 8, 2000.

64. "Electoral law amendment not anti-democratic—Duray," *CTK National News Wire*, March 8, 1998.

65. Letter from HCNM van der Stoel to Minister of Foreign Affairs Zdenka Kramplova, May 29, 1998.

66. "EU concerned about Slovakia's amendment to electoral law," *BBC Monitoring Europe—Political*, May 26, 1998.

67. "EU envoy slams democracy in Slovakia after visit," *BBC Summary of World Broadcasts*, June 22, 1998.

68. Law on election to municipal self-government bodies. Act no. 233/1998 Coll.

69. Letter from to Minister of Foreign Affairs Zdenka Kramplova to HCNM van der Stoel, July 13, 1998.

70. The new regulations defined school reports as official documents, which, according to the language law, must be issued in state language. "Education Ministry says school reports must be in Slovak," *BBC Summary of World Broadcasts*, February 3, 1997.

71. Adding to OSCE efforts to persuade the government to reverse the school certificate policy, fifty-five thousand parents of Hungarian pupils signed a petition protesting the cancellation of bilingual school certificates to Slovak education minister Eva Slavkovska, and over eleven thousand parents sent protest letters to the government. "Government receives 11,000 protest letters on minority education," *CTK National News Wire*, May 12, 1997.

72. "Ethnic Hungarians request international help over school issue," *BBC Summary of World Broadcasts,* July 4, 1997.

73. "Slovakia on same level as best EU membership candidates—Sestak," *Czech News Agency (CTK) CTK National News Wire,* May 26, 1998; "EU/Slovakia: Joint parliamentary committee goes over the Same Ground again," *Europe Information Service European Report,* May 27, 1998.

74. Council Of Europe, Committee Of Ministers, Resolution (93) 33, Invitation to Slovakia to Become a Member of the Council of Europe, Adopted by the Committee of Ministers on June 30, 1993, at the 496bis meeting of the Ministers' Deputies.

75. "An important condition of fulfilling the national interest of the state-forming nation is the protection of its language. The government will prepare a law on the state language in such a way that it satisfy European customs and the nation's requirements, and emanate from the Constitution of the Slovak Republic. In this way, the formation of dams separating members of various ethnic groups living on the territory of the Slovak Republic can be avoided. All citizens of the Slovak Republic will be provided with equal opportunities for success on the entire territory of the state."

Excerpt from the Program of the Government of the Slovak Republic, adopted January 12, 1995.

76. Letter from HCNM van der Stoel to Minister for Foreign Affairs Schenk, August 24, 1995. Letter from HCNM van der Stoel to Minister for Foreign Affairs Schenk, November 13, 1995. Parliamentary Assembly of the Council of Europe, Committee on Legal Affairs and Human Rights, Honouring of obligations and commitments by Member States of the Council of Europe, Slovak Republic, Considerations on the Act of the Slovak Republic on Its State Language in the Light of the Standards of the Council of Europe, Strasbourg, January 18, 1996, AS/jur (1996)7.

77. Surprisingly, 108 out of 142 deputies present expressed their support to the adoption of this law. The nationalist card was used to influence the vote, with some deputies observing that the territory that is now Slovakia was ruled by Hungary for one a thousand years. Zora Lasarova, who represented Meciar's HZDS, said that "anyone who votes against that bill is against the fulfillment of the Slovaks' desires and deserves public contempt." An influential factor in voting was a HZDS proposal that each deputy state his opinion out loud after his name was called, with the entire proceeding broadcast on Slovak television. The opposition parties feared being labeled anti-Slovak if they did not support the bill, and several deputies walked out before the vote in an apparent effort to avoid making a decision (Fisher 1996, 14–15). In the end, most deputies from the opposition Democratic Union (DU)—formally a "liberal" party—and the former Communists' Party of the Democratic Left (SDL) voted in favor of the language bill, although many of their amendments were rejected during parliamentary discussions. They did so, however, based on a promise that a law on minority languages would soon follow. Author's interview, Peter Weiss, SDL, February 10, 2000.

78. Letter from Minister for Foreign Affairs Schenk to HCNM van der Stoel, December 18, 1995.

79. Letter from HCNM van der Stoel to Minister for Foreign Affairs Schenk, February 26, 1996.

80. Council of Europe, Parliamentary Assembly, Committee on Legal Affairs and Human Rights, Honouring of Obligations and Commitments by Member States, Slovakia, Considerations of the Act of the Slovak Republic on Its State Language in the Light of the Standards of the Council of Europe, by Dr. Heinz Tichy, Strassbourg, January 18, 1996, AS/Jur (1996) 7.

81. Second meeting of the association council between the European Union and the Slovak Republic, Brussels, February 27, 1996, *RAPID*, February 27, 1996.

82. "As regards the connection between this law and the legitimate language rights of persons belonging to national minorities, allow me, Your Excellency, to draw your attention to the not entirely accurate quotation on your part of para. 4 in the Section 1 of the said law. Under this para., 'the usage of languages of national minorities and ethnic groups is arranged by separate laws'; that is, not 'will be dealt with' as you state in your letter. This means that the language rights of persons belonging to national minorities in the Slovak Republic are guaranteed and arranged by at least 12 legal norms, including the Slovak Constitution, to the extent corresponding with The Slovak Republic's international commitments."
Letter from Minister for Foreign Affairs Schenk to HCNM van der Stoel, April 23, 1996.

83. "Slovakia's political image different than the economic one—EU," *Czech News Agency (CTK) CTK National News Wire*, July 1, 1996; "US, EU warns Slovakia on democratic reforms," *Limited Reuters World Service*, October 21, 1996. "EU/ Slovakia: Joint parliament committee hears strong words from van den Broek," *Europe Information Service Euro-East*, June 18, 1996; "Ethnic Hungarians complain about minority rights at EU-Slovak meeting," *BBC Summary of World Broadcasts*, October 31, 1996.

84. Restricted Internal OSCE memorandum.

85. "Ministry says no need for law on minority languages—Hungarian radio," *BBC Summary of World Broadcasts*, January 24, 1997.

86. "EU warns Slovakia on minority rights," *Limited Reuters World Service*, February 14, 1997. The institutions got a boost from a March 1997 ruling by Slovakia's Constitutional Court that Hungarian did have the right to use their own language in official state contacts, although the court did not uphold many of the other language rights. "Minorities have no right to use native language in parliament," *BBC Summary of World Broadcasts*, March 6, 1998

87. By June 1997, at a joint EU-Slovak parliamentary committee meeting, the cochairman of the joint committee Herbert Boesch, said that the Slovak Republic could not count on an invitation to open talks on joining the union. The list of the sins of the current government was very long. The committee issued a statement recommending that Slovakia, inter alia, prepare legislation on the use of national minority languages by the end of November.

88. "Premier accepts country's exclusion from European integration process," *BBC Summary of World Broadcasts*, September 24, 1997.

89. The government distributed a memorandum to European institutions and embassies saying that twenty-six laws, including the Slovak Constitution, cover the

ethnic minority rights and that twelve laws concern the use of ethnic minority languages. Foreign Minister Zdenka Kramplova denied at a press conference that the memorandum meant a definitive "no" because although the government did not consider the passing of a special law necessary the memorandum "creates space for an international analysis." "If that then showed the need for such a law to be passed we are also open to such a solution," Kramplova said. In the meantime the memorandum would enable the above-mentioned problem not to be "constantly" raised by foreign partners, she added. "No need for minority language law-government," *BBC Summary of World Broadcasts*, November 6, 1997.

90. "Slovakia rejects language law bid," *Prague Post*, November 19, 1997.

91. "EU/Slovakia: Parliament committee says include Slovakia in enlargement talks," *Europe Information Service European Report*, November 28, 1997

92. Author's interview, anonymous representative of one of the institutions, 1998.

93. "EU envoy slams democracy in Slovakia after visit," *BBC Summary of World Broadcasts*, June 22, 1998

94. *RFE/RL Newsline*, June 18, 1998.

95. "Slovak Press Survey," *CTK National News Wire*, September 2, 1998.

96. "Slovakia to present its new situation at June 1999 EU summit—minister," *BBC Monitoring Europe—Political*, December 28, 1998.

97. "Ethnic languages law needed for EU entry talks," *CTK National News Wire*, March 19, 1999.

98. "Language law held up by squabble," *Slovak Spectator* June 7–13, 1999.

99. *RFE/RL Newsline*, 4 June 1999.

100. "MP appeals to ethnic Hungarians to back minority language law," *BBC Summary of World Broadcasts*, June 10, 1999.

101. "Slovak president calls on government to approve minority language bill," *BBC Monitoring Europe—Political*, June 16, 1999.

102. A SMK ideal law would touch on the legal use of minority languages at weddings, burials, in broadcasting for national minorities, and on the dubbing of video cassettes available in video rental shops in ethnically mixed territories.

103. "Nationalists demonstrate against language law," *BBC Summary of World Broadcasts*, June 25, 1999.

104. *RFE/RL Newsline*, June 28, 1999.

105. Author's interview, Tomás Strázay, Slovak Foreign Policy Association, February 8, 2000; Author's interview, Juraj Hrabko, General Director, Section on Human Rights and Minorities, Slovak Republic Government Office, February 10, 2000; Author's interview, SDL Deputy Peter Weiss, Chairman of the Foreign Affairs Committee, February 10, 2000; Michael Shafir, "Radical Politics In Post Communist East Central Europe, Part I: 'Reds,' 'Pinks,' 'Blacks,' and 'Blues', " *RFE/RL* report on East European Perspectives, 1(1) (November 3, 1999).

106. Council of Europe, Parliamentary Assembly, Committee on the Honoring of obligation and commitments by member states of the Council of Europe, Slovakia, Rapporteurs: Mr. Lesein and Mr. Leoni, Preliminary Draft Report, 23 October, 1998, AS/MON (1998) 50, paragraph 93.

107. "Hungarian ministers in Slovak cabinet solving urgent problems," *CTK National News Wire*, November 4, 1998.

108. "Amendment to law on bilingual school reports passes first reading," *BBC Monitoring Europe—Political*, January 14, 1999.

109. "Slovakia, 1998–1999. A Global Report on the State of Society," Institute for Public Affairs, 1999.

110. Author's interview, Miroslav Wlachovsky, February 7, 2000.

111. Author's interview, Gregorij Meseznikov, president of the Institute for Public Affairs, February 8, 2000.

112. Author's interview, Juraj Hrabko, General Director, Section on Human Rights and Minorities, Slovak Government, February 10, 2000.

113. Steve Kettle, "Slovakia's one-man band," *Transition*, August 23, 1996.

114. Author's interview, members of the Slovak Foreign Policy Association, February 8, 2000.

115. *East European Constitutional Review*, 6(4) (Fall 1997), Constitution Watch, a country-by-country update on constitutional politics in Eastern Europe and the ex-USSR: Slovakia.

116. Wlachovsky 1997, 46.

117. Új Szó (Bratislava/Pozsony), August 31, 1998.

118. "Full version of European Union demarche towards Slovakia," *BBC Summary of World Broadcasts*, November 30, 1994.

119. "Full text of European Parliament warning to Slovakia," *CTK National News Wire*, November 17, 1995.

120. In February 1996 on a trip to Bratislava, European External Relations Commissioner Hans van den Broek said that Slovakia would have to allow greater press freedom and respect minority rights if it wanted to take part in preparations for admission to the EU (Meseznikov 1998, 19). The Slovak-EU Association Council meeting pressured Slovakia, in a memorandum, to ratify the Slovak-Hungarian treaty and pass a law on minority languages. Second meeting of the Association Council between the European Union and the Slovak Republic, RAPID, February 27, 1996.

121. "EU strictures on Slovakia," *Financial Times*, May 30, 1997.

122. The text of the 1997 Commission opinion and other relevant documents on EU enlargement can be found on the EU enlargement website at http://europa.eu.int/comm/enlargement/index.htm.

123. "EU hands Slovakia list of membership conditions," *Reuter European Community Report*, May 29, 1997

124. "Premier accepts country's exclusion from European integration process," *BBC Summary of World Broadcasts*, September 24, 1997.

CHAPTER 7
ROMANIA: THE LONG ROAD

1. This background introduction relies heavily on East and Pontin 1997; Stan 1997; Van Houten 1998.

2. The circumstances of this incident are still debated, and there is no agreement on the exact numbers of dead or wounded. The death toll ranges from four to twelve. "Power of the pulpit; politics: Laszlo Tokes used his role as a minister to

speak against the corrupt Romanian regime. Now he speaks on behalf of Romania's fledgling democracy," *Los Angeles Times*, March 26, 1990.

3. HCNM, Remarks to the meeting of Romania's Council for National Minorities, August 18, 1993.

4. CSCE Comm. 253–Letter dated 9 September 1993 to Minister for Foreign Affairs of the Republic of Romania, Teodor Melescanu.

5. "Minorities council raises questions," *RFE/RL research report* 2(24) (June 11, 1993): 38.

6. CE, Parliamentary Assembly, Opinion 176, paragraph 10, 28 September 1993.

7. "Council of Europe delegation conducts inquiry into human rights policies," *BBC Summary of World Broadcasts*, March 31, 1994. Source: Romanian Radio, Bucharest, in Romanian 1900 gmt 28 Mar 94.

8. In May 1994, the minister of foreign affairs replied in a letter to the HCNM outlining various proposals. Minister of State, Minister of Foreign Affairs' answer to the OSCE High Commissioner on National Minorities of May 30, 1994. In October 1994 President Iliescu said in a speech to the Parliamentary Assembly of the CE that his government had submitted a draft minority law to parliament that observed the standards of the CE, the CSCE, and the UN regarding the rights of persons belonging to ethnic minorities. "Iliescu addresses Parliamentary Assembly of Council of Europe," *BBC Summary of World Broadcasts*, October 6, 1994.

9. "Five years later: Eastern Europe, Post-Communism—A special report," *New York Times*, November 26, 1994.

10. "Budapest, Bucharest in new clash over ethnic Hungarians," *Agence France Presse*, January 27, 1995.

11. "Hungarian Minority meeting criticized in Romania," *Agence France Presse*, February 19, 1995.

12. "Central Europe: Romanian-Hungarian ethnic tension flares up," *Inter Press Service*, March 6, 1995.

13. Romanian Television, January 20. 1995. Cited in "Ruling party formalizes relations with Extremists," *Transition*, April 14, 1995, 43.

14. Confidential source.

15. "Ethnic Hungarians protest at decision to replace Harghita and Covasna prefects," *BBC Summary of World Broadcasts*, July 27, 1992.

16. "RNUP supports government decision to replace prefects, criticises HDUR," *BBC Summary of World Broadcasts*, July 27, 1992.

17. "Premier Stolojan responds to questions on Transylvania and the economic reform," *BBC Summary of World Broadcasts*, July 28, 1992.

18. "Premier Stolojan responds to questions on Transylvania and the economic reform," *BBC Summary of World Broadcasts*, July 28, 1992.

19. *East European Constitutional Review*, spring 1993.

20. "Senate holds heated debate over Covasna, Harghita prefects," *BBC Summary of World Broadcasts*, March 31, 1993.

21. "Government: HDUR attempt to 'internationalise' prefect affair a 'dangerous game'," *BBC Summary of World Broadcasts*, April 5, 1993.

22. "Hungarian deputies ask Romanian parliament to mediate in dispute over prefects," *BBC Summary of World Broadcasts*, April 13, 1993.

23. "HDUR president's statements on Romania's membership request to Council of Europe," *MTI Econews*, April 30, 1993.

24. "Spokeswoman unhappy at delay in accepting Romania into Council of Europe," *BBC Summary of World Broadcasts*, May 15, 1993.

25. "Council of Europe official explains delay in granting full membership to Romania," *BBC Summary of World Broadcasts*, June 17, 1993.

26. Parliamentary Assembly of the Council of Europe, 19 July 1993, Doc. 6901, Report on the application by Romania for membership of the Council of Europe.

27. "Council of Europe delegation conducts inquiry into human rights policies," *BBC Summary of World Broadcasts*, March 31, 1994. Source: Romanian Radio, Bucharest, in Romanian, 1900 gmt 28 Mar 94

28. "Nationalists said to be pressing government to sack pro-Hungarian officials," *BBC Summary of World Broadcasts* , October 24, 1995.

29. "PDSR says CDR should not give posts to UDMR," Bucharest Radio Romania Network in Romanian, 1100 GMT 7 Nov 96, FBIS-EEU-96-218.

30. CSCE Comm. 253; Letter from HCNM van der Stoel to Romanian Minister for Foreign Affairs Teodor Melescanu, September 9, 1993; Council of Europe, Doc. 7795(Report); November 4, 1997. Honouring of obligations and commitments by Romania, Gunnar JANSSON (Finland, LDR).

31. Law on local public administration, Law No. 24, April 12, 1996.

32. Agenda 2000, Opinion on Romania's Application for Membership, European Commission, 1997, "1.2 Human Rights and the Protection of Minorities."

33. "UDMR promises support for new cabinet, reform program," Bucharest Radio Romania Network in Romanian, 1600 GMT 6 Apr 98, FBIS-EEU-98-096.

34. *East European Constitutional Review* 7(3) (summer 1998).

35. Tony Blair, Speech to the Romanian Parliament, May 4, 1999. Copy obtained from the Romanian mission to the EU in Brussels.

36. *RFE/RL Newsline*, May 26, 1999.

37. Letter addressed by Mr. Teodor Melescanu, Minister of State, Minister for Foreign Affairs of Romania, to Mr. Friedrich König, Rapporteur for Romania of the Political Affairs Committee, 22 June 1993.

38. CSCE Comm. 253, Letter dated September 9, 1993, to the Minister for Foreign Affairs of the Republic of Romania, Mr. Teodor Melescanu.

39. Report on the Application by Romania for membership of the Council of Europe, July 19, 1993, Doc., 6901, Parliamentary Assembly of the Council of Europe.

40. "Council of Europe delegation conducts inquiry into human rights policies," *BBC Summary of World Broadcasts*, March 31, 1994. Source: Romanian Radio, Bucharest, in Romanian, 1900 gmt 28 Mar 94

41. Minister of State, Minister of Foreign Affairs' answer to the HCNM of May 30, 1994.

42. Peter Humphrey, "Iliescu appeals for calm among ethnic Hungarians," *Reuters*, July 16, 1994.

43. "Europe helps Romania's ethnic dispute," *United Press International*, August 18, 1994.

44. Law No. 84/1995, Article 122 (1): "In vocational, technical, economic, administrative, agricultural, forestry, mountain-agricultural public education, as well

as in post-secondary education, specialist training is provided in Romanian, assuring also, as far as possible, the learning of the specialistic terminology in the mother tongue."

45. Ibid., Article 120.

46. "Ethnic Hungarian leader welcomes stand on education law," *BBC Summary of World Broadcasts*, July 17, 1995.

47. "Hungarians to continue protest against Education Law," *BBC Summary of World Broadcasts*, August 9, 1995.

48. HCNM, Statement on the occassion of the HCNM mission to Romania, August 28–31, 1995–September 1, 1995.

49. REF.HC/6/96, Letter dated 26 February 1996 to the Minister for Foreign Affairs of the Republic of Romania, Mr. Teodor Melescanu.

50. "Opposition tactics behind education law deal—ethnic Hungarian leader," *BBC Summary of World Broadcasts*, July 6, 1999.

51. Urgent Governmental Decree No. 36(1997) on modification of the Act on Education.

52. Urgency Ordinance n° 36/1997 referring to modifying and completing the Law of Education n° 84, 1995.

53. "President, ethnic Hungarians issue joint statement," *BBC Summary of World Broadcasts*, December 12, 1997.

54. With the departure of SDU ministers, the new administration is dominated by Prime Minister Ciorbea's Christian Democrats with NLP and DAHR as junior partners. Ciorbea now heads a minority government, which only holds 152 of Parliament's 328 seats and must rely on the SDU's 53 deputies for legislative support.

55. HCNM.GAL/1/98; Letter of March 2, 1998 to the Minister for Foreign Affairs of the Republic of Romania, Mr. Andrei Plesu.

56. "Hungarian organization to stay in government with conditions," *BBC Monitoring Europe—Political*, June 29, 1998.

57. "Iliescu Says NATO, EU Main Reason for Treaty With Hungary," Budapest MTV Television Network in Hungarian, 1700 GMT 22 Sept. 96, Lexis Nexis Database number: FBIS-EEU-96-185.

58. "Funar to withdraw PUNR ministers if Hungarian treaty signed," *BBC Summary of World Broadcasts*, March 23, 1995.

59. *East European Constitutional Review*, spring 1995.

60. "EU/Romania: parliamentary committee studies progress with membership bid," *European Report*, October 21, 1995.

61. "Commissioner Hans van den Broek visits Romania and Slovakia," *Together in Europe* 83 (February 15, 1996).

62. "A possible light at the end of the tunnel," *Transition*, September 20, 1996. The Hungarian Government and the ministry of foreign affairs officially endorsed a declaration at the conclusion of the Hungarian minority summit in Budapest calling for "the establishment of local governments and autonomy" for Hungarian minorities. The declaration also committed the Hungarian government to financially support the self-government aspirations of Hungarians abroad by allocating a percentage of the national budge to their cause. The declaration said that self-rule was vital to preserve the identity of ethnic Hungarians abroad. The West and

neighboring states reacted sharply to the government's endorsement of the declaration. Domestic criticism also built. The Horn government tried to argue that the document was not binding, but the criticism continued.

63. CE Recommendation 1201, Article 15. *East European Constitutional Review* 5(4) (Fall 1996).

64. Contrary to the treaty with Slovakia, where Slovakia's interpretation of Recommendation 1201 was only attached in an addendum, which Hungary did not sign, the Romanian treaty with Hungary incorporated this restrictive interpretation into a footnote of the treaty itself. Thus, the limitation on collective rights had more legitimacy. The following comment was added to the treaty: "the Recommendation does not concern collective rights and does not require special autonomous status to be granted on the basis of ethnic criteria."

65. "Vacaroiu stresses 'special' role of treaty with Hungary," *Bucharest Radio Romania Network*, in Romanian, 0935 16 Sep 96, FBIS-EEU-96-180.

66. "Iliescu Says NATO, EU Main Reason for Treaty With Hungary," Budapest MTV Television Network, in Hungarian, 1700 GMT 22 Sept. 96, FBIS-EEU-96-185.

67. "A possible light at the end of the tunnel," *Transition*, September 20, 1996, 29.

68. EU document: Relations between the European Union and Romania , European Union, DN: MEMO/96/12, July 2, 1996. In addition to the trade component, the agreement had an important section on political dialogue and guidelines on democratic reform, the need to sign a treaty with Hungary, the need to allow the Hungarian minority their own local administration and education in their own language, and the need to accommodate the Roma.

69. "German foreign minister's visit; Kinkel says conditions for Romania's EU entry still unfulfilled," *BBC Summary of World Broadcasts*, July 15, 1994.

70. *FRE/RL Newsline*, July 19, 1995.

71. "A possible light at the end of the tunnel," *Transition*, 20 September, 1996.

72. Hans van den Broek Member of the European Commission EU support for reform in Romania, Romanian Parliament, Bucharest, 7 March 1997, European Union, DN: Speech/97/54, July 3, 1997; *RFE/RL Newsline*, November 4, 1997.

73. "Reform in Romania too slow," *Romania Libera Online*, July 15–22, 1998.

74. Declaration by the Presidency on behalf of the European Union on Romania, January 22, 1999. The document can be found on the EU website at http://ue.eu.int/pesc/article.asp?lang=en&id=19905352.

CHAPTER 8
ALTERNATIVE EXPLANATIONS: RUSSIA, HUNGARY, AND DEMOCRATIC DEVELOPMENT

1. See the discussion of this case in chapter 5 for more details on later developments.

2. Martin Klatt, "Russians in the near-abroad.: *RFE/RL Research report* 3(32) (1994): 33–44.

3. "Latvian Chronology," *Monthly Survey of Baltic and Post-Soviet Politics*, May 1993, p. 15.

4. For example, on July 28, 1993, the U.S. Senate unanimously adopted an amendment calling on Russia to withdraw its troops from the Baltic States. On September 23, 1993 the U.S. Senate passed (97–1) the Byrd amendment, which linked aid to Russian to withdrawal of its troops from the Balkan states.

5. "The Russian President's Statement on Estonian 'ethnic Cleansing' and 'Apartheid,' " *ITAR-TASS News Agency*, June 25, 1993, as translated in the *BBC Survey of World Broadcasts*, SU/1726, June 28, 1993, p. A2/1.

6. "Yeltsin now says he plans to keep troops in Estonia," *New York Times*, July 11, 1994, A1

7. *East European Constitutional Review*, "Estonia Update," 6(1) (Winter 1997).

8. *The Monthly Survey of Baltic and Post-Soviet Politics*, Tallinn: Panor Press, Sakala Center, March, 1994.

9. Press statement by the Presidency on behalf of the European Union on the signing of the Latvian-Russian agreements on the withdrawal of Russian troops from Latvia, DN: PESC94/47, October, 5, 1994.

10. Dzintra Bungs, "Yeltsin links troop pullouts to Russian minorities," *RFE/RE*, July 6, 1994.

11. "Clinton brings help and a warning to Baltics," *Financial Times*, July 7, 1994, p. 2.

12. "Latvian withdrawal reaffirmed," *Moscow Times*, August 6, 1994; "Yeltsin issues statement condemning Latvia for ethnic intolerance," *BBC Summary of World Broadcasts*, August 8, 1994; "Russia withdraws at last," *International Herald Tribune*, September 2, 1994.

13. "Defence minister on Romanian military agreement; situation with refugees," *BBC Summary of World Broadcasts*, June 5, 1992.

14. "NATO dreams spark reconciliation; Desire to join pact credited with repairing Hungarian-Slovakian ties," *Washington Times*, April 4, 1995.

15. Statements by Hungarian and Romanian Defence Ministers, *MTI Econews*, February 4, 1995.

16. "Latvian PM calls for new education reform policy," *Baltic News Service*, August 30, 1996

17. The events of March, 1998, have been summarized as follows: "An increase in tension between the Latvian government and the Latvian Russophone population ignited a diplomatic firestorm between Latvia and the Russian Federation, during the spring quarter. The international row fractured the ruling coalition and threatened the stability of Prime Minister Guntars Krast's government. On March 3, the Russian-language newspaper, *Panorama Latvia*, posted a call for a rally near the Riga City Council building to protest a hike in city taxes. Held that day, the meeting was attended by roughly 1,000 people, primarily Russophone pensioner, who blocked one of the roads in front of the council building. Police reinforcements, called in to break up the protests, used truncheons to disperse the crowd. Images of Latvian police beating elderly men and women were filmed by several television stations and, soon thereafter, the footage was broadcast on television channels in the Russian Federation. Russian foreign Minister Yevgeny Primakov denounced Latvia's 'Flagrant violation of basic human rights,' and Moscow Mayor Yuri Luzhkov likened the treatment of Russophones in the

Latvian regime to Cambodia under Pol Pot. The Duma of the Russian Federation pressured Yeltsin to defend the rights of Russophones living in Latvia. Two weeks later, on March 16, a commemorative march of approximately 4000 veterans of the Latvian Legion took place in Riga. The German occupation forces, which recruited Latvians into the Nazi SS and the German army during W.W. II formed the legion. Although some Latvians were forced to join the legion, many joined voluntarily. . . . Some view the veterans as the heroic opponents of the soviet invaders, while others, including a large segment of the Latvian Russophone population, see them as complicit in the Nazi genocide of Latvia's Jewish and Russian populations. The government had announced that it would not involve itself in the event, and the minister of defense issued an order forbidding the participation of any military officials. Nevertheless, Juris Dalbins, high commander of the National Armed Forces, participated in the march in his uniform, and several Fatherland and Freedom Party parliamentarians—the party of Prime Minister Krasts—also attended the march. . . . Dalbins preempted a decision dismiss him and resigned. . . . On March 16, approximately 5,000 people, mostly Russophone non-citizens, attended a rally in Riga demanded the extension of the Soviet passports. . . . On March 24, amendments to the passport regulation were approved. . . . On April 1, a bomb exploded at the Riga synagogue. Nobody has claimed responsibility for the explosion, which was condemned by the president, Parliament , and the government. The child of the State Police and the chief of Riga Criminal Police were dismissed. . . On April 6, another blast went off near the Russian embassy in Riga. Again, no one claimed responsibility. In March, Russian threatened to impose economic sanctions. While many countries and international organizations condemned Yeltsin's bullying tactics, they nonetheless conceded that Latvia had to do more to integrate its Russophone population. The tensions divided the governing coalition into two factions. In early April, the minister of economics, Atis Sausnitis (DPS), stated that possible sanctions from Russia and the loss of the Russian market would be detrimental for the Latvian economy. . . . On April 3, Krasts dismissed Sausnitis from his post for, among other things, his 'panic stricken' behavior and 'hysterical remarks.' On April 8, the DPS recalled all its ministers from the Krasts government. DPS accused Krasts of exacerbating ethnic tensions, marring the image of Latvia abroad, placing his own party interests before the interests of the state, and governing with and authoritarian style."

East European Constitutional Review (Spring 1998): 15–17.

18. "Luzhkov claims Latvia committing 'genocide' against Russian-speakers," *RFE Newsline* March 30, 1998.

19. "European Union objects to any Russian sanctions against Latvia," *LETA* (Latvian National News Agency, July 20, 1998.

20. "Kremlin spokesman says Latvia must change citizenship law," *RFE Newsline*, April 24, 1998; "Baltic Council head urges Latvia to amend citizenship law," *RFE Newsline* May 14, 1998.

21. "EU warns Riga not to drag heels on granting citizenship," *RFE Newsline*, July 21, 1998.

22. "Russian Duma threatens trade restrictions if Latvia does not revoke language law," *LETA-ITAR-TASS*, July 9, 1999; "Russian State Duma backs bill on sanctions against Latvia," *Baltic News Service*, November 16, 1999.

23. "Russian parliament takes vote on expelling Estonian diplomat," *Baltic News Service*, June 7, 1995.

24. "Appeal court finds in favour of expelled Russian nationalist," *BBC Summary of World Broadcasts*, October 10, 1996.

25. Foye 1992; Van Houten 1998, p. 143.

26. "Eric Jansson, Guntars Krasts and the silent treatment," *Baltic Times*, April 23, 1998.

27. See for example, Human rights and the situation of the Russian national minority in Estonia, Council of Europe, Doc. 7671, 2 October 1996, Motion for a Resolution, presented by Mr Glotov and others.

28. "Romania's Hungarians Quit Ethnic Peacemaking Body," *The Reuter Library Report*, September 3, 1993; "Romanian Hungarians Complain to CSCE over Rights," *Reuters World Service*, August 15, 1994; "Relations with Council of Europe; CE official says Slovakia has fulfilled recommendations," *BBC Summary of World Broadcasts*, November 24, 1994; "Hungarian coalition parties to lodge complaint with Council of Europe," *BBC Summary of World Broadcasts*, February 16, 1995.

29. "Van der Stoel: Non-Estonian-speakers must have right to run for election," *Baltic News Service*, January 8, 1999; Council of Europe, Amendments to some Estonian laws violate the rights of minorities, Doc. 8315, 8 February 1999, Written Declaration No. 289.

30. In March and April, 1998, protests in Riga sharply focused attention on the citizenship law and renewed pressure from the institutions as tensions with Russia rose. For a detailed discussion of the events, see *East European Constitutional Review*, Spring 1998, 15–17.

31. *RFE/RL Newsline*, August 4, 1998.

Chapter 9
Conclusion

1. See chapter 2 for more discussion of these conditions.

2. Indeed, some interviewees for this study described how politicians would be very polite during meetings with the HCNM, only to quickly mock his suggestions after he had departed.

3. Letter to the HCNM from the Minister of Foreign Affairs of the Slovak Republic Zdenka Kramplová, Bratislava, 13 July 1998.

4. "Working group formed to submit amendments to citizenship bill," *BBC Summary of World Broadcasts*, June 30, 1994.

5. "Iliescu Says NATO, EU Main Reason for Treaty With Hungary," *Budapest MTV Television Network* (Hungarian), 1700 GMT 22 Sept. 96, FBIS-EEU-96-185.

6. "Premier Meciar speaks at the Stability Pact conference in Paris," *BBC Summary of World Broadcasts*, March 21, 1995.

7. "MP appeals to ethnic Hungarians to back minority language law," *BBC Summary of World Broadcasts*, June 10, 1999.

8. "Dispute over minority language law continues—press," *CTK National News Wire*, June 9, 1999.

9. "What the amendments mean for Latvia," *Baltic Times*, May 16, 2002.

10. Author's interview, John Packer, Assistant to the HCNM, October 1998.

11. Council of Europe, Opinion No. 183 (1995) on the application by Latvia for membership of the Council of Europe.

12. "Premier vows to restore economic stability, rules out autonomy for ethnic Hungarians," BBC Summary of World Broadcasts, March 9, 1999.

13. "Roughly 53 percent of the voters supported maintaining the amendments in the form passed by the parliament. Latvian voters approve citizenship reforms, back centre-right," *Deutsche Presse–Agentur*, October 4, 1998

14. Author's interview, Miroslav Wlachovsky, February 7, 2000.

15. Author's interviews, members of the government coalition, February 2000; author's interview, Peter Hunzik, Founder of the Hungarian Civil Liberal Party, February 9, 2000; Pridham 1999; Vachudova forthcoming.

16. *East European Constitutional Review* 6(4) (Fall 1997), "Constitution Watch, a country-by-country update on constitutional politics in Eastern Europe and the ex-USSR: Slovakia."

17. *FRE/RL Newsline*, July 19, 1995.

18. "A possible light at the end of the tunnel," *Transition*, September 20, 1996.

19. Ikenberry and Kupchan (1990) conclude that normative persuasion is insufficient to drive the socialization process, which works only in junction with the provision of material incentives. Similarly, in her work on the influence of the human rights network on Argentina and Mexico's policy Sikkink (1993) argues that "in the realm of human rights, it is the combination of moral pressure and material pressure that leads to change." Klotz (1996) also makes a similar argument about the use of norms and sanctions in South Africa.

20. This case is not part of this study, but nevertheless illustrates the type of engagement. *Activities of the CE*, 1990 Report, Strasbourg: CE Press, 1991, 31–32.

21. On durability of learning, see Levy 1994, 289.

22. "Crafting Cooperation: The Design and Effect of Regional Institutions in Comparative Perspective," conference, Harvard University, October 3–6, 2002

23. Cephas K. Lumina, "Political Conditionality and It's Implications for Human Rights," http://www.ossrea.net/announcements/cephas.pdf

24. Indeed, Botcheva-Andonova (2000) has studied environmental issues, and Shevel (2000) has studied refugee issues in a similar light.

References

Abbott, Kenneth, and Duncan Snidal. 2000. "Hard and Soft Law in International Governance." *International Organization* 54(3): 421–456.

Abele, Daniel. 1996. "Support for Minority Rights in Estonia, Latvia, Romania, and Slovakia." Dissertation, George Washington University.

Adler, Emanuel. 1998. "Seeds of Peaceful Change: The OSCE's Security Community-Building Model." *Security Communities*, ed. Emanuel Adler and Michael Barnett. Cambridge: Cambridge University Press, 119–160.

Alderson, Kai. 2001. "Making Sense of State Socialization." *Review of International Studies* 27: 415–433.

Amato, Giuliano, and Judy Batt. 1998. "Minority Rights and EU Enlargement to the East." RSC Policy Paper No 98/5, European University Institute.

Arrow, Kenneth. 1951. *Social Choice and Individual Values*. New Haven: Yale University Press.

Axelrod, Robert. 1986. "An Evolutionary Approach to Norms." *American Political Science Review* 80(4): 1095–1111.

Axelrod, Robert. 1997a. "Promoting Norms: An Evolutionary Approach to Norms." In *The Complexity of Cooperation*, ed. Robert Axelrod. Princeton: Princeton University Press, 44–68.

Axelrod, Robert. 1997b. "A Model for the Emergence of New Political Actors." In *The Complexity of Cooperation*, ed. Robert Axelrod. Princeton: Princeton University Press, 124–144.

Axelrod, Robert. 1997c. "The Dissemination of Culture: A Model with Local Convergence and Global Polarization." In *The Complexity of Cooperation*, ed. Robert Axelrod. Princeton: Princeton University Press, 148–177.

Baehr, Peter. 1997. "Problems of Aid Conditionality: The Netherlands and Indonesia." *Third World Quarterly*, 18(2): 363–376.

Bajarunas, Eitvydas, et al. 1995. "The Baltic States: Security and Defense after Independence." Chaillot Papers 19, Institute for Security Studies of Western European Union.

Bakker, Edwin. 1997. *Minority Conflicts in Slovakia and Hungary?* Capelle a/d Ijssel: Labyrint Publication.

Baldwin, David. 1971. "The Power of Positive Sanctions." *World Politics* 24: 19–38.

Barrington, Lowell. 1995. "The Domestic and International Consequences of Citizenship in the Soviet Successor States." *Europe-Asia Studies* 47(5): 731–753.

Barrington, William. 1995. "To Exclude or Not to Exclude: Citizenship Policies in Newly Independent States." Dissertation, University of Michigan.

Bernauer, Thomas, and Dieter Ruloff, eds. 1999. *The Politics of Positive Incentives in Arms Control*. Columbia: University of South Carolina Press.

Bird, Graham. 2001a. "IMF Programmes: Is There a Conditionality Laffer Curve?" *World Economics* 2(2): 29–49.

Bird, Graham. 2001b. "IMF Programs: Do They Work? Can They Be Made to Work Better? *World Development* 29(11): 1849–1865.

Birkenbach, Hanne-Margret. 1997. *Preventive Diplomacy through Fact-finding: How International Organizations Review Conflict over Citizenship in Estonia and Latvia.* Kiel: Keiler Schriften zur friedenswissenschaft.

Bloed, Arie. 1993. "Two Decades of the CSCE Process: From Confrontation to Cooperation." In *The Conference on Security and Cooperation in Europe. Analysis and Basic Documents*, ed. Arie Bloed. Dodrecht: Martinus Nijhoff. Washington, D.C.: Brookings, 1–118.

Börzel, Tanja, and Thomas Risse. 2000. "When Europe Hits Home: Europeanization and Domestic Change." *European Integration Online Papers* (EioP,) 4: 15; http://elop.or.at/eiop/texte/2000-015a.htm.

Boyce, James, and Manuel Pastor Jr. 1998. "Aid for Peace: Can International Financial Institutions Help Prevent Conflict?" *World Policy Journal* 15(2): 42–49.

Boyce, James, ed. 1996. *Economic Policy for Building Peace: The Lessons of El Salvador.* Boulder: Lynne Rienner.

Brandtner, Barbara, and Allan Rosas. 1998. "Human Rights and the External Relations of the European Community: An Analysis of Doctrine and Practice." *European Journal of International Law* 9: 468–490.

Breton, Albert, Gianluigi Galeotti, Pierre Salmon, and Ronald Wintrobe, ed. 1995. *Nationalism and Rationality.* Cambridge: Cambridge University Press.

Brody, Richard, Diana Mutz, and Paul Sniderman, ed. 1996. *Political Persuasion and Attitude Change.* Ann Arbor: University of Michigan Press.

Brown, Michael. 1997a. "The Causes of Internal Conflict." *Nationalism and Ethnic Conflict*, ed. Michael Brown. Cambridge: MIT Press.

Brown, Michael. 1997b. "The Good, the Bad, and the Ugly: Political Leaders and the Causes of Ethnic Conflict." Paper presented at the MacArthur Foundation Workshop on Case Study Methods, Harvard University, October 17–19.

Brown, Michael. 1997c. *Nationalism and Ethnic Conflict.* Cambridge: MIT Press.

Brubaker, Rogers. 1995. "National Minorities, Nationalizing States, and External National Homelands in the New Europe" *Daedalus* 124: 107–133.

Brubaker, Rogers. 1996. *Nationalism Reframed.* Cambridge: Cambridge University Press.

Burnell, Peter. 1994. "Good Government and Democratization: A Sideways Look at Aid and Political Conditionality." *Democratization* 1(3): 485–503.

Bútora, Martin, and Péter Huncik, eds. 1997. *Slovakia 1996–1997: A Global Report on the State of Society.* Bratislava: Sándor Márai Foundation.

Bútora, Martin, and Thomas W. Skladony, eds. 1998. *Slovakia 1996–1997: A Global Report on the State of Society.* Bratislava: Institute of Public Affairs.

Bútora, Martin, Grigorij Meseznikov, Zora Bútorova, and Sharon Fisher, eds. 1999. *The 1998 Parliamentary Elections and Democratic Rebirth in Slovakia.* Bratislava: Institute of Public Affairs.

Butorova, Zora, ed. 1998. *Democracy and Discontent in Slovakia.* Institute of Public Affairs, Bratislava.

Cahill, Kevin. 1996. *Preventive Diplomacy: Stopping Wars before They Start.* New York: Basic Books.

Cartwright, Dorwin, ed. 1959. *Studies in Social Power*. Ann Arbor: Research Center for Group Dynamics, Institute for Social Research, University of Michigan.

Chayes, Abrahm and Antonia Chayes, eds. 1996. *Preventing Conflict in the Post-communist World*. Washington, D.C.: The Brookings Institution.

Chayes, Abram, and Antonia Handler Chayes. 1993. "On Compliance." *International Organization* 47(2) (Spring): 175–205.

Chayes, Abram, and Antonia Handler Chayes. 1995. *The New Sovereignty: Compliance with International Regulatory Agreements*. Cambridge: Harvard University Press.

Checkel, Jeffrey T. 1997a. "International Norms and Domestic Politics: Bridging the Rationalist-constructivist Divide." *European Journal of International Relations* 3(4): 473–495.

Checkel, Jeffrey T. 1997b. *Ideas and International Political Change*. New Haven: Yale University Press.

Checkel, Jeffrey T. 1999. "Norms, Institutions, and National Identity in Contemporary Europe." *International Studies Quarterly* 43: 83–114.

Checkel, Jeffrey T. 2000a. "Compliance and Conditionality." Paper presented at the annual meeting of the American Political Science Association, Washington, D.C., August.

Checkel, Jeffrey T. 2000b. "Bridging the Rational-choice / Constructivist Gap? Theorizing Social Interaction in European Institutions." ARENA working paper 00/11. University of Oslo.

Checkel, Jeffrey T. 2001. "Why Comply? Social Learning and European Identity Change." *International Organization* 55(3): 553–588.

Chigas, Diane. 1996. "Preventive Diplomacy and the Organization for Security and Cooperation in Europe." In *Preventing Conflict in the Post-communist World*, eds. Abrahm Chayes and Antonia Chayes. Washington, D.C.: The Brookings Institution, 25–99.

Chmelar, Josef. 1937. *National Minorities in Central Europe*. Prague: Orbis.

Claude, Inis L. 1995. *National Minorities; An International Problem*, Cambridge: Harvard University Press.

Collier, Paul, et. al. 1997. "Redesigning Conditionality." *World Development* 25(9): 1399–1407.

Collier, Paul. 1997. "The Failure of Conditionality." In *Perspectives on Aid and Development*, eds. Catherine Gwin and Joan Nelson. Washington, D.C.: Overseas Development Council, 51–78.

"Constitution Watch: A Country-by-Country Update on Constitutional Politics in Eastern Europe and the Ex-USSR: Slovakia." *East European Constitutional Review* 6(4) (fall 1997). Available online at http://www.law.nyu.edu/eecr/volumes.html

Cortell, Andrew, and James W. Davis Jr. 1996. "How Do International Institutions Matter?" *International Studies Quarterly* 40: 451–478.

Cortright, David, and George Lopez, eds. 1995. *Economic Sanctions: Panacea or Peacebuilding in a Post-cold War World?* Boulder: Westview Press.

Cortright, David. 1997. *The Price of Peace: Incentives and International Conflict Prevention*. New York: Rowman and Littlefield.

Council of Europe. 2001. *Framework Convention for the Protection of National Minorities: Collected Texts*. Strasbourg: Council of Europe Publications.

Cowles, Maria, James Caporaso, and Thomas Risse, eds. 2001. *Transforming Europe: Europeanization and Domestic Change*. Ithaca: Cornell University Press.

Croft, Stuart, John Redmond, G. Wyn Rees, and Mark Webber. 1999. *The Enlargement of Europe*. Manchester: Manchester University Press.

Crumm, E. 1995. "The Value of Economic Incentives in International Politics." *Journal of Peace Research* 32(3): 313–330.

Davis, James W. 2000. "The Politics of Positive Incentives in Arms Control." *Political Science Quarterly* 115(2): 312–314

Dawisha, Karen, and Bruce Parrot. 1994. *Russia and the New States of Eurasia: The Politics of Upheaval*. Cambridge: Cambridge University Press.

Dawisha, Karen, and Bruce Parrott, eds. 1997a. *Politics, Power, and the Struggle for Democracy in South-East Europe*. Cambridge: Cambridge University Press.

Dawisha, Karen, and Bruce Parrott, eds. 1997b. *The Consolidation of Democracy in East-Central Europe*. Cambridge: Cambridge University Press.

De Witte, Bruno. 2000. "Politics versus Law in the EU's Approach to Ethnic Minorities." Working Paper RSC No. 2000/4. European University Institute.

Deutsch, Karl, and Ernst Haas. 1957. *Political Community in the North Atlantic Area: International Organization in the Light of Historical Experience*. Princeton: Princeton University Press.

Dixon, William J. 1993. "Democracy and the Management of International Conflict." *Journal of Conflict Resolution* 37(1): 42–68.

Downs, George, David Rocke, and Peter Barsoom. 1996. "Is the Good News about Compliance Good News about Cooperation?" *International Organization* 50(3): 370–406.

Doxey, Margaret. 1971. *Economic Sanctions and International Enforcement*. New York: Oxford University Press.

Doxey, Margaret. 1995. "Economic Sanctions in Contemporary Perspective." In *Economic Sanctions: Panacea or Peacebuilding in a Post-Cold War World*, ed. David Cortright and George Lopez. Boulder: Westview Press, 98–100.

Dreifelds, Juris. 1996. *Latvia in Transition*. Cambridge: Cambridge University Press.

Drezner, Daniel. 2000. "Bargaining, Enforcement, and Multilateral Sanctions: When Is Cooperation Counterproductive?" *International Organization* 4(1): 73–102.

Duffield, John. 1992. "International Regimes and Alliance Behavior: Explaining NATO Counter Force Levels." *International Organization* 46: 819–855.

Dumas, Lloyd. 1990. "Economics and Alternative Security: Toward a Peace-keeping International Economy." In *Alternative Strategy: Living without Nuclear Deterrence*, ed. Burns Weston. Boulder: Westview Press, 137–175.

East, Roger, and Jolyon Pontin. 1997. *Revolution and Change in Central and Eastern Europe*, rev. ed. London: Pinter Publishers.

Elster, Jon. 1982. *Nuts and Bolts for the Social Sciences*. Cambridge: Cambridge University Press.

Estonaez, Martin. 1995. "The Protection of National or Ethnic, Religions and Linguistic Minorities." In *The European Union and Human Rights*, ed. Nanette Neuwal and Allan Rosas. Cambridge: M. Nijhoff, 133–163.

Evangelista, Matthew. 1995. "The Paradox of State Strength: Transnational Relations, Domestic Structures, Security Policy in Russia and the Soviet Union." *International Organization* 49: 1–38.

Evans, Peter, Harold Jacobson, and Robert Putnam. 1993. *Double-edged Diplomacy: International Bargaining and Domestic Politics.* Berkeley: University of California Press.

Evans, Peter. 1993. "Building and Integrative Approach to International and Domestic Politics." In *Double-edged Diplomacy: International Bargaining and Domestic Politics,* eds. Peter Evans, Harold Jacobson, and Robert Putnam. Berkeley: University of California Press, 397–430.

Farrell, Henry, and Gregory Flynn. 1999. "Piecing Together the Democratic Peace: The CSCE, Norms, and the 'Construction' of Security in Post–Cold War Europe." *International Organization* 53(3): 505–535.

Fearon, James, and Alexander Wendt. 2002. "Rationalism v. Constructivism: A Skeptical View." In *Handbook of International Relations,* eds. Walter Carlsnaes, Thomas Risse and Beth Simmons. London: Sage, 52–72.

Fearon, James. 1994. "Domestic Political Audiences and the Escalation of International Disputes." *American Political Science Review* 88(3) (September): 577–592.

Fearon, James. 1998. "Bargaining, Enforcement, and International Cooperation." *International Organization* 52(2): 269–305.

Fierke, Karin, and Antje Wiener. 1999. "Constructing Institutional Interests: EU and NATO Enlargement." *Journal of European Public Policy* 6 (December): 721–742.

Finnamore, Martha. 1996. *National Interests in International Society.* Ithaca: Cornell University Press.

Finnemore, Martha, and Kathryn Sikkink. 1998. "International Norms Dynamic and Political Change." *International Organization* 52(4): 887–917.

Finnemore, Martha. 1993. "International Organizations as Teachers of Norms: The United National Educational, Scientific, and Cultural Organization and Science Policy." *International Organization* 47: 565–597.

Finnemore, Martha. 1996. *National Interests in International Society.* Ithaca: Cornell University Press.

Fisher, Roger. 1981. *Improving Compliance with International Law.* Charlottesville: University Press of Virginia.

Foundation on Inter-Ethnic Relations. 1997. "Bibliography on the OSCE High Commissioner on National Minorities: Documents, Speeches and Related Publications." The Hague, Netherlands.

Franck, Thomas. 1990. *The Power of Legitimacy Among Nations.* New York: Oxford University Press.

Fric, Pavol, et al. 1993. *The Hungarian Minority in Slovakia.* Prague: EGEM.

Gallagher, Tom, 1995. *Romania after Ceausescu: The Politics of Intolerance.* Edinburgh: Edinburgh University Press, c1995.

Gallagher, Tom. 1997. "Nationalism and Post-Communist Politics: The Party of Romanian National Unity, 1990–1996." In *Romania in Transition,* ed. Lavinia Stan. Brookfield, Vt.: Dartmouth, 25–47.

Galtung, Johann. 1997. "On the Effects of International Economic Sanctions: With Examples from the Case of Rhodesia." *World Politics* 19(3): 378–416.

Geistlinger, Michael, and Aksel Kirch. 1995. *Estonia—A New Framework for the Estonian Majority and the Russian Minority.* Wien: Braumuller.

Gelazis, Nida M. 2000. "The Effects of EU Conditionality on Citizenship Policies and Protection of National Minorities in the Baltic States / San Domenico di Fiesole, Italy. Robert Schuman Centre Working Paper RSC No. 2000/68. European University Institute.

George, Alexander, and Timothy McKeown. 1984. "Case Studies and Theories of OrganizationalD." *Advances in Information Processing in Organizations.* Greenwich: JAI Press.

Gilbert, Christopher, Andrew Powell, and David Vines. 1999. "Positioning the World Bank." *The Economic Journal* 109 (November): F598–F633.

Gilbert, Christopher, Raul Hopkins, Andrew Powell, and Amlan Roy. 1997. "The World Bank and Conditionality." *Journal of International Development* 9: 507–516.

Gilbert, Geoff. 1996. "The Council of Europe and Minority Rights." *Human Rights Quarterly* 18(1): 160–189.

Goertz, Gary, and Paul Diehl. 1992. "Toward a Theory of International Norms." *Journal of Conflict Resolution* 36: 634–666.

Goldstein, Judith, and Robert Keohane, eds. 1993. *Ideas and Foreign Policy.* Ithaca: Cornell University Press.

Gottlieb, Stuart. 1997. "Authoritarian Structures and International Aggression." Paper presented at the MacArthur Foundation Workshop on Case Study Methods, Harvard University, October 17–19.

Gourevitch, Peter. 1978. "The Second Image Reversed: The International Sources of Domestic Policies." *International Organization* 32: 881–912.

Gower, Jackie. 1999. "EU Policy to Central and Eastern Europe." *Back to Europe: Central and Eastern Europe and the European Union*, ed. Karen Henderson. London and Philadelphia: UCL Press , 3–19.

Grabbe, Heather, and Kirsty Hughes. 1998. *Enlarging the EU Eastwards.* London: Royal Institute of International Affairs.

Grabbe, Heather. 1999. "A Partnership for Accession? The Implications of EU Conditionality for the Central and East European Applicants." Robert Schuman Centre Working Paper 99/12, European University Institute.

Grabbe, Heather. 2001. How Does Europeanization Affect CEE Governance? Conditionality, Diffusion and Diversity. *Journal of European Public Policy* 8(6): 1013–1031.

Groft, Stuart, John Redmond, G. Wyn Rees, and Mark Webber. 1999. *The Enlargement of Europe.* Manchester: Manchester University Press.

Gurr, Ted; with contributions by Barbara Harff, Monty Marshall, and James Scarritt. 1993. *Minorities at Risk: A Global View of Ethnopolitical Conflicts.* Washington, D.C.: United States Institute of Peace Press.

Haas, Earnest B. 1958. *The Uniting of Europe: Political, Social and Economic Forces, 1950–1957.* Stanford: Stanford University Press.

Haass, Richard. 1997. "Sanctioning Madness." *Foreign Affairs* 76(6): 74–86.

Hardin, Russel. 1995. "Self Interest, Group Identity." *Nationalism and Rationality*, ed. Albert Breton, Gianluigi Galeotti, Pierre Salmon, and Ronald Wintrobe. Cambridge: Cambridge University Press, 14–42.

Harsanyi, John. 1962. "Measurements of Social Power, Opportunity Costs, and the Theory of Two-person Bargaining Games." *Behavioral Science* VII(January): 67–80.

Hawkins, Darren. 1997. "Domestic Responses to International Pressure: Human Rights in Authoritarian Chile." *European Journal of International Relations* 3(4): 403–434.

Henderson, Karen, ed. 1999a. *Back to Europe: Central and Eastern Europe and the European Union.* London and Philadelphia: UCL Press.

Henderson, Karen. 1999b. "Slovakia and the Democratic Criteria for EU Accession." *Back to Europe: Central and Eastern Europe and the European Union*, ed. Karen Henderson. London and Philadelphia: UCL Press, 221–240.

Hill, Fiona, and Pamela Jewett, 1994. *Back in the USSR: Russia's Intervention in the Internal Affairs of the Former Soviet Republics and the Implication for United States Policy towards Russia.* Cambridge: Harvard University Press.

Hoffmeister, F. 1998. *Menschenrechts- und Demokratieklauseln in den vertraglichen Aussenbesiehungen der Europäishchen Gemenshaft.* Berlin: Springer.

Hollis, Wendy. 1999. *Democratic Consolidation in Eastern Europe: The Influence of the Communist Legacy in Hungary, the Czech Republic, and Romania.* Boulder: East European Monographs.

Horak, Stephan M. 1985. *Eastern European National Minorities, 1919–1980: A Handbook.* Littleton, Colo.: Libraries Unlimited.

Horowitz, Donald. 1985. *Ethnic Groups in Conflict.* Berkeley: University of California Press.

Huber, Konrad. 1994. "The CSCE's New Role in the East: Conflict Prevention." *RFE/RL Research Report* 31: 23–30.

Hufbauer, Gary, Jeffrey Scott, and Kimberly Elliot. 1990. *Economic Sanctions Reconsidered: History and Current Policy*, 2nd. ed. Washington, D.C.: Institute for International Economics.

Hurd, Greame. 1999. "The Baltic States and EU Enlargement." In *Back to Europe: Central and Eastern Europe and the European Union*, ed. Karen Henderson. London and Philadelphia: UCL Press, 259–273.

Hurlburt, Heather. 1997. "Gaining Leverage for International Organizations." In *The Price of Peace: Incentives and International onflict Prevention*, ed. David Cortright. New York: Rowman and Littlefield, 225–242.

Ikenberry, John, and Charles Kupchan. 1990. "Socialization and Hegemonic Power." *International Organization* 44: 283–315.

Jackson Preece, Jennifer. 1998. *National Minorities and the European Nation-states System.* Oxford: The Clarendon Press.

Joensson, Christer. 1990. *Communication in International Bargaining.* New York: St. Martin's Press.

Johnston, Iain. 2001. "Treating International Institutions as Social Environments." *International Studies Quarterly* 45(4): 487–516

Joo, Rudolf, ed. 1994. *The Hungarian Minority's Situation in Ceausescu's Romania.* Boulder: Social Science Monographs.

Kahler, Miles. 1998. "Rationality in International Relations." *International Organization* 52(4): 919–994.

Kant, Immanuel. 1948. "Essay on Eternal Peace." Reprinted in Carl Joachim Friedrich, *Inevitable Peace*. Cambridge: Harvard University Press, 284–285.

Katzenstein, Peter, Robert Keohane, and Stephen Krasner, eds. 1999. *Exploration and Contestation in the Study of World Politics*. Cambridge: MIT Press.

Katzenstein, Peter. 1996. *The Culture of National Security: Norms and Identity in World Politics*. New York: Columbia University Press.

Keck, Margaret, and Kathryn Sikkink. 1998. *Activists beyond Borders*. Ithaca: Cornell University Press.

Kellas, James. 1998. *The Politics of Nationalism and Ethnicity*, 2nd ed. New York: St. Martin's Press.

Kemp, Walter, ed. 2001. *Quiet Diplomacy in Action: The OSCE High Commissioner on National Minorities*. Boston: Kluwer Law International.

Keohane, Robert. 1984. *After Hegemony: Cooperation and Discord in the World Political Economy*. Princeton: Princeton University Press.

Keohane, Robert. 1988. "International Institutions: Two Approaches." *International Studies Quarterly* 32: 379–396.

Keohane, Robert. 2002. "Ironies of Sovereignty: The European Union and the United States." *Journal of Common Market Studies* 40(4): 743–765.

Keohane, Robert, and Marc Levy. 1996. *Institutions for Environmental Aid: Pitfalls and Promise*. Cambridge: MIT Press.

Keohane, Robert, and Joseph Nye, Jr. 1977. *Power and Interdependence. World Politics in Transition*. Boston: Little, Brown.

Killick, Tony. 1996. "Principals, Agents and the Limitations of BWI Conditionality." *The World Economy* 16: 211–229.

Killick, Tony, with Ramani Gunatilaka and Ana Marr. 1998. *Aid and the Political Economy of Policy Change*. London: Routledge.

King, Gary, Robert Keohane, and Sidney Verba. 1994. *Designing Social Inquiry*. Princeton: Princeton University Press.

Klotz, Audie. 1996. "Norms and Sanctions: Lessons from the Socialization of South Africa." *Review of International Studies* 22: 173–190;

Koh, Harold Hongju. 1997. "Review Essay: Why Do Nations Obey International Law?" *The Yale Law Journal* 106 (June): 2599–2660.

Kolar, Othmar. 1997. *Rumanien und seine nationalen Minderheiten: 1918 bis heute*. Wien: Bohlau.

Krasner, Stephen. 1977. "Domestic Constraints on International Economic Leverage." In *Economic Issues and National Security*, eds. Klaus Knorr and Frank Trager. Lawrence, Kansas: Allen Press, 160–181.

Krasner, Stephen. 1978. "United States Commercial and Monetary Policy: Unraveling the Paradox of External Strength and Internal Weaknesses." In *Between Power and Plenty*, ed. Peter Katzenstein. Madison: University of Wisconsin Press, 51–88.

Kreps, D. M. 1992. "Corporate Culture and Economic Theory." In *Perspectives on Positive Political Economy*, eds. J. E. Alt and K. A. Shepsle. London: Cambridge University Press, 90–143.

Lauristin, Marju, Peeter Vihalemm, Karl Erik Rosengren, and Lennart Weibull. 1997. *Return to the Western World: Cultural and Political Perspectives on the Estonian Post-communist Transition*. Tartu, Estonia : Tartu University Press.

Leandro, Jose, Hartwig Schafer, and Gasper Frontini. 1999. "Towards a More Effective Conditionality: An Operational Framework." *World Development* 27(2):285–299.

Legro, Jeffrey. 1997. "Which Norms Matter? Revisiting the "Failure" of Internationalism." *International Organization* 51: 31–63.

Levy, Jack. 1994. "Learning and Foreign Policy: Sweeping a Conceptual Minefield." *International Organization* 48(2): 279–312.

Lieven, Anatol. 1993. *The Baltic Revolution*. New Haven: Yale University Press.

Liliana Botcheva-Andonova. 2000. "EU Institution, Transnational Networks, and the Politics of the Environment in Eastern Europe." Paper delivered at the Annual Meeting of the American Political Science Association, Marriott Wardman Park, August 31–September 3.

Linz, Juan, and Alfred Stepan. 1996. *Problems of Democratic Transitions and Consolidation: Southern Europe, South America and post-Communist Europe*. Baltimore: The Johns Hopkins University Press.

Linz, Juan. 1970. "An Authoritarian Regime: Spain." In *Mass Politics*, eds. Erik Allardt and Stein Rokkan. New York: The Free Press, 251–283.

Long, William L. 1996. *Economic Incentives and Bilateral Cooperation*. Ann Arbor: University of Michigan Press.

Losman, Donald. 1979. *International Economic Sanctions: The Cases of Cuba, Israel, and Rhodesia*. Albuquerque: University of New Mexico Press.

Lovatt, Catherine. 1999. "Romania's Partial Progress in Minority Issues." *Central Europe Review* 1(2) (July 5); available on line at http://www.ce-review.org/99/2/lovatt2.html.Macartney, C. A. 1934. *National States and National Minorities*. London: Oxford University Press.

Macartney, C. A. 1934. *National States and National Minorities*. London: Oxford University Press.

Manas, Jean. 1996. "The Council of Europe's Democracy Ideal and the Challenge of Ethno-national Strife." In *Preventing Conflict in the Post-communist World*, eds. Abrahm Chayes and Antonia Chayes. Washington D.C.: Brookings Institution, 99–144.

Mansfield, Edward. 1995. "International Institutions and Economic Sanctions." *World Politics* 47: 575–605.

March, James G., and Johan P. Olsen. 1989. *Rediscovering Institutions: The Organizational Basics of Politics*. New York: The Free Press.

March, James G., and Johan P. Olsen. 1998. "The Institutional Dynamics of International Political Orders." *International Organization* 52(4): 943–969.

Marshall, Monty. 1993. "States at Risk: Ethnopolitics in the Multinational States of Eastern Europe." In Ted Gur, with Barbara Harff, Monty Marshall, and James Scarritt, *Minorities at Risk: A Global View of Ethnopolitical Conflicts*. Washington, D.C. : United States Institute of Peace Press, 173–216.

Martin, Lisa, and Beth A. Simmons. 1998. "Theories and Empirical Studies of International Institutions." *International Organization* 52: 729–757.

Martin, Lisa, and Kathryn Sikkink. 1993. "U.S. Policy and Human Rights in Argentina and Guatemala, 1973–1980." In *Double-edged Diplomacy: International Bargaining and Domestic Politics*, eds. Robert Evans, Harold J. Jacobsen, and Robert Putnam. Berkeley: University of California Press, 330–362.

Martin, Lisa. 2000. *Democratic Commitments*. Princeton: Princeton University Press.

Martinez-Vasquez, Jorge, et al. 2001. "IMF Conditionality and Objections: The Russian Case." *American Journal of Economics and Sociology* 60(2): 501–517.

McElroy, Robert. 1992. *Morality and American Foreign Policy*. Princeton: Princeton University Press.

Mego, Anthony. 1999. *Nationalist Rhetoric and Political Competition in Slovakia: December 1989–June 1992*. Dissertation, University of Alabama.

Melwin, Neil. 1995. *Russians beyond Russia: The Politics of National Identity*. London: Royal Institute of International Affairs.

Meseznikov, Grigorij, Michal Ivantysyn, and Tom Nicholson, eds. 1999. *Slovakia 1998–1999: A Global Report on the State of Society*. Bratislava: Institute of Public Affairs.

Michalchuk, Daniel. 1999. *Minority Rights as Preventive Diplomacy: OSCE-Sponsored Legal Reform and the Prevention of Ethnic Conflict in Post-communist Countries*. Masters thesis, Carleton University, Canada.

Mill, John Stuart. 1923. *Principles of Political Economy*. London: Longmans Green.

Mitchell, Ronald B. 1994. "Regime Design Matters. International Oil Pollution and Treaty Compliance." *International Organization* 48(3): 425–458.

Moravcsik, Andrew. 1993. "Introduction." In *Double-edged Diplomacy: International Bargaining and Domestic Politic*, eds. Robert Evans, Harold J. Jacobsen, and Robert Putnam. Berkeley: University of California Press, 3–42.

Moravcsik, Andrew. 1994. "Why the European Community Strengthens the State: Domestic Politics and International Cooperation." Paper presented at the annual meeting of the American Political Science Association, New York, September 1–4.

Moravcsik, Andrew. 1995. "Explaining International Human Rights Regimes: Liberal Theory and Western Europe." *European Journal of International Relations* 1: 157–189.

Muiznieks, Nils. 1993. *The Baltic Popular Movements and the Disintegration of the Soviet Union*. Dissertation, University of California, Berkeley.

Muiznieks, Nils. 1996. "Minority Policy: The Case of Latvia." Paper for the Workshop on Cultural Diversity, Conference on Governance and European Integration, Rotterdam, May 28–30.

Munuera, Gabriel. 1994. "Preventing Armed Conflict in Europe." Chaillot Paper 15/16. Institute for Security Studies, Western European Union, Paris.

Nadelman, Ethan. 1990. "Global Prohibition Regimes: The Evolution of Norms in International Society." *International Organization* 44: 479–536.

Nelson, Joan, and Stephanie Engelton. 1992. *Encouraging Democracy: What Role for Conditioned Aid*. Overseas Development Council, Policy Essay No. 4. Washington, D.C.: Overseas Development Council.

Nelson, Joan. 1996. "Promoting Policy Reforms: The Twilight of Conditionality?" *World Development* 24: 1551–1559.

Norgaard, Ole, et al. 1999. *The Baltic States after Independence*. 2nd ed. Cheltenham, UK: Edward Elgar.

Nye, Joseph. 1987. "Nuclear Learning and U.S.–Soviet Security Regimes," *International Organization* 41: 371–402.

Opalski, Magda, and Piotr Dutkeiwicz. 1996. *Ethnic Minority Rights in Central Eastern Europe*. Ottawa: Canadian Human Rights Foundation.

Opalski, Magdalena, et al. 1994. *Ethnic Conflict in the Baltic States—The Case of Latvia*. Kingston, ON: Kashtan Press.

Oudenaren, Van J. 2001. "The Limits of Conditionality: Nuclear Reactor Safety in Central and Eastern Europe, 1991–2001." *International Politics* 38(4): 467–497.

Oye, Kenneth. 1992. *Economic Discrimination and Political Exchange. World Political Economy in the 1930s and 1980s*. Princeton: Princeton University Press.

Özkirimli, Umut. 2000. *Theories of Nationalism*. New York: St. Martin's Press.

Pabriks, Artis. 1999. *From Nationalism to Ethnic Policy: The Latvian Nation in the Present and in the Past*. Berlin: Berliner Interuniversitare Arbeitsgruppe "Baltische Staaten."

Pape, Robert. 1997. "Why Economic Sanctions Do Not Work." *International Security* 22(2): 90–137.

Payne, Rodger. 2001. "Persuasion, Frames and Norm Construction." *European Journal of International Relations* 7(1): 37–61.

Pearson, Raymond. 1993. *National Minorities in Eastern Europe, 1848–1945*. New York: St. Martin's Press.

Phinnemore, David. 1999. "The Challenges of EU Enlargement: EU and CEE Perspectives." In *Back to Europe: Central and Eastern Europe and the European Union*, ed. Karen Henderson. London and Philadelphia: UCL Press, 71–88.

Pinder, John. 1997. "The EC and Democracy." In *Building Democracy: The International Dimension of Democratization in Eastern Europe*, eds. Geoffrey Pridham, Eric Herring, and George Sanford. London: Leicester University Press, 119–143.

Plakans, Andrejs. 1997. "Democratization and Political Participation in Post-communist Societies: The Case of Latvia." In *Democratization and Authoritarianism in Postcommunist Societies: 1, The consolidation of democracy in East Central Europe*, eds. Karen Kawisha and Bruce Parrot. Cambridge: Cambridge University Press, 245–289.

Pourchot. Georgeta. 1997. "Mass Media and Democracy in Romania." In *Romania in Transition*, ed. Lavinia Stan. Brookfield, Vt.: Dartmouth, 67–90.

Pridham, Geoffrey, and Tatu Vanhanen. 1994. *Democratization in Eastern Europe; Comestic and International Perspectives*. New York: Routledge.

Pridham, Geoffrey. 1997. "The International Dimensions of Democratization: Theory, Practice and Inter-regional Comparisons." In *Building Democracy? The International Dimensions of Democratization in Eastern Europe*, rev. ed., eds. G. Pridham, E. Herring and G. Sanford. London: Leicester University Press, 7–29.

Pridham, Geoffrey. 1999. "Complying with the European Union's Democratic Conditionality: Transnational Party Linkages and Regime Change in Slovakia, 1993–1998." *Europe-Asia Studies* 51(7): 1221–1244.

Putnam, Robert. 1988. "Diplomacy and Domestic Politics: The Logic of Two-level Games." *International Organization* 42: 427–60.

Rady, Martyn C. 1992 *Romania in Turmoil: A Contemporary History*. New York: IB Tauris.

Raitz von Frentz, Christian. 1999. *A Lesson Forgotten: Minority Protection under the League of Nations*. New York: St. Martin's Press.

Ram, Melanie H. 1999. *Transformation through European Integration: A Comparative Study of the Czech Republic and Romania*. Dissertation, George Washington University.

Ratner, Steven. 2000. "Does International Law Matter in Preventing Ethnic Conflict?" *New York University Journal of International Law and Politics* 32(3): 591–698.

Raustila, Kal, and Anne-Marie Slaughter. 2002. "International Law, International Relations and Compliance." In *The Handbook of International Relations*, eds. Walter Carlsnaes, Thomas Risse, and Beth Simmons. London: Sage, 528–552.

Reinicke, Wolfgang. 1996. "Can International Financial Institutions Prevent Internal Violence? The Sources of Ethnonational Conflict in Transitional Societies." In *Preventing Conflict in the Post-communist World*, eds. Abrahm and Antonia Chayes. Washington, D.C.: Brookings Institution, 281–338.

Risse, Thomas. 1999. "International Norms and Domestic Change: Arguing and Communicative Behavior in the Human Rights Area." *Politics and Society* 27(4): 529–559.

Risse, Thomas. 2000. " 'Let's Argue!' Communicative Action in World Politics." *International Organization* 54(1): 1–39.

Risse, Thomas, and Kathryn Sikkink. 1999. "The Socialization of International Human Rights Norms into Domestic Practices: Introduction." In *The Power of Human Rights: International norms and Domestic Change*, eds. Thomas Risse, Stephen Ropp, and Kathryn Sikkink. Cambridge: Cambridge University Press, 1–38.

Risse, Thomas, Stephen Ropp, and Kathryn Sikkink, eds. 1999. *The Power of Human Rights: International Norms and Domestic Change*. Cambridge: Cambridge University Press.

Risse-Kappen, Thomas. 1994. "Ideas Do Not Float Freely." *International Organization* 48(2): 185–214.

Risse-Kappen, Thomas. 1995. "Democratic Peace—Warlike Democracies? A Social Constructivist Interpretation of the Liberal Argument. *European Journal of International Relations* 1: 491–517.

Rosas, Allan. 1999. "The Role of the Universal Declaration of Human Rights in the Treaty Relations of the European Union." Unpublished Manuscript.

Rose, Richard, et al. 1994. *Nationalities in the Baltic States: A Survey Study*. Glasgow, Scotland: Centre for the Study of Public Policy, University of Strathclyde.

Rosencrance, Richard. 1987. *The Rise of the Trading Star*. New York: Basic Books.

Ross, Michael. 1996. "Conditionality and Logging Reform in the Tropics." In *Institutions for Environmental Aid: Pitfalls and Promise*, eds. Robert Keohane and Marc Levy. Cambridge: MIT Press, 167–198.

Ross, Michael, and Fairman, D. 1996. "Old Fads, New Lessons: Learning from Economic Development Assistance." In *Institutions for Environmental Aid: Pitfalls and Promise*, eds. Robert Keohane and Marc Levy. Cambridge: MIT Press, 29–52.

Rosting, Helmer. 1923. "Protection of Minorities by the League of Nations. *American Journal of International Law* 17: 641–642.

Ruggie, John Gerard. 1998. "What Makes the World Hang Together? Neo-utilitarianism and the Social Constructivist Challenge." *International Organization* 52(4): 855–885

Rummel, Reinhardt. 1996. "The European Union's Politico-Diplomatic Contribution to the Prevention of Ethno-National Conflict." In *Preventing Conflict in the Post-communist World*, eds. Abrahm Chayes and Antonia Chayes. Washington, D.C.: The Brookings Institution, 197–235.

Schelling, Thomas. 1960. *The Strategy of Conflict*. Cambridge: Harvard University Press.

Schelling, Thomas. 1966. *Arms and Influence*. New Haven: Yale University Press.

Schelling, Thomas. 1978. *Micromotives and Macrobehavior*. New York: W. W. Norton

Schimmelfennig, Frank. 2000a. "International Socialization in the New Europe: Rational Action in an Institutional Environment." *European Journal of International Relations* 6(1): 109–139.

Schimmelfennig, Frank. 2001. "The Community Trap: Liberal Norms, Rhetorical Action, and the Eastern Enlargement of the European Union." *International Organization* 55(1): 47–80.

Schimmelfinnig, Frank. 2002. "Costs and Conditionality. The Uneven International Socialization of Central and Eastern Europe." Paper prepared for IDNET/ARENA Workshop, International Institutions and Socialization in the New Europe, European University Institute, February.

Schraeder, Peter. 1994. "Elites as Facilitators or Impediments to Political Development? Some Lessons from the 'Third Wave' of Democratization in Africa." *The Journal of Developing Areas* 29(1): 69–91.

Shannon V. P. 2000. "Norms Are What States Make of Them: The Political Psychology of Norm Violation." *International Studies Quarterly* 44(2): 293–316.

Shevel, Oxana. 2000. "International Influences on Refugee Policies and Practices: The Case of the UNHCR in Russia." Paper delivered at the annual meeting of the American Political Science Association, Marriott Wardman Park, August 31–September 3.

Sikkink, Kathryn. 1993a. "Human Rights, Principles Issue-networks, and Sovereignty in Latin-America." *International Organizations* 47: 411–441.

Sikkink, Kathryn. 1993b. "The Power of Principled Ideas: Human Rights Policies in the United States and Western Europe." In *Ideas and Foreign Policy*, eds. Judith Goldstein and Robert Keohane. Ithaca: Cornell University Press, 139–172.

Simmons, Beth A. 2000. "Compliance in International Relations." Prepared for delivery at the annual meeting of the American Political Science Assocation, Washington, D.C., August 31–September 3.

Smith, Karen. 1998. "The Use of Political Conditionality in the EU's Relations with Third Countries: How Effective?" In *European Foreign Affairs Review* 3: 253–74.

Snyder, Glenn, and Paul Diesing. 1997. *Conflict among Nations: Bargaining, Decision Making, and System Structure in International Crises*. Princeton: Princeton University Press.

Stan, Lavinia, ed. 1997. *Romania in Transition*. Brookfield, Vt.: Dartmouth.

Stokke, Olav. 1995. *Aid and Political Conditionality*. London: Frank Cass.

Strhan, Milan, and David Daniel. 1994. *Slovakia and the Slovaks*. Bratislava: Gold-press.

Susskind, L. 1994. *Environmental Diplomacy: Negotiating More Effective Global Agreements*. London: Oxford University Press.

Szomolanyi, Sona, and Grigoruj Meseznikov. 1994. *The Slovak Path of Transition to Democracy*. Bratislava: Slovak Political Science Association and Interlingua.

Taras, Ray. 1993. "Conclusion: Making Sense of Matrioshka Nationalism." In *Nations and Politics in the Soviet Successor States*, eds. Ian Bremmer and Ray Taras. Cambridge: Cambridge University Press, 513–538.

Mandelbaum, Michael, ed. 2000. *The New European Diasporas : National Minorities and Conflict in Eastern Europe*. New York: Council on Foreign Relations.

Tismaneanu, Vladimir. 1996. "Tenuous Pluralism in the Post-Ceaucescu Era." *Transition* 2(26) (December 27). Accessible online at http://www.tol.cz/look/Transition/home.tpl?IdLanguage-1&IdPublication-8&NrIssue-50&NrSection-1&NrArticle-3804

Tismaneanu, Vladimir. 1997. "Romanian Exceptionalism? Democracy, Ethnocracy, and Uncertain Pluralism in Post-Ceausescu Romania." In *Politics, Power, and the Struggle for Democracy in South-east Europe*, eds. Karen Dawisha and Bruce Parrott. New York: Cambridge University Press, 413–451.

Tsebelis, George. 1995. "Decision Making in Political Systems: Veto Players in Presidentialism, Parliamentarism, Multicameralism, and Multipartyism." *British Journal of Political Science* 25: 289–326.

Underdal, Arild. 1998. "Explaining Compliance and Defection: Three Models." *European Journal of International Relations* 4 (March): 20–23.

U.S. Congress, Commission on Security and Cooperation in Europe. 1992. *Russians in Estonia : Problems and Prospects*. Washington, D.C.: CSCE.

Vachudova, Milada Anna. 2001. "The Leverage of International Institutions on Democratizing States: Eastern Europe and the European Union." Robert Schuman Center working paper, 2001/33.

Vachudova, Milada. 1997. "The Systemic and Domestic Determinants of the Foreign Policies of East Central European States after 1989." Dissertation, University of Oxford.

Vachudova, Milada Anna. 2004. *Europe Undivided: Democracy, Leverage, and Integration since 1989*. Oxford: Oxford University Press.

Vachudova, Milada Anna, and Tim Snyder. 1997. "Are Transitions Transitory? Two Types of Political Change in Eastern Europe since 1989." *East European Politics and Societies* 11: 1–35.

Van der Stoel, Max. 1999. "Reflections on the Role of the OSCE High Commissioner on National Minorities as an Instrument of Conflict Prevention." In OSZE Jahrbuch. Baden-Baden: Nomos.

Van Evera, Stephen. 1997. *Guide to Methods for Students of Political Science*. Ithaca: Cornell University Press.

Van Houten, Pieter. 1998. "The Role of a Minority's Reference State in Ethnic Relations." *Archives Europeennes de Socieologie. European Journal of Sociology. Europaisches Archiv fur Soziologie* 39(1): 110–146.

Verdery, Katherine. 1993. "Nationalism and National Sentiment in Post-Socialist Romania." *Slavic Review* 52(2): 179–203.

Vermeersch, Peter. 2002. "Ethnic Mobilization and the Political Conditionality of European Union Accession: The Case of the Roma in Slovakia. *Journal of Ethnic and Migration Studies* 28(1): 83–101.

Wagner, R. Harrison. 1988. "Economic Interdependence, Bargaining Power, and Political Influence." *International Organization* 42: 461–483.

Weidenfeld, Werner. 2000. "Erweiterung ohne Ende? Europa als Stabilitätsraum strukturieren." *Internationale Politik* 55(8): 1–10.

Weiner, Robert. 1997. "Democratization in Romania." In *Romania in Transition*, ed. Lavinia Stan. Brookfield, Vt.: Dartmouth.

Waltz, Kenneth. 1979. *Theory of International Politics*. New York: McGraw-Hill.

Welsh, David. 1993. "Domestic Politics and Ethnic Conflict." In *Ethnic Conflict and International Security*, ed. Michael Brown. Princeton: Princeton University Press, 43–60.

Whitefield, Stephen. 1993. *The New Institutional Architecture of Eastern Europe*.New York: St. Martin's Press.

Whitehead, Laurence. 1996. "International Aspects of Democratization." In *Transitions From Authoritarian Rule: Comparative Perspectives*, eds. Guillermo O'Donnel, Phillippe Schmitter, and Laurence Whitehead, Baltimore: The Johns Hopkins University Press, 3–46.

World Bank. 1997. *A Framework for World Bank Involvement in Post-Conflict Reconstruction*. Washington, D.C.: The World Bank.

Wright, Jane. 1996. "The OSCE and the Protection of Minority Rights." *Human Rights Quarterly* 18(1): 190–225.

Young, Oran R. 1979. *Compliance and Public Authority: A Theory with International Application*. Baltimore: The Johns Hopkins University Press.

Young, Oran R. 1992. "The Effectiveness of International Institutions: Hard Cases and Critical Variables." In *Governance Without Government: Order and Change in World Politics*, eds. J. N. Rosenau and E. O. Czempiel. Cambridge: Cambridge University Press, 160–194.

Young, Oran. 1979. *Compliance and Public Authority: A Theory with International Applications*. Baltimore: The Johns Hopkins University Press.

Zaagman, Rob. 1999. "Conflict Prevention in the Baltic States: The OSCE High Commissioner on National Minorities in Estonia, Latvia, and Lithuania." ECMI Monograph 1. Flensburg: European Centre for Minority Issues.

Zettelmayer, Jeanne O. 2001. "International Bailouts, Moral Hazard and Conditionality." *Economic Policy* 16(33): 407–432.

Index

Abele, Daniel, 210n.4
Abikis, Dzintars, 212n.43, 215n.71
accession partnerships, 19, 119, 206n.45
admission process, 175. *See also* membership; changes required before, 191; cost-benefit analysis of requirements in, 209n.27; gradual, 46–47; implementing global policy priorities with, 195; incremental, 189; steps in, 186–187; structure of, 191
agriculture reform, EU in, 19
Ahtisaari, Martti, 221n.28
aid conditionality, 9–10, 173–174; evaluation of, 193; failure of, 39–40
Aldermane, Eizenia, 218n.112
Aliens' Law (Estonia), 109–110, 111–113, 220n.6, 224n.66, 224n.68; amendments of, 112–113
Amato, Giuliano, 9–10, 173
Andreyev, Viktor, 98–99
Annan, Kofi, 170
aquis communitaire, 192
Argentina: human rights network in, 39
arms control: positive incentives in, 10, 204n.14
assimilation, 5
Association of Workers of Slovakia (ZRS): in Slovakian language legislation, 129
Atkinson, David, 147
Austria: Freedom Party of, 11
authoritarian leadership, 12; conflicting with Western democratic standards, 135–136; in domestic policy, 50–51; effects of on international efforts, 175; in institutional influence, 184–185; role of, 65–66; in Slovakia and Romania, 14–15
authority: in pro-norm behavior, 33
Axelrod, Robert, 32–33

Baehr, Peter, 9
Bajarunas, Eitvydas, 166
Baldwin, David, 10
Baldwin, James, 21
Balkan States: membership candidacy of, 193

Balladur, Edourard, 122
Baltic States, 11–12. *See also* Estonia; Latvia; citizenship policies of, 193–194; ethnic friction in, 85; fear of Russian reintegration of, 166–167; Russian troop withdrawal from, 238n.4; Russian troops in, 167–169; Russia's influence in, 165–166, 172–173
bargaining theory, 208n.19
Barrett, Geoffrey, 218n.117
Barrington, William, 173
Batt, Judy, 9–10, 173
behavioral change. *See also* policy change: aggregate, 207n.1; durability of, 191–192; as outcome, 29–30; required before admission, 191
beliefs: in behavior change, 29; in policy change, 36
benchmarking, 20t
Berlin, Congress of 1978, 5
Bernauer, Thomas, 10, 188, 204n.14, 208n.14
Berzins, Gundars, 215n.66
Bildt, Carl, 111
bilingual education, 115, 138; for minorities in Romania, 153; in Slovakia, 127–128, 229n.71
bilingual signs: in Romania, 140, 147–149
Bird, Graham, 9
Birkavs, Valdis, 88, 89, 178, 212n.48, 217n.98; in Latvia's language law revisions, 82
Birzniece, Inise, 218n.107
Blair, Tony: in Latvia's language law revisions, 83; in minority language use in Romania, 149; negotiating Bosnian support, 41; Romanian parliament speech of, 208–209n.26
Boesch, Herbert, 231n.87
Bohemia, 116
Bosnia: European cooperation in, 41
Botcheva-Andonova, 241n.24
Bottolfs, Heidi, 212n.45
Boyce, James, 10, 40, 189
Brennan, Neil, 220n.17